Literature and Politics
in the Age of Nero

Literature and Politics
in the Age of Nero

J. P. Sullivan

Cornell University Press

ITHACA AND LONDON

First published 1985 by Cornell University Press.
Published in the United Kingdom by
Cornell University Press Ltd., London.

International Standard Book Number 0-8014-1740-6
Library of Congress Catalog Card Number 84-14278
Printed in the United States of America
Librarians: Library of Congress cataloging information
appears on the last page of the book.

The paper in this book is acid-free and meets the guidelines for
permanence and durability of the Committee on Production Guidelines
for Book Longevity of the Council on Library Resources.

UXORI MEAE

JUDITH LEE GODFREY

PRO PATIENTIA ET DILIGENTIA

HOC OPUS

Contents

Preface   9

Abbreviations   15

CHAPTER I

Propaganda, Politics, and Patronage   19

CHAPTER II

Callimachean Critiques: Nero and Persius   74

CHAPTER III

The Stoic Opposition? Seneca and Lucan   115

CHAPTER IV

Court Politics and Petronius   153

EPILOGUE

Literature and Politics in the Flavian Era   180

APPENDIX

Chronology of the Neronian Age   197

Selected Bibliography   201
Index   209

[7]

And has not a profound observer of human affairs declared, *Ex privatis odiis respublica crescit*, individual hatreds aggrandize the republic. This miserable philosophy will satisfy those who are content, from private vices, to derive public benefits. One wishes for a purer morality, and a more noble inspiration.

Isaac D'Israeli
Literary Quarrels of Authors (1812)

Die wahre Kritik liegt im Verständnis.

J. J. Bachofen

Preface

This book is based on the Charles Beebe Martin Lectures delivered at Oberlin College in March 1976 under the title "Literary Politics in the Age of Nero." The title could as well have been "Literary Politics" or "Political Literature in the Age of Nero," but I hope that my particular, and here limited, focus on the writings of this period will define itself in the course of the discussion. I fear my audience at that time will find little resemblance between the lectures and the text here printed, as much scholarly work relevant to the subject has since appeared in journals. The temptation to make the book a full history of Neronian literature, or indeed politics, was easily resisted, because so many treatments, admittedly of each of them separately, already exist. But the selected aspects of the period that I have discussed may add to the conventional picture of Nero *artifex* and his ambience.

The whole represents an extension of some of my earlier work on Petronius and Persius in their Neronian context, but here I take a somewhat broader view and present in more detail the interaction of literature, criticism, and court politics during this period. The new title more accurately represents my topic, for the book deals not only with literature and politics in the usual sense but also with certain critical controversies of the time which sometimes had political implications.

For some these disparate aspects may seem difficult to unite, but literature, particularly ancient literature, has to be understood in its historical context before we can judge it. Only then may we transcend the historical context and place a particular work firmly in the *musée imaginaire* of Western art which T. S. Eliot conjured up for us, where every new work of art affects our estimation of those that preceded it, and where, I would add, every rediscovered work of art, newly understood perhaps, should affect our judgment of what came after it.

The so-called New Critics, for their own salutary purposes, have fostered in us a feeling that each work of art is an object to be examined *in vacuo*. Our critical gaze is to be focused on the work of art itself and on nothing more, not the personality of the artist, not the molding pressures of the time or the genre or the tradition. But this nonhistorical approach surely applies only to the artistic judgment we make or to the syncopated Gallic pipings stimulated by the text, not to the deep understanding we must *first* have, the inwardness that is far more difficult to achieve with works in a foreign or ancient language written at periods hardly accessible to us by native wit alone. Only a handful of lyric poems seem to be exempt from such limitations. How could one understand, to take an extreme instance, the genesis and jagged development of Ezra Pound's *Cantos* without a knowledge of twentieth-century history, Pound's own personal crises, and much more besides? More recently, of course, the poststructuralist school in France, notably in the work of Foucault, Barthes, and Derrida, has advocated the critical abolition of the author, who thus becomes a mere meeting-point of various cultural and historical forces and influences, which may be neglected in favor of intellectual musings prompted by the text.

Perhaps under the influence of this trend in English and French studies, recent critics of classical literature, for their own different reasons, have tended to examine the extant literary works in a similar isolation. Some superficial references may be explained and some considerations of model and genre adduced, but we are generally left with the impression that most of the great Greek and Roman artists, granted their human motives of writing for fame and their willingness to use contemporary material, simply sat down and produced the best work they were capable of in their chosen literary form and left it at that. Problems such as the relationship of Vergil and Horace to Augustus and Maecenas are swiftly burked. Such an approach, with the aid of semiotics, may indeed deepen our understanding of, even pleasure in, the text itself, but for my present purposes I have preferred the older critical tradition of Vico, Herder, and those nineteenth-century French critics such as Michelet, Renan, Sainte-Beuve, and Taine who looked at literary works in terms of their historical origins first. I would argue that all superior art, art that is not purely derivative, is a triumph over almost intractable *données*: the poverty of subject or language, the lack or excess of models, the deadening weight of a tradition, or the uncharted path that faces the avant-gardiste. Art is the product of a human being, a human being subject to the pressures of his or her personal, literary, political, and indeed economic environment. Artists may transcend the crippling effect of such influences, but we cannot assume that such influences did not actively affect the nature of their art. Art is not produced in a vacuum, but in a matrix. The age of Nero is therefore a particularly fruitful period for the study of the interrelation of these forces, both because of the mass of literature it produced and because of our documentation of the pressures exerted on individual writers.

It is true that the evidence is tenuous and some imaginative leaps must be made which rely on the literary politics of later eras, not least the twentieth century, when propagandism left behind its earlier religious sense in favor of more worldly creeds and history came to be regarded as the propaganda of either victors or, with increasing frequency, the vanquished. The tenuousness of the evidence is not quite as daunting as its interpretation. A Gadamerian attitude is all one can offer against the conclusion of one skeptic, Barry Baldwin, who in an article on Seneca and Petronius suggested that "reconstructing the various nuances of influence and jockeying for position at Nero's court is a pastime akin to contemporary China-watching from wall posters" (1981) 139.

The topic, however selectively treated, is still so large that I have tried to keep to a minimum the number of notes, references, and works cited. I have preferred to adduce only the most important or seminal items from my predecessors and have chosen to refer, where possible, to some recent work that contains the necessary references to the previous literature rather than repeat that tedious and meritorious labor. I thank the editors of *Transactions of the American Philological Association*, the *American Journal of Philology*, and H. D. Evjen, ed., *Mnemai: Classical Studies in Memory of Karl K. Hulley* (Scholars Press, 1984) for permission to adapt for Chapters 1, 2, and the Epilogue, respectively, material that appeared in different form in those sources. I also express my thanks to Cambridge University Press and the Librairie Arthème Fayard, Paris, for permission to print some quoted material.

For the citations of individual works necessary for my argument or as guides to further exploration, I have adopted the sensible practice of the social sciences; the notes give simply the author's name, the date of the publication, and the page number. Fuller details may then be found in the bibliography. So, for example, Rose (1971) refers to K.F.C. Rose, *The Date and Author of the Satyricon* (Leiden, 1971). I have used arabic numerals to indicate the particular page or pages I am citing. The literature on the period, both historical and critical, is voluminous and I have therefore omitted many works consulted (with or without profit). The most comprehensive survey is to be found in Imperatore (1978), and for later work, Cizek (1982). I hope I have given credit where credit is due. The translations are my own.

I have many debts to acknowledge. First of all, that to the Trustees of the Charles Beebe Martin Lectureship, who invited me to give these lectures and who were kind enough to allow me to defer my acceptance of their invitation until I could lay down my administrative duties at the State University of New York at Buffalo. Nathan A. Greenberg and his colleagues were most kind in making my stay at Oberlin a pleasant one. I am indebted to the State University of New York at Buffalo for a sabbatical year that allowed me to devote my full time to the preparation of the lectures. I am similarly grateful to the University of California for a short sabbatical in 1981 that allowed me to reflect further on the problems. Clare Hall, Cambridge, and Wolfson College, Oxford, generously elected me to visiting fellowships and provided the congenial company and conditions of work necessary for academically profitable periods of time. Part of the earlier research was facilitated by a senior fellowship from the National Endowment for the Humanities.

My individual acknowledgments for help and comfort are necessarily many. The works of Ahl, Bradley, Cizek, Griffin, MacMullen, and Rose (cited in the Bibliography) saved me a great deal of labor while provoking in me a good deal of thought, and Sir Ronald Syme's *Tacitus* was, as usual, a mine of information. The original draft of the lectures was scrutinized, in whole or in part, by several friends, among whom I especially mention Frederick Ahl, Mary Beard, Keith Bradley, Michael Coffey, John Crook, Allan Kershaw, William McDermott, Joyce Reynolds, Gareth Schmeling, and Robin Seager. I am grateful also to Sir Ronald Syme, who read over the manuscript at a critical stage. These readers not only saved me from many errors, but suggested further avenues of exploration down which I have taken a few cautious steps, while I was revising the text and supplementing the notes with references to the later secondary literature. Some useful scholarly help was provided by Ernst Badian, Glen Bowersock, Anthony Bullock, Howard Clarke, Georg Luck, L. D. Reynolds (whose text of Seneca I have adopted wherever possible), and the publisher's anonymous readers. In various practical ways I am indebted to Robert Littman, Gordon Snell, and Maeve Binchy, who provided peaceful hospitality during the final writing; to my wife, Judy Godfrey, who typed the first version of the lectures; and to Randi Glick, who produced the final version from a much-corrected manuscript. I owe particular thanks to Allan Kershaw for reading the proofs. For the remaining mistakes, omissions, and dubious deductions from the fragile evidence the responsibility is entirely mine. These coadjutors, however, helped me test the maxim *nescit vox missa reverti*.

J. P. SULLIVAN

Santa Barbara, California

Abbreviations

For Latin and Greek authors I have followed the practice of the
dictionaries of Lewis and Short and Liddell-Scott-Jones. For classical and archaeological periodicals I have usually followed the conventions of *L'Année Philologique*. The following abbreviations for
standard works of reference may be noted:

ANRW   H. Temporini et al., eds., *Aufstieg und Niedergang der römischen
           Welt* (Berlin, 1972–)
Anth.   R. Riese, ed., *Anthologia Latina* I (Leipzig, 1893)
AP   *Anthologia Palatina*
CAH   *Cambridge Ancient History* (Cambridge, 1923–39)
CIL   Corpus Inscriptionum Latinarum (Berlin, 1862–)
HRR   H. Peter, ed., *Historicorum Romanorum Reliquiae*, vol. 2 (Leipzig,
           1906)
KP   K. Ziegler, ed., *Der Kleine Pauly* (Stuttgart, 1964–75)
OCD[2]   N.G.L. Hammond and H. H. Scullard, eds., *The Oxford Clas-
           sical Dictionary*, 2d ed. (Oxford, 1970)
PIR[2]   E. Groag and A. Stein, eds., *Prosopographia Imperii Romani*, 2d
           ed. (Berlin, 1933–)
RE   A. Pauly, G. Wissowa, and W. Kroll, *Realenzyklopädie der klas-
           sischen Altertumswissenschaft* (Stuttgart, 1893–)

Literature and Politics
in the Age of Nero

CHAPTER I

Propaganda, Politics, and Patronage

Tacitus and Pliny are in agreement that literature does not flourish under tyranny; we, with our greater cumulative experience of man's endurance and ingenuity, may feel more sympathy with Jorge Luis Borges's remark: "A dictatorship is good for writers. Censorship challenges them to make their points with ever greater care and subtlety." From an economic point of view, Phoebe Sheavyn's comment on the literary profession in the Elizabethan age is valid also for Roman times: "The prevalence of a system of private literary patronage has usually coincided with the existence of a despotic or at least highly aristocratic and oligarchical form of society. In such a society alone is the bounty of individual benefactors a necessity." Certainly the connection between literature, patronage, and politics and between art, economics, and political advancement has been frequently observed in both occidental and oriental cultures. The rewards, penalties, and rivalries associated with these relationships are nowhere more clearly seen than in the Neronian period.[1]

---

1. Of course, the Neronian period is not unique in this respect; there is evidence of similar phenomena in the Flavian and Antonine periods. For the hostile relationship between Statius and Martial for example, see Heuvel (1937) 299. Nor was the Augustan age distinguished by literary harmony; for the evidence on the feud be-

Because of the many lamentable failures of works of art with a message, of poems and novels with partisan content, we are tempted to think that art and contemporary propaganda cannot mix. Longer ideological, religious, or aesthetic perspectives whether pagan, Christian, or Jewish, conservative or socialist, artistic or realistic, may be embodied in enduring works of imagination, but what is too time-bound, we feel, is sure to end in artistic failure. But perhaps the opposite is the case. The work of art that is not rooted in its historical reality is more likely to be a failure, because it will feed on nothing but the imitation of past literature without understanding the pressures and the intellectual immediacy that generated its models. The fusion of the writer and his or her age produces the artistic tension that ensures both comprehension by contemporaries and continued appreciation, perhaps of a different sort, by later generations. The historical element becomes elevated to the status of artistic matter, but the original impetus and enthusiasm necessary for a work's continuing attraction lives on long after the historical matrix has become remote for later audiences. The *Aeneid* survives as a revered classic because Vergil grappled with contemporary issues, not just with Homer.

Nearer our own times, in that recognizable, if less respectable, genre of fantasy, it is arguable that Swift's *Gulliver's Travels* and Orwell's *Animal Farm* owe some of their power to the genuine concern of their authors with, respectively, English church and state politics and the visible horrors of contemporary totalitarian regimes. Similarly, in Neronian literature, Lucan, an author greatly admired by more percipient ages than ours, produced a revolutionary work of art because his historical vision confronted issues of contemporary importance, and Petronius, if set firmly in the ambience of the Neronian court circle, becomes more comprehensible and impressive as an artist *because* of his involvement in contemporary life than if we place him in some

---

tween Horace and Propertius, see Sullivan (1976) 12; Syme (1978) 178. For post-Augustan political patronage, see Williams (1982) 3; for the rewards, White (1982) 50; for the economic structure of patronage in Elizabethan England, Sheavyn (1967) 8.

second-century milieu, as a whole school of Italian scholars continues to do, where his *Satyricon* becomes only an amusing, if historically learned, exercise of ingenuity.

The Neronian age, without denying due honor to Flavian or Antonine literature, is surpassed only by the Augustan age for the number and fertility of the poets and prose writers it produced or encouraged. The roll call is long: Seneca, Lucan, Persius, Petronius, Silius Italicus, Calpurnius Siculus, Columella, the Elder Pliny, the Greek epigrammatists Lucillius and Nicarchus. The Stoic philosophers Annaeus Cornutus and Musonius Rufus are represented by extant works; the works of many others have perished or, if they survive at all, survive only in anonymous, fragmentary, or citational form, for example, the *Einsiedeln Eclogues* or the fragmentary papyrus on the *Bellum Actiacum* recovered at Herculaneum.[2] Sometimes, like literary ghosts, they haunt the pages of the Elder Pliny or Tacitus or, worse yet, late grammarians and scholiasts. The list could be longer and of course some of the writers, literary or technical, had taken up their avocation before the artistic young prince had succeeded Claudius in 54. Some, such as Martial, may have begun their literary work under Nero, even though they are now considered Flavian authors.[3]

Martial is an interesting case. From his epigrams we may date his arrival in Rome to around 65, although his first extant published book was not to appear until 80. This was the dramatically successful *Liber de Spectaculis*, a selection of the epigrams he had written on the hundred days of games given by Titus to celebrate the opening of the magnificent Flavian amphitheatre,

---

2. The casualties include such authors as Calpurnius Statura, Thrasea Paetus, Agrippina, Domitius Corbulo, Publius Arteius, Curiatius Maternus, Caesius Bassus (the greatest lyric poet since Horace), Verginius Flavus, Verginius Rufus, Cluvius Rufus, Gaius Lucilius Iunior, Fabius Rusticus, Servilius Nonianus, Antistius Sosianus, Larcius Licinus, Fabricius Veiento, Curtius Montanus, Tiberius Claudius Balbillus, Lucius Antistius Vetus, Claudius Agathurninus, Petronius Aristocrates, Remmius Palaemon, the mime writer Catullus, the tragic author Pomponius Secundus, and the authors of the popular Atellan farces. For the details, see Bardon (1956) 123.

3. There must have been enough poetic activity under Claudius also to justify Seneca's jibes at the *poetae novi* (*Apoc.* 12).

the Colosseum. The worldwide fame he claims in 85 (1.1) indicates that he had not been inactive or unsuccessful in his pursuit of patronage. He refers to previous *libelli* in his preface to Book 1 and to an amateur archivist who preserved his *juvenilia* (1.113). His obscurity in our period may be due to the timing of his arrival in the capital. As a well-educated young Spaniard—and Spaniards fared well under Nero—he would have gained access to what was left of the literary circle of Seneca and Lucan, but these writers and patrons were now out of favor with the court and so hardly able to promote him to imperial notice. For obvious reasons all of Martial's references to Nero are hostile in tone. His praise of Seneca and Lucan, however, is to be seen in 1.61; 4.40; 7.44; 7.21, 22; 14.194 and his connection with Lucan's widow, Argentaria Polla, continued, as is clear from the poems addressed to her on the occasion of Lucan's birthday (7.21, 23).

The mention of Martial prompts also some reference to the thriving interest in Greek epigram under Nero and indeed earlier. Lucillius and Nicarchus are clearly Neronian, but so also may be Cerealius and Straton. The latter is the author of the *Musa Puerilis*, a collection of pederastic epigrams by no means alien to the age of Petronius—the poet even uses the novelist's theme of impotence (e.g. *AP* 12.208, 215, and 240).[4] Lucillius and Nicarchus left about 140 surviving epigrams between them, so no investigation of the Neronian literary renaissance should overlook the developments in Greek epigram at this period, even though their interaction with politics is only tangential. Their part in the *critical* controversies of the period is discussed in Chapter II.

The Greek epigrammatists were doubtless as avid for patronage and reward as most indigent Latin authors and were therefore as complimentary to their prospective or actual patrons in their different ways. Lucillius, for example, wrote epigrams on Nero's dramatic performances and mocked those actors who did

---

4. See Keydell (1952) 498; Maxwell-Stuart (1972) 215.

three of Nero's favorite parts badly, a delicate intimation that Nero had performed them well.

In no small measure the credit for this literary renaissance must be given to Nero himself. It may even be said, without much exaggeration, that his devotion to the arts cost him his life and his throne. "Qualis artifex pereo!" he murmured shortly before he killed himself. Unfortunately for him, a pacific emperor who added little territory to the Empire and who managèd to close the Temple of Janus for a time,[5] he did not count among his many enthusiasms a taste for military leadership or for inspection tours of his legions in the provinces. Although it is only a popular legend that Nero fiddled while Rome burned, he did perhaps recite his own lines on the destruction of Troy as the city blazed.[6] In another display of poor judgment, despite the urgings of his freedman Helios, he left Rome on 25 September for Greece and lingered there from October 66 till January 68, while massive discontent from various causes and among various elements of the state festered unchecked.[7] Greece, he said, was the only nation that truly appreciated his artistic gifts.

His aesthetic bent contributed in another way to his downfall. It fostered the philhellenism whose overt and histrionic manifestations added to the outrage of the senatorial class: the public performances on the stage, the disregard of imperial dignity, and the involvement of members of the upper classes in such un-Roman activities—all these intensified the aristocratic dislike of this most recent and dubiously accredited scion of the Julio-Claudian dynasty. Other ancient rulers, no doubt, had shared Nero's enthusiasm for the arts. Ptolemy Philopator had been inordinately preoccupied with poetry and literary criticism to

5. For the usual policy of negotiation rather than war with Parthia, see Syme (1958) 492, and for the most ambitious face that can be put on Nero's foreign policy and his annexations of minor vassal states, Cizek (1982) 321.

6. For discussion of this rumor, Bradley (1978) 234; another inappropriate recital of part of this work took place at a public religious festival, according to Dio 62.18.

7. For a brief summary of the grievances in the Empire and the army, Brunt (1959) 533.

the neglect of his regal duties, but Hellenistic models could provide no mitigating excuses for a Roman emperor.[8]

Yet the young Nero had begun his reign auspiciously enough. In his first speech on attaining the purple, a speech ghostwritten for him by his tutor Seneca, he had promised to rule *ex praescripto Augusti*.[9] Few had been deceived about the realities of power in Augustan times. The political state created by Augustus was always and inevitably on the side of the reigning monarch, just as the earlier Republican constitution was tipped on the side of nobility and wealth. The first princeps tried cautiously to conceal those realities under constitutional veils. He had been conciliatory toward the senatorial upper classes and the iron fist was carefully covered by the velvet glove. Yet the natural tendency of the principate to absolute monarchy, aided by the supineness (or realism) of many members of the senate, was openly hastened by Nero, particularly after 62, once he felt the basic lack of sympathy among them for his style of life and nonpolitical ambitions. Up until 62, for instance, Nero had chosen his consuls with careful regard for the senate. The consular *fasti* point to the inclusion above all of the senatorial aristocracy. Between 55 and 60 the consuls *ordinarii* were all sons of imperial consulars and sometimes boasted patrician descent or old Republican nobility; these provided three out of four of Nero's own consular colleagues and occasionally belonged to families who had suffered under earlier emperors.[10]

Nero was now moving toward what appeared to some as a monarchy of the Hellenistic type and to others something worse, the capricious rule of a Caligula. The image of the great Ptolemaic patrons of arts and letters with their libraries, court poets, and divine status proved too much of a temptation.[11] Nero hankered after the Glory that was Greece: the senators looked back

---

8. For Ptolemaic patronage and the encouragement of arts and sciences, Fraser (1972) 305.

9. Tac. *Ann.* 13.4; Suet. *Nero* 10.

10. Ginsburg (1981) 51; for the change, Syme (1980) 35.

11. For the fullest discussion of this aspect of Nero's ambitions in which he seemed almost to emulate the now infamous Marcus Antonius, see Cizek (1982) 84, 121, 353.

to the Grandeur that was Rome—particularly as embodied in the senate. The high point of Nero's reign, when he was exercising his power most confidently, was the period between 60 and 65, between the two *Neronias*. It ended, however, with ominous signs of what was to come. One of the consequences was the Pisonian conspiracy. This led in turn to justified or indiscriminate treason trials and purges of the senatorial order, and hence further embitterment, fear, and an even more poisoned atmosphere among the upper classes. Nero, like his successor Domitian whose fear or paranoia drove him to similar excesses, might well complain that the dangers were real enough,[12] but when the purges extended to the army (with the elimination of three important generals, Scribonius Rufus, Scribonius Proculus, and Domitius Corbulo) Nero was tempting fortune, even if in hindsight less dalliance in Greece and swifter action in the final crisis might have saved him.

The dramatist Ernst Toller wrote that "history is the propaganda of the victors" and as Nero was a loser, it is small wonder that the senatorially biased histories that have survived make Nero out to be a monster. Yet Josephus and Martial[13] suggest that there were also histories that put Nero in a far more favorable light; indeed for many years after his death parts of the Empire awaited his miraculous return with hope and credulity.[14] Sue-

12. Domitian's remark applies also to Nero; *condicionem principum miserrimam aiebat, quibus de coniuratione comperta non crederetur nisi occisis* (Suet. *Dom.* 21); Domitian's own artistic enthusiasms did not, however, distract his attention from the army and frequent tours of military duty.

13. Josephus *AJ* 20.154–55; Mart. 3.20.4. Greek writers especially, such as Plutarch, Pausanias, Dio Chrysostom, and Flavius Philostratus, were biased in Nero's favor because of his grant of freedom to Greece, although it was almost immediately rescinded by Vespasian; cf. e.g. Plut. *Mor.* 567 f. On the legend of Nero, see Grant (1970) 206; Cizek (1982) 17.

14. One example of the mixed reaction to Nero's death is the success of a certain Terentius Maximus who, as late as 79, capitalized on his resemblance to Nero in appearance and in his vocal and instrumental talents. He managed to raise an increasing number of followers on his progress to the Euphrates and was greeted hospitably by Artabanus and the Parthians, when he took refuge with them, a small sign of Nero's personal success in his quietist frontier policies (Dio 66.19.3; Suet. *Otho* 7; *Orac. Sibyll.* 4, 130–39). But there were at least three such pretenders (Tac. *Hist.* 2.8); see Bradley (1978) 294 for the most recent discussion and further references. On Nero's popularity among the lower classes, Tac. *Hist.* 1.16; see Yavetz (1969) 24, 120.

tonius even records censoriously (*Otho* 7) that the masses hailed Otho as Nero when he was making his bid for power and Otho did nothing to reject the association. Significantly, the unknown author of the *Octavia* has to go out of his way to stress Nero's alienation from the people in 62.

The emperor's artistic and personal extravagances, however agreeable to the people, played an obvious part in alienating the senatorial and equestrian orders, and the memory of the murder of his stepbrother Britannicus, his mother Agrippina, and finally his wife Octavia, would reinforce—or rationalize—this disaffection. It should be stressed that even if the sexual excesses involving both men and women, as luridly described by Suetonius and more than hinted at by Tacitus, were not exaggerated, these activities, however shocking to our modern sensibilities, would have had little adverse effect on the imperial image. None of the Julio-Claudians is given a clean bill of moral health by Flavian propaganda or by the prurient Suetonius; the latter-day reader should remember that the Romans, anticipating some of Freud's theories about the polymorphous perversity of human sexuality, assumed that most if not all men were fundamentally bisexual, as is evident from Catullus, Tibullus, Petronius, and Martial.[15] Moreover, a master's absolute power of life and death over his slaves, a power only gradually and minimally diminished by progressive imperial legislation, adds a dimension to the picture of Roman morality (or immorality) that is well-nigh incomprehensible to a Judeo-Christian society. By Roman standards Nero was hardly a sexual monster; his affections, whether for Acte, Poppaea Sabina, or Sporus, ran relatively deep. But such histrionic gestures as his mock-marriage to Pythagoras in 64, even if explicable, would be more offensive to Roman *gravitas* than the alleged homosexual relationship itself, as Tacitus' disgusted tone makes clear.[16]

15. For a more detailed discussion of contemporary Roman attitudes as exemplified by Martial, see Sullivan (1979) 88.

16. Tacitus even hints that Nero was a passive homosexual, perhaps unlikely since he was attracted to Sporus because of his resemblance to Poppaea; for the references,

Our purpose here, however, is not to rehabilitate Nero as a man and a ruler, but to examine some features of his reign and his character that helped mold the literature of his day. It is ironic that nothing proves the power of literature more than the fact that the accepted picture of Nero himself is the hostile depiction conveyed to later generations by Tacitus, Suetonius, Dio Cassius, and the anonymous author of the *Octavia*.[17]

The evidence for Nero's own artistic activity, or his encouragement in various ways of the activity of other writers and artists, is to be found in all of our chief sources. Tacitus notes his early and lively interest in carving, painting, and singing (not to mention his passion for horses). The historian even grudgingly recognizes in him an educated talent for versifying.[18] Nero's artistic impulses found even more ambitious and grandiose areas than literature for their exercise. His public and private building was architecturally and culturally revolutionary. By 61 he had built and dedicated a complex of a gymnasium and hot baths in order to unite Greek cultural and athletic activities with the standard bathing habits of imperial Rome.[19] After the great fire of 64 had partly destroyed the *Domus Transitoria*, itself an ambitious project, Nero with the aid of two technologically innovative architects and engineers, Severus and Celer, set to work on the *Domus Aurea*, an architectural masterpiece, which deployed in dramatic new ways light and shadow, space and color, in an urban pastoral setting.[20] Centuries later the surviving murals served as an inspiration to the painters of the Renaissance. Because he

---

see *KP*, s.vv. *Sporus* and *Pythagoras* (4). For plausible explanations of Nero's aberrant sexual behavior, see Cizek (1982) 39, 41.

17. Naturally, Nero's short-lived persecution of Christians did nothing to help his reputation with posterity and his expected return was assimilated to the imminent advent of Antichrist by the early church. Patristic and medieval literature added to the macabre portrait.

18. *Ann.* 13.3: *Nero puerilibus statim annis vividum animum in alia detorsit: caelare, pingere, cantus aut regimen equorum exercere; et aliquando carminibus pangendis sibi elementa doctrinae ostendebat.* The sneers at Nero's preference for poetry over oratory accord ill with the argument of the *Dialogus*.

19. Suet. *Nero* 52 and Tamm (1970) 16.

20. Boethius (1960) 94; Ward Perkins (1956) 209; for a fuller bibliography, Bradley (1978) 169.

took such a dedicated amateur's interest in painting and sculpture, his agents combed the empire for the finest statues available to adorn his great creations.[21]

Even his coinage embodied Nero's aesthetic sensibilities. Early coins of his reign may or may not reflect power struggles between Agrippina and Nero's protective advisers, but once his creative proclivities were given free rein and a suitable opportunity arose, as during the eventful year of 64 with the first minting of *aes* coinage, the designs seem to reflect the effervescence of the imperial artist. Between 64 and 66, along with a major coinage reform there is a profusion of striking issues and types,[22] a numismatic renaissance which does not change significantly with Nero's departure for Greece and his preoccupation with even higher artistic matters. (This may be evidence for his personal involvement with the coin designers and craftsmen during the two previous years.) The political advertisements for himself, such as the radiate crown on the *aes* issues evoking memories of Augustus, should not be overlooked: even art of this kind had its tangible benefits.[23]

It is not surprising that Nero should be so interested in literary matters, particularly poetry. He had been tutored first by the learned Alexandrian pedagogue Chaeremon, author of a history of Egypt and other works; this man would scarcely have failed to draw attention to his native city's greatest poetic luminary, Callimachus. His other teacher was one of the most brilliant writers of the age, Seneca, who is credited with four books of poetry as well as the authorship of several tragedies extant under his name.[24] Surprising only are the lengths to which Nero was to take this early enthusiasm and training and the subsequent

---

21. Tac. *Hist.* 1.37; *Ann.* 15.45, 16.23; D. Chr. *Orat.* 31.148–50; *CIL* 6.9741. Some of his agents are known: Polyclitus, Calvia Crispinilla, Vatinius, Aegialus, and Acratus, but anonymous procurators of his were also active (Plut. *Galb.* 4.1). Statues were acquired from Olympia, Athens, Thespiae, Pergamum, and elsewhere; see Bradley (1978) 189.

22. See Sutherland (1951) 164; for illustrations, Sutherland (1974) 164; cf. Grant (1958) 27; Mattingly and Sydenham (1923) 21.140; Mattingly (1965) clxv.

23. See Grant (1950) 183; in general, Hannestad (1976) 107; Huss (1978) 129.

24. See note 50 below; for Chaeremon, also a Stoic, see *PIR*² C706.

impact they had on the public. Seneca had, almost literally, written his way out of exile and into a position of great wealth and even greater influence at court. With such an example before them, contemporaries with similar aspirations would not be slow to realize that other than aesthetic benefits were conferred by the practice of literature. It was Nero's interest in horseflesh as well as his connections with Agrippina that helped Ofonius Tigellinus to become coprefect of the Praetorian Guard in 62,[25] but even before that, avenues to success and power through catering to Nero's enthusiasms had been visible to his contemporaries.

That Nero's enthusiasm was genuine and that he really wrote poetry himself is guaranteed by Suetonius (*Nero* 52), who was able to inspect some rough drafts that came into his hands, presumably when he had access to the imperial archives. Perhaps these were drafts presented to the literary circle Nero established in 59, which went into session after dinner.[26] Tacitus' remarks are worth quoting in full for their sneering innuendo and their uncharacteristic disdain of literary artifice:

> ne tamen ludicrae tantum imperatoris artes notescerent, carminum quoque studium adfectavit, contractis quibus aliqua pangendi facultas necdum insignis erat. hi cenati considere simul et adlatos vel ibidem repertos versus conectere atque ipsius verba quoquo modo prolata supplere, quod species ipsa carminum docet, non impetu et instinctu nec ore uno fluens. (*Ann.* 14.16)

But the emperor did not wish his stage talents to be his only avenue to fame. He affected also an enthusiasm for poetry. He brought together round him associates with some ability in versification, whose talents had not yet attracted public attention. After dinner they all sat down and strung together verses they had brought along to the meeting or had improvised on the spot, and they

---

25. Tac. *Ann.* 13.3.3; cf. Griffin (1976) 448. Those who rise to power rarely depend on one factor alone; native ability and connections, as well as a real or pretended rapport with Nero's artistic or grosser interests, play a part in political advancement. For a softening of the harsh outlines of the conventional portrait of Tigellinus, see Roper (1979) 346.

26. For an earlier discussion of this circle, see Sullivan (1969) 453.

aided Nero in his own efforts, whether they were drafts or extemporizations. This is obvious from the very impression given by his poems: no vitality, no inspiration, and an inconsistent tone.

Tacitus is prejudiced against all Nero's artistic interests because he thought them excessive; we must therefore consider his verdict moot and prefer that of Martial who speaks of Nero's poetry as well known in some circles and of Nero himself as *doctus* (8.70.8). We may, however, surmise that the help was not one-sided. Nero was supposed to have a pretty knack for extempore composition, that highly esteemed art which he had been taught by Seneca himself.[27] There were not only poetry workshops, but also lyre recitals at Nero's house. His instrumental skills were honed by one of the most famous musicians of the day, Terpnus, who used to give him lessons, also after dinner. This was his preparation for entering the contests which he himself established, the *Ludi Iuvenales* of 59 and the *Neronia* of 60 and 65.[28] At the first of these new festivals named after himself, a third of the performance was devoted to *mousikē*, including poetry and oratory, and quite eminent men contended. Not unexpectedly Nero won the prize for the lyre. Often the contests were of a theatrical kind and we can compile a doubtlessly incomplete list of the dramatic roles in which Nero particularly fancied himself. It would include the incestuous Canace in labor, Orestes as matricide, the blind Oedipus, Hercules insane,

27. Suet. *Nero* 42. For the impromptu oratory, see Tac. *Ann.* 14.55. This particular talent was as highly prized in Neronian times as in any period. Remmius Palaemon (Suet. *De Gramm.* 23), Lucan, and Titus (a good poet according to Plin. *NH* 2.89, 5 *praef.*) were famous for it, and in Petronius' *Satyricon* two characters, Agamemnon and Eumolpus, preen themselves on their instant verses (*Sat.* 5, 109.8). The satirist Lucilius was the first we know of to boast of such a facility (Hor. *Serm.* 1.4.9–10). The Greek poet, Archias, had a similar talent, cf. Cic. *Arch.* 18; Cic. *Orat.* 194. Its continuing popularity is evident from Martial's epigrams and Statius' *Silvae*. As a cultural amusement it may be likened to the Japanese fondness for extempore *haiku* at picnics, often combined with artistic sketches.

28. It is possible to make too much of these first *Neronia*, as does Toynbee (1942) 83, who wished to transfer to them the *Apocolocyntosis*, Calpurnius' *Bucolica*, the second of the *Carmina Einsiedlensia*, and part of Lucan's *Pharsalia*. Bagnani (1954) 66 wished to ascribe to them the publication of part of Petronius' *Satyricon*, but in what class could it have been entered? Against these views, Momigliano (1944) 96, Rose (1966) 379.

Thyestes, Alcmaeon (one of the *Epigoni* in the expedition against Thebes who slew his own mother and went mad), Antigone, Melanippe, the pregnant daughter of Chiron, Niobe (unless she was the theme of a song), possibly Nauplius avenging his son's death, and the Theban hero Capaneus.[29] The frequently violent, if not bizarre, character of such male and female parts would be hardly reassuring to senators already offended by the whole idea of a stage-struck emperor.[30] Moreover, performances were often official occasions, which were to culminate in the many contests Nero entered during his triumphal tour of Greece in 66 and 67, when he won no less than 1,808 prizes and dedicated the wreaths on the Capitol.

This circle that Nero had formed in 59 deserves more attention than it customarily receives. Nero was twenty-one by this date, fretting under his mother's domination and perhaps the restraining influences of Seneca and Burrus. The latter two may have felt that this interest in poetry was a harmless enough occupation. At any rate, Seneca's nephew Lucan may have been recalled from his studies in Athens to join the circle.

Tacitus, as we have noted, is rather slighting about the productions of this coterie, but can he have seen them all? The very existence of such a circle is surely proof of Nero's genuine, if jealous, literary interests. Moreover, philosophical debates varied the poetic diet, even if inconclusive dialectic and sectarian squabbles rather than the pursuit of truth provided the interest and amusement. Tacitus has informed us sardonically that there was no dearth of apparently serious philosophers in attendance. What Tacitus may have overlooked, however, is that membership of this circle often led to admission into Nero's *consilium principis* and, where appropriate, to high office and other tan-

29. Lucill. *AP* 11.185, 254; Plin. *NH* 14.5; Suet. *Nero* 20.21; Juv. 8.228 f.; Dio 63.9.4, 10.2; Philostr. *Vit. Apoll.* 5.8; see Bradley (1978) 133.

30. This is not the place to discuss the psychological significance of Nero's choice of parts, but apart from the blaspheming warrior Capaneus, who was unsuccessful in battle, none of them are what one might describe as heroic and the themes of pregnancy and matricide are conspicuous. For the popularity of such themes at the time, see *AP* 11.185, 189, 253, 254 (Lucillius).

gible prizes. The candidates for membership should therefore be carefully scrutinized.

The consul of 65, M. Julius Vestinus Atticus, whose barbed jokes, based on close intimacy with Nero, eventually led to his downfall during the Pisonian purges (Tac. *Ann.* 5.68), need not detain us long. More important for literature is M. Cocceius Nerva, the future emperor (96–98). Born between 30 and 35, he was only a few years older than Nero, but the emperor hailed him as the Tibullus of his day and seems to have had a high respect for his criticism, even if we reject Martial's flattering picture of the emperor handing over his earlier, risqué poems in fear and trembling.[31] The significant aspect of Nerva's career is his vigorous part in the suppression of the Pisonian conspiracy. He and Tigellinus were honored not only with triumphal insignia but also with triumphal statues in the Forum and the imperial palace. Nerva became praetor in 66. In view of the sensitivity of the Pisonian conspiracy and the need for absolute confidence in the investigators, we may conclude that Nerva was high in Nero's councils. Is it not possible that his interest in poetry, which Martial indicates had declined with time, if it was ever serious at all, was a large factor in cementing the reciprocal friendship?

Another future emperor who was part of the circle and who also seems really to have admired Nero's compositions was Aulus Vitellius. His earlier successful career suffered no setback under Nero and evidence of his participation in Nero's literary activities is to be seen in his presidency at the *Neronia* and his loyal demand for a recital from the *liber dominicus* after he became emperor himself. Suetonius comments on his closeness to Nero,[32] which must have had some literary connections, otherwise he would not have been honored with so important a function as presiding over a festival of the arts.

31. Mart. 8.70; 9.26. This would not justify the characterization of Nero's circle as "a group of experts to help him" in writing poetry, Syme (1958) 515; this is to misunderstand the nature and purpose of Roman *recitationes* and modern "poetry workshops." For Nerva's own poetry, see further Plin. *Ep.* 5.3.5, where a long list of distinguished writers of *lusus* and *versiculi* is given.

32. Suet. *Vitell.* 4–11; his sacrifices in Nero's honor are recorded (Tac. *Hist.* 2.95).

Yet a third ruler of Rome may have been a member of the circle. This was the future emperor Titus (79–81), who would have been seventeen years old in 59. He had been a close friend and schoolmate of Britannicus, but Nero must have been assured of his loyalty or captivated by his artistic talents: a ready orator in Latin and Greek, an equally accomplished poet in both those languages, Titus was notable also for his skill at extemporization. He was in addition a good singer and a trained and agreeable musician.[33] Perhaps his martial abilities helped, but after holding military tribunates he received a quaestorship and subsequently in 67 the command of a legion in Judea. Would we know of his peacetime poetic talents unless they were displayed at court in his youth? After 64 or thereabouts he was immersed in military matters or civil administration.

Ti. Silius Italicus, author of the *Punica*, who died in 101 at the age of seventy-five, was also probably a member of this circle. Born about 26, he appears to have been a gratuitously active or overly loyal prosecutor at this period (Plin. *Ep.* 3.7). He later had to live this down, but it indicates a closeness to Nero, which his consulate in 68 would seem to confirm. It is perhaps significant that he supported Vitellius, who retained his affection for Nero, in the succession struggles of that complicated year.

Despite modern doubts, it is not implausible that Bücheler was right in attributing to Silius the *Ilias Latina* on the basis of the acrostics *ITALICUS . . . SCRIPSIT* at the beginning and end of the poem.[34] The work certainly belongs to the period before 69, as there is a flattering reference to the Julian house (*Augustumque genus claris submitteret astris*) between vv.899–902 (cf. vv.236, 483). The retelling in much abbreviated form of

33. Suet. *Titus* 3: *Latine Graeceque vel in orando vel in fingendis poematibus promptus et facilis ad extemporalitatem usque; sed ne musicae rudis, ut qui cantaret et psalleret iucunde scienterque.*

34. See Mueller (1860) 481; Bücheler (1880) 390, who was supported by Doering and Munk; on the close similarity of the metrical patterns of the *Ilias Latina* and the *Punica*, Duckworth (1969) 140; for the Alexandrian nature of the work, see Chapter II. *OCD*² (s.v.) contests the attribution; *KP* is wisely neutral on the subject. Neither entry takes account of the echoes of Lucan in the poem. Plessis (1885) xiii was responsible for the theory that it was written by a schoolmaster.

epic themes, mythological or historical, may seem curious to us, but two examples survive in Petronius' *Satyricon*, namely the *Troiae Halosis* and the *Bellum Civile*. And these abridgments are not the ancient equivalents of our condensations of wordy modern novels. They have their own slant and their own preoccupations. As we shall see, the author of the *Ilias Latina* was influenced by Alexandrian poetic interests, the dominant influence in Neronian poetic circles, as well as by Vergil and Ovid. Granted that the metrical patterns of the hexameters conform closely to Silius' later epic poem on the war with Carthage, the *Punica*, this attribution to a middle-aged courtier rather than to a schoolmaster cannot be excluded. In any case, as Silius was a devoted and loyal friend of Nero's who blossomed later as an epic poet, it is unlikely that he did not participate, however prentice his hand, in the court's literary activities.

A. Fabricius Veiento, another minor writer, also rose to high honors and influence under Nero. He was, then and long after, a friend of Nerva's and as praetor he had to take some interest in, and action about, one of Nero's other enthusiasms, chariot racing. His only known publication was the *Codicilli*, a slanderous exercise in a long-lived genre which seems based on a practice going back to Augustan times and earlier, the misuse of wills and testaments for malicious purposes. Petronius, another member of the court circle, found it convenient for his posthumous vengeance on Nero.[35] Fabricius, however, attacked sena-

---

35. The *codicilli* written by Petronius on his last night have puzzled commentators. Tacitus reports (*Ann.* 16.19): *ne codicillis quidem, quod plerique pereuntium, Neronem aut Tigellinum aut quem alium potentium adulatus est: sed flagitia principis sub nominibus exoletorum feminarumque et novitate cuiusque stupri perscripsit, atque obsignata misit Neroni*. Petronius, it has been assumed from this passage, had decided not to add flattering codicils to his will, as others had done to save part of their estates for their legitimate heirs. But as his will would therefore certainly be invalidated, what is the point of adding *anything* to his will? It should be noted also that Tacitus says nothing of a will: he speaks merely of *codicilli*. Older commentators argued that these *codicilli* contained in fact the *Satyricon*, which was then taken to be a satire on Nero and other members of the court—an improbable interpretation of Tacitus' words and an impossible evaluation of the *Satyricon*—revived unfortunately by Williams (1978) 289. I would suggest that the document Petronius composed on his last night had at least one contemporary precedent, the *Codicilli* of Fabricius. Tacitus tells us (*Ann.* 14.50): *haud dispari crimine Fabricius Veiento conflictatus est, quod multa et probrosa in*

tors and priests, probably for their lackadaisical attitude to religion and ritual, and despite Nero's known fondness for satire and, indeed, tolerance of lampoons against himself, he may have gone too far and provoked serious hostility. His enemies seized the opportunity to accuse him of abuse of his position at court, the selling of offices and state privileges. Nero therefore transferred the case to his own jurisdiction and Fabricius was exiled. It was probably for these corrupt practices that Fabricius was punished rather than for his libels; for why should Nero at this time care about the sensitivities of the senate?[36]

Another literary, or at least literate, man was the consular Cluvius Rufus. He is known best for his later, well-informed, but doubtless revisionist history of Nero's reign and beyond. He obviously had a place in the circle, because he was Nero's impresario for his stage appearances even in Greece and therefore must have demonstrated the appropriate artistic leanings. He may of course have feigned them, as one suspects Nerva did, but there is firm evidence that he wrote, appropriately enough, a treatise on the theatre, which would have been a sure way to Nero's heart. We cannot determine whether Nero was responsible for his consular rank. Josephus attributes the status to him in 41 (if the allusion at *AJ* 91 really is to our Cluvius Rufus). This would put him in his early or mid-sixties when he intro-

---

patres et sacerdotes composuisset iis libris quibus nomen Codicillorum dederat. We know from Suetonius (*Aug.* 56) that it was not uncommon for wills to contain much uninhibited criticism and free speech: (Augustus) *de inhibenda testamentorum licentia ne quidquam constitueretur, intercessit.* Probably Fabricius had elevated this feature of some wills to the level of a satirical pamphlet. There is a trace of this literary form in Varro's *Testamentum* or περὶ διαθηκῶν (*Sat. Men.* 82, frr. 543–46, ed. Bolisani). One might adduce as later examples the *Testamentum Porcelli* (c. A.D. 250, a humorous version of the form), François Villon's *Testaments*, or even John Donne's *The Legacy.* Such a form might appeal to Petronius for his own vengeful attack on Nero's sexual grossness and tastelessness, since Fabricius' work was circulated and much read (*conquisitos lectitosque*). Despite the ambiguity of the word *codicilli* and Tacitus' vague reference, it would be preferable to assimilate Petronius' last opus to Fabricius' *Codicilli* rather than to any last minute codicils to a real will. Notice also that Tacitus separates Seneca's dying demand to review his will and his dictated last words for publication (*Ann.* 15.62, 63).

36. As we shall see later, trials for treasonous libels were far less common under Nero than they were in the reigns of Tiberius and Domitian. On Fabricius Veiento, see further McDermott (1970).

duced Nero to his audiences, a somewhat frail impresario. It is perhaps better to surmise that it is more likely that Josephus was mistaken or deliberately anachronistic in giving him the honor, than that Nero, with his passion for youth, made such an oldster responsible for his fanfare.[37]

Another member of the circle, at least in 62 and probably much later, was C. Calpurnius Piso. This is odd, perhaps, but Piso, until enemies began their insinuations against both Seneca and himself, had been an apparently close supporter and friend of the emperor. He was no Stoic and not remotely likely to be a champion of *prisca virtus* or Republican *libertas*. Piso was a kindly, easy-going man with social and physical graces, and a taste for luxury and ostentation. He perhaps shared with Nero, if we may judge from his choice of a wife, that *nostalgie de la boue* that makes its victims stoop to conquer and find those mates attractive who are still in other men's arms. His histrionic pretensions were to some as offensive as the emperor's musical performances (Tac. *Ann.* 15.65). Like Otho, he was eminently fitted for a place in Nero's affections and pleasures—and equally unsuited for the purple. His intimacy with Nero was such that it was proposed by the conspirators in 65 that Nero be struck down in Piso's lovely villa at Baiae, as the emperor enjoyed his visits there and took few precautions (Tac. *Ann.* 15.32). Calpurnius Siculus is the best candidate for the authorship of the *Laus Pisonis*, the work of a young poet on the make if ever there was one; this presents a picture of Piso eulogizing the emperor and thanking him before the senate for his consulate. Although Piso's forte was oratory, he also wrote light verse and lyrics and shared with Nero a fondness for the lyre, an accomplishment of which few senators would be proud.[38] The author addresses him, not unnatu-

37. On Cluvius' history and dating, Syme (1958) 293; *HRR* has the fragments. For his work on the theatre, Plut. *Quaest. Rom.* 107 (= *Mor.* 289 c); in general, cf. *RE* 1207 (17).

38. For a disapproving description of his character, Tac. *Ann.* 15.48; he showed a romantic rather than Roman affection at the end for his disreputable wife, Satria Galla. He had taken her from another man's bed, as Nero had taken Poppaea Sabina from Otho (*Ann.* 15.59): *testamentum foedis adversus Neronem adulationibus amori uxoris*

rally, as a potential patron. Nor need we doubt his success. Calpurnius in the *Eclogues* makes it clear that such financial assistance
from his pseudonymous patron might fuel the larger ambition
of bringing one's literary work to the attention of Nero himself,
the most munificent patron of all. And Nero, like many artists
susceptible to flattery, would not find disagreeable the fulsome
praise of the imperial beauty and talents which decorated the
aurea aetas he had inaugurated. Calpurnius Siculus must await
longer and later discussion, but his testimony indicates that the
future conspirator was an eager and active participant, in various
ways, in the literary activity of the court.

It cannot be presumed, of course, that all the members of Nero's
artistic circle had political ties and ambitions or became intimately involved in the sensitive political policymaking of the
aula Neronis. Apart from the technical trainers, who received
handsome rewards, there were the intellectuals caustically mentioned in Tacitus' account and perhaps also such practicing poets
as Caesius Bassus, the younger friend and editor of Persius.[39]
Quintilian mentions him after Horace in somewhat dismissive
tones, implying that there were better lyric poets—such as Statius?—among Quintilian's contemporaries. But merit is not always the only key to entrance into amateur poetic workshops;
and, given Nero's generosity, there could be other more mun-
dane expectations as well as hopes for advancement in the *cursus
honorum*.

The most significant member of Nero's circle in the eyes of
later critics was, of course, Lucan. With his precocious poetic

---

*dedit, quam degenerem et sola corporis forma commendatam amici matrimonio abstulerat.
nomen mulieri Satria Galla, priori marito Domitius Silus: hic patientia, illa impudicitia
Pisonis infamiam propagavere.* For Piso's oratory and praise of the emperor, *LP* 69–71;
for his verses and musical accomplishments, *LP* 163–76. Seel (1969) in his Introduction reviews the arguments that it is C. Calpurnius Piso rather than his brother
Lucius (consul with Nero in 57 before the formation of the circle) who is the addressee of the effusion. Gallivan (1974) 290 argues that there is still room for unat-
tested consuls from this period. For further confirmation of Seel's view, see now
Reeve (1984) 42.

39. Caesius Bassus' life ended with the eruption of Vesuvius, so his dates are c.
37–79. He may be the author of a derivative treatise on meter dedicated to Nero
(Keil *Gramm. Lat.* vi. 255–72).

gifts and, more importantly, his uncle Seneca's influence at court, he was introduced early to the circle, and it was in this ambience no doubt that there developed the friendly competition with Nero described in the Voss Life. One of Lucan's rewards for his talents and initial friendship with Nero was a premature quaestorship and an augurate. Lucan's poetic output, considering that he died in his twenty-sixth year, is staggering, even when we allow for his talent in extempore composition and later his anger with Nero.[40] He treated the perennial theme of Troy in his *Iliacon*; he churned out epigrams and ten books of miscellaneous poems (the *Silvae*), which may have included a famous address to his devoted wife, the *Adlocutio ad Pollam*. For our purposes it is enough to point to the *Laudes Neronianae* of 60 as evidence of the friendship that was to sour into treason and seditious libels by 64. The cause alleged was Nero's jealousy of Lucan's poetic genius, which prompted a deliberate affront; Nero walked out on Lucan during one of his recitations in the presence of the senate. The poet's reaction with a scurrilous attack on Nero and his new cronies is recorded by Suetonius in his mutilated life of Lucan: *sed et famoso carmine cum ipsum tum potentissimos amicorum gravissime proscidit*. The ban on further publication of the *Pharsalia* after the first three books is supposedly further evidence of that jealousy. A pleasant piece of gossip, but Nero, surrounded by admiring claques, is unlikely to have been so pusillanimous. More probably, Lucan's connection with the Stoic circles in which L. Annaeus Cornutus and Persius moved and the strong Republican sympathies visible in even the first books of his poem on the Civil War would have alarmed the political sensitivities of the princeps. Nor would there have been lacking new members of the circle, hostile to even the waning influence of Seneca and his family, to point this out. A prime candidate would be Petronius.

T. Petronius Niger, Nero's arbiter of elegance, joined the circle

---

40. For a judicious survey of his production before and after the break with Nero, Ahl (1976) 333.

later, before or after his suffect consulship in 62, when he had already shown himself a successful governor of Bithynia.[41] Indeed he achieved such influence with Nero that he aroused the jealousy of Tigellinus, who engineered his downfall. If admission into this circle was a proven road to rapid political and material advancement as well as a more informal influence on Nero's decisions, then we have one plausible explanation for the rapid growth in the number of poetasters and other amateur writers that we hear of in Persius' first satire: *scribimus inclusi, numeros ille, hic pede liber* (1.13). When poetry is fashionable in palaces and leads to political influence, the number of poetasters is bound to grow, witness the literary activity in England at the courts of Henry VIII and Elizabeth I.

Persius, young though he was when he died in 62, was not naive. He was taught the tenets of Stoicism by the politically aware Annaeus Cornutus, who was Lucan's teacher also, and he enjoyed the friendship of the historian Servilius Nonianus. Persius connects public decline with moral decay, and he left some laudatory verses on the Elder Arria, his distant relative and the wife of Caecina Paetus; she had nobly committed suicide with her condemned husband. The verses the poet wrote might have resembled the epigram (1.13) of his admirer, Martial, on the death of the same gallant lady, but they may have been more explicit about the reasons for her suicide. At any rate, his literary executor, Cornutus, suggested their destruction and in editing the poet's literary *Nachlass*, his close friend Caesius Bassus presumably rejected them.

Nero's genuine devotion to literature, to dramatic performance, to declamation, and to the other arts, did not blind him to

41. The generally accepted date is 62 (probably May–August), so Syme (1958) 538. Gallivan (1974) 290 argues for July 63. Ginsburg (1981) 57 argues for the accepted date; cf. Eck (1981) 228. The evidence for the suffect consulships of Q. Manlius Tarquitius Saturninus and T. Petronius Niger is *Tab. Herc. Ins.* V no. 22 (no longer in situ), published by Pugliese Carratelli (1946) 381. Most of the evidence for the identification of the Arbiter with T. Petronius Niger is presented by Rose (1971) 38, Wistrand (1962) 129, 189.

their political usefulness.[42] All emperors knew that their power, indeed their very survival, depended on controlling, or at least not alienating, various political forces in Rome. Obviously the most important was the army, but the senate and even the populace, the *plebs*, were dangerous factors to ignore and each emperor had to make up his mind how he rated the potential perils in each quarter. Augustus took pains to conciliate the senate, as did Nero at the opening of his reign, but most emperors, unlike modern authoritarian regimes, were equally careful to provide the populace with a primitive form of social welfare, *panem et circenses*, in Juvenal's notorious phrase. Nero was particularly assiduous about this; he was jealous of everyone who could touch the heart of the masses.[43] After the great fire of Rome, he threw open his gardens and various public places to house the homeless and, in order to dispel any unassuaged suspicion in the inhabitants of Rome that he was responsible for the conflagration, he took elaborate and cruel measures to blame it on that heretical Jewish sect, the Christians.[44]

One obvious way to enhance his popularity and his safety was to capitalize on his own enthusiasm for the stage and the circus by providing spectacular entertainments: gladiatorial games were not perhaps as common as the people would have wished, but races and theatrical performances of both the popular and serious variety were congenial to ruler and ruled alike. Because the mob also liked their emperors to have the common touch, Nero's frequent artistic and sporting appearances and his obvious delight in them, however repulsive they might seem to the dignified senatorial and equestrian classes, were natural means of winning the hearts and minds of the masses.[45] If these exhibi-

---

42. See Manning (1975) 164, Huss (1978) 129, and in general Yavetz (1969) 120.

43. Suet. *Nero* 53; Tac. *Ann.* 13.31.

44. Tac. *Ann.* 15.34. Lucan's *De Incendio Urbis* clearly incorporated the canard that Nero was responsible for the arson (Stat. *Silv.* 2.7.60–62: *dices culminibus Remi vagantis/infandos domini nocentis ignes*). Nero's direct responsibility for the fire is also alleged by the author of the *Octavia*, so the unfounded slander had taken firm root very early.

45. See Suet. *Nero* 10 for Nero's interest in declamation, which may indicate greater oratorical abilities than Tacitus concedes (*Ann.* 13.3) and may account for his banish-

tions included members of the aristocracy, at Nero's irresistible urging, this confirmed further Nero's rapport with the people. His chariot racing in 59 was greatly applauded, as we know from Tacitus' sour comment that the entertainment-hungry crowd is delighted if the emperor shares its tastes. This helped stimulate no doubt his establishment of the *Ludi Iuvenales* and *Neronia*. Tacitus records the excellent reception Nero received even at the second *Neronia* in 65: the crowd clearly could not get enough of him. Indeed Vitellius, when he was emperor, took a leaf from Nero's book, as it were, when he had a flute player at a banquet play something from the *liber dominicus*, Nero's collection of *cantica*, and he applauded vigorously to cash in on Nero's still existent popularity with the crowd. Not surprisingly, the first impersonator of Nero appeared with a lyre. Fronto was later to approve of Nero's policy, stressing that it was politically important for an emperor to be concerned about performers on the stage and in the circus, because he knows that the loyalty of the Roman people is retained by the corn doles and lavish entertainments.[46] Of course Nero's artistic talents, however welcome to the Roman people, were greeted even more tumultuously in Greece and the Greek-speaking areas of Italy, such as Naples, where drama and music were then as now the objects of lively passion.

Nero was not alone, of course, in stimulating this artistic renaissance. We can distinguish a number of literary (and intermittently political) gatherings apart from the emperor's own.[47] The potential of such circles for political and social reform and dissent had been pointed out by Tiberius. There was also a more mischievous side to such gatherings, which may account for

---

ment of the famous rhetor Verginius Flavus (*Ann.* 15.71), and for his popular poetry readings in the theatre. Only in the case of the executions of the slaves of Pedanius Secundus did Nero risk an unpopular action and this was probably due to his general sensitivity about dangers to himself (Tac. *Ann.* 14.39–44). Dio's claim (62.18) that Nero stopped the corn dole in 64 seems unlikely, but if true, then it was uncharacteristic and due to financial exigencies.

46. Fronto *Princ. Hist.* 17.
47. These will be discussed later; see also note 57.

Domitian's hostility to them.[48] It was at a particularly crowded dinner, given by P. Ostorius Scapula, that Antistius Sosianus, now praetor, recited his slanderous poems against Nero in 62. Cossutianus Capito, Tigellinus' son-in-law, promptly accused him of treason (Tac. *Ann.* 14.48). Nero, who was normally tolerant of such abuse (Suet. *Nero* 39) and not above writing scurrilous verse himself, allowed the infamous *lex maiestatis* to be revived for the first time in his reign and Antistius was banished by the senate (Tac. *Ann.* 14.49). This is the only Neronian case documented of prosecution for offensive writing under the provisions of the *lex maiestatis*.

All this illustrates the sometimes dangerous connection between writing and power, a connection Seneca had seen long ago. Debarred from Nero's poetry workshop presumably because of his established reputation, he had therefore infiltrated his young nephew Lucan into it, even though, to judge from his education under Cornutus and from the *Pharsalia*, the young Stoic was politically antipathetic to all that Nero represented. There can be little doubt then, that until 62 and his forced, or voluntary, retirement from court, Seneca took a great interest in the literary activities of Nero's court. His position of influence with the literary-minded prince had been reinforced by his ghostwriting of Nero's speeches, such as those on behalf of the fire-ravaged colony of Bononia, for Apamea after its earthquake, as well as for the freedom of Rhodes and Ilium.[49] Seneca's continued flow of literary work, erotic verses and epigrams, or serious tragedies and scientific and philosophical treatises— even if we discount the overt political cast of some of them, such as the *De Ira* and *De Clementia*—is usually credited to the great gratification he found in writing and in philosophical exposition, but it may often be explained, as we shall see, by extrinsic motives. Seneca, the tutor who had diverted his pupil's attention

---

48. Tac. *Ann.* 3.54: "nec ignoro in conviviis et circulis incusari ista et modum posci". Cf. *Agr.* 2.3: *adempto per inquisitiones etiam loquendi audiendique commercio.*

49. Quint. *Inst.* 8.5.18; Tac. *Ann.* 13.3, cf. Bradley (1978) 60. Ghostwriting was common in antiquity, as the surviving texts of some of the Attic orators prove.

from Cicero so that his own style might shine the brighter, could not have afforded to overlook the power to be gained by those who were admitted to these gatherings. In fact, two of the charges made by his enemies later in 62 were that Seneca claimed sole honors for eloquence and had also started writing verse more frequently now that Nero had developed an affection for it.[50] The implication is that Seneca had written more verse either as contributions to Nero's more general literary entertainments or to counteract the literary predominance of Nero's newer intimates by his own independent productions. Seneca naturally would try to safeguard his standing with the artistically minded emperor by writing. In view of Nero's predilection for the stage and dramatic recitals, it is not unreasonable to date *some* at least of Seneca's tragedies to the period after 59 rather than place them all earlier. These then could be part of the poetry his enemies are referring to.[51] Certainly in Tacitus' account, Seneca's accusers

---

50. Tac. *Ann.* 14.52. Information about Seneca's many lost works can be gleaned from such diverse sources as Martial, Aulus Gellius, St. Jerome, Tertullian, St. Augustine, Lactantius, and St. Martin of Braga: a twenty-second book of the *Epistulae Morales*; correspondence with Caesonius Maximus and Novatus (this in ten books); the *De Situ Indiae* and the *De Situ et Sacris Aegyptiorum* (unless this was a section of the dialogue *De Superstitione*); a treatise on marriage; the *De Amicitia*; a youthful biography of the elder Seneca; the *De Fortuitis* or *De Remediis Fortuitorum* (a badly mutilated and altered version of which survives); a treatise *De Moribus* as well as collections such as *Proverbia Senecae* and *Sententiae Rufi* (Seneca's dying words?); a bad version of his *De Formula Honestae Vitae* uttered by St. Martin of Braga; see Bickel (1905) 505. For Seneca's poems, see Quint. *Inst.* 10.1.129; Plin. *Ep.* 5.3 (erotic verses, which would be appropriate enough in Neronian circles); Tacitus *Ann.* 14.52; Prisc. *lib.* 7.759 (ed. Putsch), where it is stated that the poems were originally in four books. For a general discussion of the chronology see Münscher (1922).

51. The evidence for dating Seneca's tragedies is scanty at best. Quint. *Inst.* 8.3.31 points to Seneca's giving readings of some in the early fifties in competition with Pomponius Secundus and the echoes of *Hercules Furens* in the *Apocolocyntosis* would date that play at least to before or in 54. But there has been an unspoken assumption that all the plays have to be located in one period of Seneca's lifetime, although we know that the dates of, say, Euripides' documented dramas are spread over a period of thirty-five years. Fitch (1981) has argued, using stylistic criteria, that the tragedies may be divided into three rough chronological groups: an early set (*Agamemnon, Phaedra,* and *Oedipus*); a middle set (*Medea, Troades,* and *Hercules Furens*); and a late set (*Thyestes* and *Phoenissae*). Fitch concludes that the plays represent "not a brief flirtation with Melpomene, but rather an interest to which Seneca returned over a number of years" (307). This leaves room for speculation about the motives behind this intermittent rekindling of interest in writing tragedy, but it would seem then that part at least of Seneca's admirable and justly admired dramatic *oeuvre* was a

had urged Nero to rid himself of a vain and pretentious guide, which suggests that the philosopher had until this time tried to retain his original position as the director and molder of Nero's literary tastes. His praise for a line of Nero's verse in the *Naturales Quaestiones* (2.5.6) wistfully recalls his former status as chief critic. An attack on Seneca's *literary* gifts seems indicated by Seneca's temporary modesty about them in 62, when he offered to lay down his power and riches and retire.[52] He terms them *studia in umbra educata*, the ancient equivalent of reflections from the ivory tower. Their reputation, he claimed, was due solely to their supposed help in educating the young prince. From this date on, Seneca withdraws from court life, devoting himself to writing, valetudinarianism, or sightseeing in the more fashionable parts of Campania.

The death of Burrus and the philosopher's semiretirement meant that Nero fell under the influence of advisers very different from those he formerly had, and Lucan either became a casualty of Nero's jealousy and changing tastes or, more likely, his ideological bias led to the break with the court. Among the imperial advisers would be those who espoused political, philosophical, and literary principles very different from those of the Annaean family. The most odious example must surely be Vatinius, described by Tacitus as "a brat from a cobbler's shop." A native of Beneventum, he played the licensed buffoon with Nero and his reckless accusations against completely innocent members of the upper classes brought him enormous influence, wealth,

---

formidable contribution to the Neronian literary renaissance, for which the emperor may take some direct or indirect credit. Exact chronological dating is of course more difficult, cf. e.g. Costa (1973) 7. If Calder (1976a) 27 is correct in seeing an allusion to the *Medea* (vv.35–36) to Nero's plan to drive a canal through the Isthmus of Corinth (begun in 66), this might date the play to 64–65, but such an allusion may be purely fortuitous and, in any case, there are several allusions to the Isthmus in Neronian literature—the expensive and unrealistic project may have been much discussed long before it was actually started.

52. Browne (1968) 17 believes that some of Seneca's large estates were in fact confiscated by Nero, basing his argument on *P.Oxy. inv.* 3B36/G (3–4), datable to 25 October A.D. 62. A *misthōtēs* is running Seneca's property in Egypt (cf. Rostovtzeff [1957] 2.671, 3.25), but the use of *misthōtae* or tenants-in-chief was not unusual on both imperial and private estates in this area; see Crawford (1976) 49.

and power to harm, until he was crushed by Curiatius Maternus who discredited him with literary weapons.[53]

Ofonius Tigellinus and Faenius Rufus at this period replaced Burrus as co-commanders of the Praetorian Guard, and the philosophy that, in its Roman form, differed in so many ways from Stoicism began to gain influence after 62. Epicureanism was to have its representatives not only in Calpurnius Piso, but also in Petronius. It is most unlikely that the refined tastes of the *arbiter elegantiae* would not be felt in the literary and critical activity of the court.[54]

The success of Tigellinus, the former horse breeder, and his victory in some sort of power struggle with Petronius in 66, illustrate that Nero would give preferment or, where that was not feasible, material largesse to those who shared his less literary tastes.[55] Nero and the future emperor Otho again exhibited their common *nostalgie de la boue* in their habit of wandering through the less reputable parts of the city and beating up or harassing such vulnerable citizens as they encountered.[56] Later they vied with each other in the extravagance of their entertainment and Otho abetted Nero in his affair with his future wife Poppaea Sabina, his reward (or punishment) being a quaestorian command of the praetorian province of Lusitania. What the rewards were of Nero's other *louche* associates in vice, whose names and perversities were carefully catalogued by Petronius on his deathbed for transmission to Nero, we do not know. We may surmise that they were generous, to judge from the gifts lavished on the lyre players Terpnus and Menecrates, the gladiator

---

53. Tac. *Ann.* 15.34: *sutrinae tabernae alumnus . . . optimi cuiusque criminatione eo usque valuit, ut gratia pecunia vi nocendi etiam malos praemineret;* cf. Tac. *Dial.* 11. Martial, in his squibs against a cobbler (*cerdo*) who put on airs and gladiatorial exhibitions may have Vatinius in mind (Mart. 3.16; 59; 99).

54. For Petronius' general behavior and luxury, see Tac. *Ann.* 16.18–19; Plin. *NH* 37.20; Plut. *Mor.* 60 d–e.

55. See Syme (1958) 743.

56. Suet. *Nero* 26; *Otho* 2. In Hellenistic times Antiochus Epiphanes (nicknamed Epimanes, the madman) went in for somewhat more harmless forms of this behavior, mixing and drinking with the lowest classes and resident aliens, cf. Athen. 10.439; Polyb. 26.480–85.

Spiculus, and the imperial banker Paneros (Suet. *Nero* 30). Discretion was important, however; Silia, a senator's wife and Petronius' alleged informant, was exiled for her loose tongue. One must add that not all of Nero's new advisers seem to have reached their positions on the basis of their literary credentials: Caesennius Paetus, Petronius Turpilianus, Vibius Crispus, and the vigorous orator Eprius Marcellus have left no trace of poetic leanings.

In the case of the last, one might speculate that oratory too might provide a road to success under Nero, given his interest in declamation. Persius, of course, attacks contemporary oratory (1.83–91) because, like the decadent poetry of the period, it sacrificed content to artifice, a charge supported by the Elder Seneca (*Controv.* 9 *praef.* 1–2) and Tacitus (*Dial.* 20.2). But this might apply more to the practitioners of rhetoric than to those who had to hold their own in dangerous senatorial debates or serious legal cases in the courts. The rewards of political oratory were certainly great enough, since Eprius received five million sesterces for his part in the legal persecution of Thrasea Paetus (Tac. *Ann.* 16.33.2).

What were the other literary and political circles outside the palace?[57] An easily identifiable group is that of the Calpurnii, whose most prominent member was C. Calpurnius Piso, the archconspirator in 65. Its philosophical bias was probably Epicurean, its literary views conservatively classical, and its politics initially cooperation with the imperial regime. Stoic circles existed also, such as that of Thrasea Paetus in which Persius and Cornutus moved. It is important, however, not to make these circles too discrete. Movement between them was easy; guests overlapped. It is in these circles that the aspiring poet would find his rich patron; that new literary enterprises could be tried out; that subversive or libelous writings could get their first hearing. Although it would be fruitless to list even the identifiable circles,

---

57. See Cizek (1972) 56, 67, 415, for speculation about their number, nature, and activities; for a more cautious view of similar circles, White (1978) 74. Cizek may somewhat exaggerate their number, cohesiveness, and ideological activity.

the patrons, and their close or intermittent associates, what must be stressed once more is the poetic, philosophic, and even political writing they encouraged and their potentialities for propaganda, the molding of opinion, and even the fashioning of plots.

We can reconstruct the intellectual activities of these circles fairly easily. First, there was technical philosophy involving Stoicism, Epicureanism, and Cynicism, to which we may add philological questions—did the same author write the *Iliad* and the *Odyssey*?[58] Second, political discussion revolving round *libertas*, Republicanism, and the principate. Third, there were impromptu or rehearsed poetic productions—Persius gives us a scathing picture of the pretentiousness of some of these efforts. Fourth, and most dangerous because of the prevalence of informers, scurrilous verses and satire were directed at enemies, the senate, or even the emperor himself. Apart from the *Apocolocyntosis* of Seneca, we know little enough of the form these malicious and personal literary attacks took. As we noted earlier, Curiatius Maternus used one of his dramas to break the power of the odious, long-nosed Vatinius, but this would have been an exception, even if the boast is true. Nero, on the other hand, had insulted the flabby Afranius Quintianus in a more direct way, driving him into the arms of the Pisonian conspirators.[59] Lucan in turn had written a similar *probrosum carmen* about the emperor and his associates and we have already glanced at the cases of Antistius Sosianus and Fabricius Veiento.[60]

As a counterbalance, there are the complimentary effusions of Calpurnius Siculus, which give us a fair picture of a young poet aspiring rather obviously to fame and fortune. Calpurnius Siculus, at various places in the seven pastoral eclogues, claims that his real desire is literary fame rather than money (or position), a protestation we may take with a grain of salt. Perhaps a freedman, or the son of a freedman, he had presumably gained entry

58. Cf. Sen. *Brev. Vit.* 13.2, basically an attack on Claudius' intellectual interests.
59. Tac. *Ann.* 15.49: *Quintianus mollitia corporis infamis et a Nerone probroso carmine diffamatus contumeliam ultum ibat.*
60. See Tac. *Dial.* 11.2; *Ann.* 15.34; Suet. *Vit. Lucan.*; Tac. *Ann.* 15.49, 14.48, 14.50.

to Calpurnius Piso's salon and repaid his patron with the effusive praises we still possess. There, it will be remembered, the youthful poet praised Piso's ancestry, his eloquence, his amiability, his courtesy to the emperor during his consulship, his culture, his poetic and musical accomplishments, even his skill at Roman chess. Piso is to be his Maecenas. But that is not all. Calpurnius has even higher hopes. In the *Eclogues*, he asks "Meliboeus," that is, Piso, to bring his verse to the attention of Nero and crown the favors he has already done him.[61] And it is here that such otherwise insipid court poetry catches our attention by sounding certain political notes.

Before we can appreciate these themes, we must look at the first and prime example of literary polemic and propaganda in the Neronian age—Seneca's *Apocolocyntosis*.[62] Seneca—or the

61. It has been argued by Sarpe (1819) that "Meliboeus" is really Seneca, also a generous patron, because of the reference to natural science (*Ecl*. 4.53–55), but Piso had his serious side also (*LP* 138, 190). Would a Calpurnian connection be excluded by, or exchanged for, Annaean patronage? Other identifications are with L. Calpurnius Piso, consul with Nero in 57; he, however, does not seem to have been as versatile, talented, or as close to Nero. Columella and M. Valerius Messala Corvinus, consul with Nero in 58, are also unlikely candidates; see Hubaux (1930); *RE* (s.vv. *C. Calpurnius Piso* and *T. Calpurnius Siculus*). For the common authorship of the *Laus Pisonis* and the *Eclogues* on stylistic grounds, see Duckworth (1969) 96; Cizek (1972) 67. Seel (1969) argues unconvincingly for Lucan's authorship of the *Laus*, but his discussion and bibliography are useful. In his review of the book, Kenney (1972) 279 pointed to the predilection in both works for the "golden line" and its variants, noting especially the constellation at *LP* 70 (*abAB*), 71 (*abBA*), 73 (*abAB*). The arguments of Champlin (1978) 95 for a Severan date are not convincing to me nor to Mayer (1980) 175, Townend (1980) 166, or Wiseman (1982) 57. The stylistic and metrical criteria, the evidence of the comet (vv.77 ff.), the stress on *clementia* (v. 59), and the connection of Calpurnius Siculus with Calpurnius Piso through the *Laus Pisonis* are all glossed over by Champlin. The constant and not unjustified *fear* of civil war rather than its very recent occurrence may explain Calpurnius' mention of *civilia bella* (*Ecl*. 1.49–50). The reference to *Philippos* (ibid.) takes us back to the great Civil War, still a live topic in Neronian times as the *Pharsalia* proves. See the following discussion and notes 63–65.

62. The attribution of the *Apocolocyntosis* is still doubted by some scholars, so the evidence may be briefly laid out. Dio Cassius (60.35) tells us: συνέθηκε . . . καὶ ὁ Σενέκας σύγγραμμα ἀποκολοκύντωσιν αὐτὸ ὥσπερ τινὰ ἀποθάνατισιν ὀνομάσας. . . . The best manuscript, the ninth-century Sangallensis 569, has the title *Divi Claudii apotheosis per saturam*; the others offer such variants as *Ludus de morte Claudii Caesaris*. This has cast some doubt on the Senecan authorship, particularly as the work has no specific reference to Claudius' metamorphosis into a gourd (κολοκύνθη). But the satire is clearly the work of a practiced poet and prose writer;

unknown author—had revived the semiserious genre of Menippean satire, as practiced earlier in Latin by Varro, in order to launch a scathing attack on the recently dead emperor Claudius, and to offer a brief but fulsome eulogy of the new young princeps Nero. The piece has been criticized by later generations for its bad taste, particularly since Seneca had written Nero's speech to the senate in praise of his dead adoptive father, but by Swiftian standards it is comparatively mild.

The plot is simple: Claudius is dying slowly and Mercury urges the Fates to speed his exit. Claudius proceeds to heaven; he is announced to Jupiter, who sends Hercules to interrogate him. A sort of senatorial debate is then held in the council of the gods on whether Claudius should be elevated to divine status. In the course of this Jupiter, and finally Augustus, speak, the latter being vehemently against the proposal. Mercury then escorts the rejected Claudius to the underworld, observing the joyful funeral of the dead emperor on the way. On their arrival, the outraged victims of Claudius hale him before the tribunal of Aeacus and accuse him of murder. He is then condemned to attempt to throw dice from a broken dice box for eternity, but Caligula appears and successfully claims him as his slave.

The work ends rather abruptly. Was Seneca in a hurry or even tired of it? It reflects the prejudices and objections held by the senatorial class against the late emperor. Seneca satirizes Claudius' penchant for enfranchising provincials; for his subjection to his freedmen (not to his wives, of course, as Agrippina, Nero's mother, was Seneca's protector); for his excessive preoccupation with legal work; and for his private kangaroo courts (as

---

Seneca had both political and personal reasons for such an attack. He was the ally of Agrippina and her son's tutor and he naturally resented the long exile imposed on him by Claudius. As for the title, it is argued elsewhere that *Apocolocyntosis* does not concern the transformation of a man into a gourd but the attempted elevation of a fool into a god and the title had best be translated as "The Deification of Claudius the Clod," see Sullivan (1977) 207. Other explanations are of course possible. Linguistic resemblances to Petronius' *Satyricon*, also in part Menippean satire, tend to confirm the attribution. Moreover, what would be the point of there being two pamphlets with the same intention appearing at the same time? See Athanassakis (1973) 139 for further discussion and bibliography.

[49]

the senators conceived them). His scholarly pursuits and low tastes in amusement are jeered at, as are his grotesque appearance and speech. The number of his judicial victims is no doubt exaggerated but, whatever the score, the intention of the references is criticism of imperial attacks on the privileges and security of the upper class. As Nero, in the opening days of his reign, had promised to govern in the manner of Augustus, it was natural for Seneca to put into Augustus' mouth the vicious foray on Claudius' alleged misrule, his blatant departure from the Augustan model of government. This is one of the most significant elements in the satire. The compliments to the young Nero are short, if handsome enough:

> mutatur vilis pretioso lana metallo;
> aurea formoso descendunt saecula filo . . .
> "ne demite, Parcae,"
> Phoebus ait, "vincat mortalis tempora vitae
> ille mihi similis vultu similisque decore
> nec cantu nec voce minor. felicia lassis
> saecula praestabit legumque silentia rumpet. . . .
> talis Caesar adest, talem iam Roma Neronem
> aspiciet. flagrat nitidus fulgore remisso
> vultus et adfuso cervix formosa capillo."
> (4.1)

The cheap wool changes to precious metal; the golden ages descend in a beautiful thread . . . "Fates, don't stint!" says Apollo, "Let him exceed the span of mortal life; he is like me in face and glory and not my inferior in song and voice. He will bring happy generations to weary men and break the silence of the laws. . . ." [Like the morning and evening star, like the sun,] so will Caesar appear and so now will Rome see Nero. His bright face glows with its clustering locks.

The new emperor, however, was only seventeen. The main purpose of the satire is to arouse in the senatorial and equestrian classes relief and gratitude for the demise of Claudius, and acceptance of the passing over of Britannicus, his legitimate son, in favor of his adoptive son Nero. Equally important, however, are the propaganda motifs Seneca introduces: Augustan principles, the new Golden Age, peace, justice, beauty, and culture. Some of these are the notes echoed by Calpurnius Siculus in the *Eclogues*.

The propaganda on the subject of peace was, incidentally, sincere to a large degree. Nero was one of the more pacifist emperors. He had little interest in conquest—or, unfortunately for him, the army. After much discouragement and some futile hard-line attempts at expansion of the empire in the East, he secured a settlement with Parthia over the Armenian question by 63. He made some initial attempts to rationalize the frontiers in Britain and, despite the rebellion of Boudicca that threw the province into a turmoil, he chose finally, on the advice of his envoy Polyclitus, a policy of conciliation. There were even reports that he might pull out of that troublesome province (Suet. *Nero* 18). Toward the end of his reign there is some evidence of possible adventurism in the East again, but one may question whether the plans were serious or were merely an attempt to restore his battered imperial image. He added the title "Imperator" to his name only at the end of his life, and clearly his annexations, Lesser Armenia and Pontus Polemoniacus, were minor by comparison with those of later emperors such as Trajan.

The interesting aspect of the *Apocolocyntosis* for our purpose, then, is that a Neronian ideology has been established from the start: an image had been created by Seneca, which aspirants to fame, fortune, and power had to incorporate into their more personal flattery of Nero's good looks, godlike presence, or poetic skills. We may now see how this is reflected in the actual writing of Calpurnius Siculus, who may stand as one in place of many examples of the typical "court" poetry of the period, that is to say, poetry one of whose prime aims is flattery of the emperor and whose motivation, besides fame, is social or political advancement and pecuniary reward. The collection can be dated to early in Nero's reign.[63] The three "courtly" poems of Calpur-

63. That 58 is the approximate date (at least for *Eclogue* 7) is clear from the references to a handsome young poet-emperor who has put on a splendid series of public games in a wooden amphitheatre with dazzling innovations and events: for the *munus Neronis*, see Townend (1980) 166. This can only be Nero; there are refer-

[51]

nius' seven extant pastorals (1, 4, and 7) illustrate, by their po-
sitioning, the poet's real purpose. Theocritus' *Idylls* and Vergil's
Eclogues are the models, one of the many indications of the type
of poetry favored in Nero's and perhaps other contemporary
literary circles.

Calpurnius begins by complaining that the Muses had been
niggardly toward him and he had been about to emigrate (or
return) to Spain when he had attracted the notice of "Meliboeus." The identification of this patron is of little moment for
our present concerns, as all the candidates moved in the same
circles and all had access to the emperor, and it is Nero who is
now the poet's chief interest and focus. Whoever he was, "Meliboeus" had helped him, and perhaps got him an official job in
Rome, as "Corydon" gratefully records (vv.4.29 ff.).

The poems are frankly imitative of their older models, although some recent critics have made considerable artistic claims
for them. Their contemporary interest lies in such passages as
1.33 ff., concerning the prophecy found on a beech tree by Corydon and Ornytus and put there by Faunus;

> aurea secura cum pace renascitur aetas
> et redit ad terras tandem squalore situque
> alma Themis posito iuvenemque beata sequuntur
> saecula, maternis causam qui vicit Iulis.
> (1. 42–45)

> The Golden Age is reborn, bringing untroubled peace, and kindly
> Justice, her dusty mourning gone, returns to earth at last: ages of
> happiness are led in by the young man who fought, and won, the
> case for his mother's Troy.

Here we have the bold assertion that the youthful Nero, whose
claim to be a Julian and so, unlike Claudius, a direct descendant

---

ences to his recent accession and, among other things, to the comet of 54, fresh in
men's memories (*Ecl.* 1.77 ff., cf. Suet. *Claud.* 46; Dio 60.35; Plin. *NH* 2.25.92).
This is taken as signaling the end of Claudius' tyranny and the beginning of a new
Golden Age. The reference to reserved equestrian seats in the theatre might indicate
the year 63, but this was an old tradition, going back to the *Lex Roscia* of 67 B.C.,
which was frequently breached, much to Martial's amusement, and almost as frequently reinstated by law under such emperors as Nero and Domitian, again providing Martial with material for jokes.

of Augustus, will bring back the Golden Age of that ruler just as he has already restored their privileges to Troy and to the goddess from whom the Julian line and Agrippina, Nero's mother, claimed descent. The slur on the Claudian element of the dynasty of the Caesars is also to be found in the similar dismissal of Claudius' claims to legitimate rule in Augustus' speech in the *Apocolocyntosis* (10).

The prophecy continues with the anticipation of peace over the world under divine governance.[64] The motif of *clementia*, soundly struck in Seneca's earlier and lengthy philosophical work on the topic, reverberates in the next lines.

> candida pax aderit; nec solum candida vultu,
> qualis saepe fuit quae libera Marte professo,
> quae domito procul hoste tamen grassantibus armis
> publica diffudit tacito discordia ferro:
> omne procul vitium simulatae cedere pacis
> iussit et insanos Clementia contudit enses.
> (1.54–59)

Fair Peace will come, not fair of face alone, such as she often was when, though free from open war and with distant enemies tamed, she still in guerrilla warfare destroyed the national harmony with undercover steel. Clemency has ordered every vice of pretended peace to distant exile and blunted the mad swords.

The promises made to the senate by Nero immediately after Claudius' death are woven into the next sequence:

> nulla catenati feralis pompa senatus
> carnificum lassabit opus, nec carcere pleno
> infelix raros numerabit Curia patres. plena
> quies aderit, quae stricti nescia ferri
> altera Saturni referet Latialia regna,
> altera regna Numae, qui primus ovantia caede
> agmina, Romuleis et adhuc ardentia castris
> pacis opus docuit iussitque silentibus armis

64. For a detailed discussion of this and the lines (vv.46 ff.) dealing with Bellona, see Wiseman (1982) 58.

inter sacra tubas, non inter bella, sonare.
iam nec adumbrati faciem mercatus honoris
nec vacuos tacitus fasces et inane tribunal
accipiet consul; sed legibus omne reductis
ius aderit moremque fori vultumque priorem
reddet, et afflictum melior deus auferet aevum.
(1.60–73)

No funeral procession of a senate in chains will make the executioners' task a weary one nor will the unlucky senate chamber count but a senator here and there, while the jail is full. Domestic tranquillity will be complete and, ignorant of the drawn sword, will bring back for the second time the reign of Saturn in Latium and again the reign of Numa, who first taught the work of peace to armies that triumphed in slaughter and were still afire from the campaigns of Romulus; and it was he who first stilled the clash of arms and bade the trumpets sound in holy ceremonies, not in war. Now no more will the consul buy the shadowy image of political office and silently accept worthless fasces and an empty platform; but total justice will be here with the return of law and she will restore the former customs and appearance of the law courts, and a kindlier deity will end the era of oppression.[65]

The promise is that the senate will be properly respected, freed from the bloody caprice of Claudius, whose thirty-five senatorial victims had been carefully enumerated in the *Apocolocyntosis* (14) when the list of charges against him had been read before the tribunal of Aeacus. The return of power to the consuls seems to allude to Nero's award of consulships in the early years of his reign to various members of Republican and aristocratic families. The instauration of normal procedures to the law courts as opposed to the eccentric operation of them imputed to Claudius

---

65. The final lines of poem seem to be a poetic and obscure allusion to the common hope for an untroubled transition from one emperor to his successor, see Townend (1980) 166. For other interpretations, see Verdière (1954) 239, and for a more sympathetic analysis of these self-seeking effusions, see Leach (1973) 53. I cannot agree with Leach that "in the final poem of the collection, the poet gives strong indications that he has already lost faith in the better aspects of Rome's new hope" (56). This is totally at odds with the eulogistic thrust of the collection. Its somewhat mendicant note actually reinforces the aspirations of the first elegy.

reflects again part of Nero's initial platform as *Augustus redivivus*, and the poet proudly proclaims:

> scilicet ipse deus Romanae pondera molis
> fortibus excipiet sic inconcussa lacertis.
> (1.84–85)

A god himself will for sure take up in his strong arms the massive burden of the Roman state.

This allusive and occasionally oblique eulogy of the youthful Nero is just one of several passages one could choose from the three "court" poems. The others are derivative pastorals about shepherds and their lady-loves, interspersed with singing matches and advice on herding animals. But the passages quoted repeat many of the themes of the *Apocolocyntosis* and indeed of the *De Clementia*. This philosophical work was written about 55–56; it is therefore very close to the most plausible date for the *Eclogues*, namely 56–58. The motif of the Golden Age returning to earth was of course a theme dusted off from Augustan propaganda[66] and it fits well into the criticism of Claudius' bad treatment of the senate and his abuse of the law courts; but, above all, there is the praise of peace, a theme sounded also in *Eclogue* 4, which is deliberately modeled on Vergil's fourth eclogue addressed to Asinius Pollio:

> ab Iove principium, si quis canit aethera, sumat,
> si quis Atlantiaci pondus molitur Olympi:
> at mihi, qui nostras praesenti numine terras
> perpetuamque regit iuvenili robore pacem
> laetus et *augusto* felix arrideat ore.
>
> (82–86)

Let the poet begin with Jove if he sings of Olympus or takes up the burden of the sky supported by Atlas, but for me, the one who rules our lands with his visible godhead and guides perpetual

---

66. Cf. e.g. Verg. *Aen.* 6.792–93; 8.324–25. The best general summary of Augustus' "reorganization of opinion" is still Syme (1939, 1960) 251, 459.

peace with his youthful strength, may he, in his happiness and good fortune, smile upon me with his *august* lips.

The singing shepherds, now they have struck the appropriate general themes, go even further in support of official policies and promises. Corydon, after professing that his work would be more ambitious if he had an estate and pastures of his own, asks Meliboeus if he thinks his poetry creditable enough to bring it to the divine emperor's attention, since Meliboeus has entree to "the inner shrine of Palatine Apollo," where poetry recitals were held. Corydon then compares Meliboeus to Maecenas, who dictated Vergil's development from the *Eclogues* to the *Georgics* and then to the *Aeneid*. This would serve to reinforce the claim of Nero to be restoring by his principles of government the Golden Age of Augustus, when munificence went hand in hand with justice.

The so-called *Einsiedeln Eclogues* provide a further insight into the literary and political warfare of the period and thus into the activity of the various circles described above. Metrical and formal considerations suggest that these are from two different pens.[67] The second, for example, with its first words *quid tacitus, Mystes?* deliberately recalls the opening of Calpurnius' *Eclogue* 4, the centerpiece of the collection (*quid tacitus, Corydon . . . ?*) in order to present a critical variation on the praises of the new Golden Age inaugurated by Nero.[68] Echoes and allusions to Calpurnius' oeuvre make clear the author's intention, which is to cast doubt on the propaganda themes sounded by Calpurnius, the return of the Golden Age with peace, justice, and prosperity established again on earth under Nero-Apollo (v.38). The theme of the pastoral is expressed by Mystes, whose name suggests someone who has been initiated and so knows more than the common herd:

> curae mea gaudia turbant,
> cura dapes sequitur, magis inter pocula surgit

67. Korzeniewski (1971) 4; Korzeniewski (1966) 344; for a metrical analysis, see Duckworth (1965) 95, who also attributes them to two different authors.
68. Korzeniewski (1966) 353.

et gravis anxietas laetis incumbere gaudet. . . .

(2.2–5)

worries trouble my joys, worry attends my feasts, and rises even more in my cups, and deep anxiety likes to lie heavy on my happy thoughts. . . .

Unfortunately the *Eclogue* breaks off before Mystes has a chance to explain his anxiety fully, but we can readily surmise that there was a political or philosophical serpent in the Neronian Garden of Eden.[69] Too established a peace, too widespread a prosperity, would have its dangers too and could lead to moral decadence, a note frequently sounded in imperial writers: Mystes even says, "satietas mea gaudia vexat" (v.9).[70] The poem was probably written early in Nero's reign as an indirect response to the optimistic flattery of Calpurnius and others, but there is no evidence for our assuming a political hostility in the writer. Such a rehandling of a poetic theme, which as we shall see later in the case of Petronius, was an important part of Neronian literary activity, would not be unacceptable in the court and other circles.

This, however, is not the case with the first *Einsiedeln Eclogue*, which is probably to be dated to late 64 or 65, after the fire of Rome. This might well have emerged from a literary circle, such as that of Calpurnius Piso, where the pastoral had been used for political and propagandizing purposes earlier. A suitable irony would be to couch adverse comment on Nero in the same form, particularly now that Piso himself was becoming estranged from Nero. Again, the central poem of Calpurnius' collection is the model, although there are less direct verbal allusions in this work to the earlier poet. The choice of Midas as one of the interlocutors is perhaps significant, both as indicating the ironic intentions of the poem—who would choose such a bad judge?—and because of a persistent connection of Nero with this mythical figure, best known for his greed for gold and his bad artistic taste.[71] The formal structure of the poem is conventional, a con-

---

69. Fuchs (1958) 363.

70. For the theme, cf. e.g. Sen. *Controv.* 1 praef. 7 ff.; Sen. *Ep.* 71.15; Plin. *NH* 2.117; Tac. *Agr.* 11.4; Juv. 6.292 ff.

71. Cf. Ov. *Met.* 11.90–146; Pers. 1.119–21; for a fuller discussion of the connection, see Sullivan (1983) 7.

test between Thamyras and Ladas. Thamyras desires to sing Nero's praises; Ladas sings of Apollo, god of music, a theme Thamyras quickly incorporates into his own song by identifying Nero with the god: *hic vester Apollo est!* (v.37). Hard on these words comes the satiric exaggeration of Nero's poetic talents and vanity with almost unmistakable allusions to Nero's alleged burning of Rome, a topic constantly associated with Nero's Trojan epic and particularly with its probable conclusion in the capture of Troy.

> tu quoque, Troia, sacros cineres ad sidera tolle
> atque Agamemnoniis opus hoc ostende Mycenis:
> iam tanti cecidisse fuit! gaudete ruinae
> et laudate rogos: vester vos tollit alumnus!
> (38–41)

You also, Troy, must raise your sacred ashes to the stars and display this work to Agamemnon's Mycenae! Now your destruction was worth such a price! Rejoice in your collapse and praise your funeral pyres: your nursling raises you up!

The sarcastic note of the poem with this veiled allusion to Nero's youthful speech by which he secured exemption from all public taxes for the inhabitants of Troy (Tac. *Ann.* 12.58) is surely confirmed in the last five lines that survive:

> ergo ut divinis implevit vocibus aures,
> candida flaventi discinxit tempora vitta
> Caesareumque caput merito velavit amictu.
> haud procul Iliaco quondam non segnior ore
> stabat et ipsa suas delebat Mantua cartas.
> (45–49)

Then when [Nero] filled all ears with his divine voice, [Homer] removed the golden wreath from his white temples and crowned Caesar's head with the covering he had earned. Not far away stood Mantuan Vergil, once no poor competitor for the poet of the *Iliad*, and he tore up his works with his own hands.

The sycophantic pastorals of Calpurnius Siculus had been

written in obvious hopes of lucrative patronage from Nero and Thamyras seems to hint at this when he remarks:

> praeda mea est, quia Caesareas me dicere laudes
> mens iubet: huic semper debetur palma honori.
>
> (15–16)

The loot is mine, because my heart bids me sing Caesar's praises: the palm must always go to this homage.

Not even Nero would have missed this slighting allusion, should the anonymous parody of Calpurnius have come to his attention.

This is just one literary genre practiced in Neronian circles and we can see that not even in the idealized countryside are politics divorced from poetry and song, if they ever were. The significance of the pastoral on the development of propaganda and as a convenient vehicle for appeals to patrons should not be underestimated. The distancing effect of the artificial milieu and the convenient use of humble personae served to conceal blatant flattery and damaging criticism alike. Perhaps Theocritus began the tradition with his praise of Ptolemy Philadelphus and his approaches to Hiero II of Syracuse (*Idylls* 17 and 16); Vergil certainly continued it with his subtler praise of Augustus, but it has to be confessed that Calpurnius outdoes them both in his eulogies of Nero and of Calpurnius Piso. Apart perhaps from tradition, why would pastoral poetry provide a tempting and convenient mode for such personal and political allusions?[72] The answer to this may be partly supplied when we come to examine the literary and aesthetic preferences and the dominant style of the age of Nero.

The *Apocolocyntosis* and the *Eclogues* are two fairly substantial works that mix adulation of the present emperor with denigration of his predecessor in different proportions with different techniques. Another important work, written only slightly later than our chosen period, fills much the same function through the medium of a more elevated genre, namely tragedy. This is

72. For the sometimes regrettable consequences of these experiments, see Rosen-meyer (1969) 123.

the pseudo-Senecan *Octavia*, our only extant *fabula praetexta* and an important work for historical and other reasons.[73]

Although it lacks the exuberant melodrama of the genuine tragedies of Seneca, it has some not inconsiderable literary merits; the play is carefully crafted with symmetrically balanced scenes, fast action and dialogue, dramatic irony, and a moving denouement.[74] The work makes no attempt to hide its great dependence on the language, verse technique, and philosophy of Seneca himself. Indeed, to flesh out the minor, if significant, part the philosopher plays in the action, he is given a monologue that tries to incorporate as many of his philosophical views as can be made relevant to the theme of the play: most notably, his pessimistic reflections on Fortune (vv. 897 f., 924 ff.); popular favor (792 ff.); the cyclic nature of the cosmos (285 ff.); the deterioration of mankind through the generations after the Golden Age; the coming destruction and eventual reformation of the human race (391 ff.); the curses of luxury and wealth with the corruption and conflict they bring (418 ff.); and the community of natural blessings in the reign of Saturn, the era of justice, honor, and peace, which will only return in the progress of time (395 ff.).

The action of the play is set in the year 62, when Nero's first wife, Claudia Octavia, is being divorced by Nero, after nine years of loveless marriage, at the age of twenty-two; this is to enable him to marry Poppaea Sabina, whose wedding night is, for dramatic purposes, juxtaposed with Octavia's departure to exile in Campania and eventual death on Pandateria. The plot of the play turns on whether Nero can be swayed by popular opinion, by Seneca, or by the significantly unnamed prefect of the Praetorian Guard to change his decision. The emperor is inexorable and the tragedy moves on to its inevitable end. Poppaea's reappearance in the last part of the play presents the audience

---

73. See Kragelund (1982) and Barnes (1982) for discussions of the dating of the play, which supersede such earlier assemblages of the evidence as that by Giancotti (1954).

74. See Sutton (1983), who analyzes its careful structure.

with the ill-omened and gloomy triumph of the usurper before Octavia departs into exile on a ship offstage, an unseen vessel with the unmistakable symbolism of the Ship of Death. To add more portentous dimensions to the unfolding of the simple action, the ghost of Agrippina is introduced to predict in convincing detail the actual manner of Nero's death:

> veniet dies tempusque quo reddat suis
> animam nocentem sceleribus, iugulum hostibus
> desertus ac destructus ac cunctis egens.
> (vv.629–32)

> The day and time will come when for his crimes
> His guilty life he'll pay, his neck to foes
> Present, alone, destroyed, of ev'rything bereft.

The main purpose of the play, it has been suggested, is to present a moving description of the sad fate of Octavia by a sympathetic observer.[75] Octavia, however, may well have been dead about seven years before the earliest possible date of its completion and arguments for its near-contemporary composition are implausible. The best interpretation is to view the play as a fierce denunciation of the character and crimes of the late emperor, incorporating, however, strong criticism of the folly and cruelty of his mother and his adoptive father, the next to last ruler from the Julio-Claudian dynasty.[76] It is, in fact, an indictment of the whole Julio-Claudian line including Augustus, who is painstakingly damned by Nero's harsh characterization of his reign and his so-called clemency (vv. 504 ff.).

This is easy enough to prove. The opening soliloquy of Octavia bemoaning her unhappy fate is heavily larded with condemnations of Nero (*tyrannus*, v.33) and Agrippina (*saeva noverca*, v.21). The latter is accused of wholesale treachery including the murder of her husband (v.25). On the other hand, Octavia's

75. So Herington (1961).
76. Marti (1945) 216 assesses it rightly as "a diatribe against Nero," but clings to the view that the play is by Seneca. See also Marti (1952) passim.

mother Messalina is depicted as just another tragic, if somewhat misguided, victim of imperial caprice; she is quite unlike the scandalous figure who emerges from the pages of Tacitus and Juvenal. The catalogue of Nero's crimes is carefully built up as the play progresses. First Octavia's nurse adds to the list the execution of his own mother and the poisoning of his adopted brother Britannicus (vv. 45–46). She elaborates on his cruel treatment of his wife, who will allude later to his intimidation of her in forbidding mourning for her dead parents and brother. Octavia as the tragic heroine serves as the occasion for, and the focus of, the author's bitter resentment of Nero and so she is given another tirade against him as a tyrant more savage than wild beasts (vv. 86 ff.), driven by hatred of the *nobiles*, the pathetic remnants of the Republican consular aristocracy. He is an atheist and a misanthrope, guilty of hubris and ingratitude in slaying his mother despite her gift of empire. Octavia (vv. 101 ff.) rehearses the different wrongs done to her from all quarters: her mother's murder, the criminal elimination of her father, the fratricidal death of her brother, the hateful actions of her husband, and her dependence on a slave. Death would be preferable to close intimacy with such a vain and brutal tyrant (*tumidi et truces vultus tyranni*, vv. 109–10). She complains of the hauteur of Nero's mistress, glamorous in her Claudian spoils, and again reminds the audience that Nero is a matricide who tried to drown his mother before putting her to the sword. Now, she claims, her victorious rival hovers around her bridal chamber, burning with hate and demanding the head of Nero's legitimate wife in payment for her sexual favors (vv. 125–33).

No help can come from her father's shade, since he had sacrificed his own flesh and blood to a usurper who entered the family through his marriage, the marriage that had spawned another host of evils: bloodlust and murder, plots and ambition for the purple. The specific crimes stemming from Agrippina's incestuous marriage to Claudius are again listed: Britannicus and Octavia's former fiancé Junius Silanus both done to death, the latter committing suicide once faced with trumped-up charges

(vv. 147–50).[77] The unscrupulous scramble for the succession to imperial power and the reluctance of Octavia to enter the proposed marriage alliance are linked with the poisoning of Claudius and the brilliant promise and ancestral legitimacy of Britannicus (*modo sidus orbis, columen Augustae domus,* v.168). The nurse's commentary is even-handed in its discrediting of Claudius, Agrippina, and Nero together; for all their internecine struggles and differences, they are still to be lumped together as the last important and disastrous scions of the Julio-Claudian line.

Octavia threatens suicide, but the nurse points to her popularity with the citizenry and the power of the people (*vis magna populi est,* v.184): the populace disapproves of the divorce. This aspect of the play, "power to the people," will come up later (vv.647, 786, 792) and seems based on some tenuous facts (cf. Tac. *Ann.* 14.59; Suet. *Nero* 35.2).

The nurse's hope that Octavia may yet triumph over Poppaea, because passionate love soon dies while marital affection endures, brings no comfort to the victim. She pours imprecations on Nero's head and recalls the comet of 60, which she interprets as a sign of divine anger and imminent disaster for all nations under the sway of this impious leader; indeed, she expresses amazement that this destructive enemy of gods and subjects alike, the murderer of brother and mother, still sees the light of day. Can it be that the sovereign Father hesitates to strike down the adopted son of Claudius, now the tyrant of the world and a moral blot on Augustus' scutcheon (v.251)?

Octavia gives vent to a measured condemnation of her mother Messalina's mad folly in attempting an illicit and adulterous union with all its disastrous consequences for herself and her children. The chorus now enters and deplores the divorce, which would end the marriage that had legitimated Nero's accession. The chorus deliberately disregards Nero's charges that Octavia was

---

77. The incest motif is noted by Sutton (1983) 38, but it is not stressed enough. Significantly L. Junius Silanus Torquatus was accused of incest with his sister (Sen. *Apoc.* 8; Tac. *Ann.* 12.48, cf. *PIR* [1897] 559). In the play the charge is suppressed (*criminis ficti reus*); it is Julio-Claudian incest that must remain center stage.

sterile by urging her to have children. It even alludes, somewhat untactfully on the surface of it, to the legally incestuous bond between Nero and his wife in a reference to Jupiter and Juno, another union of brother and sister. The allusion, however, is part of the far-reaching strategy of the play. The chorus chides itself for its cowardly behavior in the face of Britannicus' death and recalls the manful and martial virtues of the Roman people in the days of the kings and the decemvirate. The familiar instances of Lucretia, Tullia, and Verginia from the history of tyranny in Rome are quickly connected with Nero's sustained and unfilial attempts to secure his mother's death, an overly detailed narrative of which is presented in the choral lyrics. The culmination is Agrippina's famous final appeal to be stabbed in the womb. The staunchly Republican sentiments and examples are surely not introduced by the author without a purpose and they must be taken into account by any interpreter of the play. It is worth observing, however, that this stress on the quondam merits and power of the populace differ from Seneca's views on the desirability of a moderate and law-abiding monarchy (*Ben.* 6.15.4; *Clem.* 1.3.3).

After the chorus exits, Seneca comes on stage to compare his present distress unfavorably with his exile in Corsica. This scene gives the writer a chance to display his familiarity with Senecan philosophy in a speech, which of itself should eliminate Seneca as a candidate for authorship. The dramatic purpose is to prepare us for the ensuing debate scene between the sage and benevolent guardian and his wayward and cruel pupil over the fate of Octavia. Here Nero will serve as his own accuser by providing the audience with damning evidence against himself, a technique cleverly used in the *Apocolocyntosis* when the indictment against Claudius is presented from all sides and out of his own mouth.

Nero first curtly orders the anonymous commander of the Guard accompanying him to despatch someone to bring him the heads of Rubellius Plautus and Faustus Cornelius Sulla, both *nobiles* related to him and now exiles in Asia and Massilia, re-

[64]

spectively. They are dangers to the regime: they had been accused this year by Ofonius Tigellinus of treasonous conspiracy. In sharp gnomic dialogue, Seneca argues for clemency and Nero for repression. Nero now expostulates at greater length: his life is in danger; Plautus and Sulla were backing mutiny among the troops and enjoyed massive popular support, so they must be eliminated along with Octavia, who will now tread in the steps of her brother. With dramatic irony he expresses his policy: *quicquid excelsum est, cadat* (v.471). But who is loftier than Nero, the audience is left to wonder, and who has further to fall?

Seneca responds with a sketch of the duties of a good prince and revives the theme of Augustan harmony, the *concordia ordinum* under a just and peaceful ruler, themes that had been so profitably deployed in the propaganda at the beginning of Nero's reign. But the emperor's hostility to the senate flashes out in his answer: Rome and the senate will be his slaves, so heaven wills and fear dictates. He refers contemptuously to *cives . . . claro tumentes genere* (v.496), presumably the old aristocracy who resented Nero's promotion of *novi homines*, and points to the death of Julius Caesar by the dagger of the ungrateful Brutus. Like himself, Augustus had executed and proscribed nobles, young and old, during the period of the triumvirate and set up the dripping heads of his victims in the Forum. His brutality had ceased only after Philippi, the Sicilian war, and the conquest of Egypt. He did not put up his sword till his enemies were all dead. Even then he ruled by fear and with the loyalty of his armies. Nero will do the same to achieve the same glory and found with his own offspring a similar ruling house (vv.530–32). Dramatic irony runs through this spectacle of Nero's self-exposure, and the unwitting condemnation of his model emperor.

Seneca wants that offspring to be Octavia's, but Nero is adamant against Seneca's impassioned defense. Nero knows, as did everyone, of Octavia's distaste for him (vv.540–41). Poppaea's beauty, the only attribute the chorus can bring up in her favor when showing its sympathy to her later (vv.762 ff.), makes her a fit and destined queen for him. Seneca tries another tack and speaks of the loyalty to Octavia among the grieving people.

The heat of Nero's denial that his actions are of any concern to the masses may be of significance here, if we take seriously the propaganda of the Year of the Four Emperors. Seneca presses on him the high expectations the people have of their ruler; Nero refuses to concede anything to popular power or demands (*male imperatur, cum regit vulgus duces*, v. 579): strange language were it coming from Nero in real life, since, as Tacitus frequently alleges, he would do almost anything to please the masses and his affection for them was usually returned. The emperor's more normal attitude is inadvertently shown by the author, when Nero says he has already been too slow in gratifying the wishes of the people: Poppaea has inside her womb a pledge of his love and a part of himself (vv. 591 f.). His daughter, of course, was to die at the beginning of 63, and the audience would be well aware of this.

The sudden entry of the shade of Agrippina is a veritable coup de theatre. The function of her monologue is to bring out for the reader the full implications of the dramatic irony in Nero's optimistic speeches. She predicts the death of Poppaea as a direct result of her criminal marriage and through Agrippina's own lust for revenge (vv. 595–97). Once more the most shocking of Nero's crimes, matricide, is recalled. The penalties awaiting the tyrant in hell (vv. 610, 620) precede the clear and detailed prediction of the manner of his death (vv. 629–31).

This interlude is followed by the return of Octavia with the chorus. The main point to be noted in her lamentation is the reminder once again that she is officially the sister of Nero (*soror Augusti, non uxor ero*, v. 658), another example of the obsessive theme of incest that runs throughout the play. The chorus, although accepting the inevitability of Octavia's expulsion, brings in another recurring theme of the play when it exclaims:

> ubi Romani vis est populi,
> fregit claros quae saepe duces,

dedit invictae leges patriae,
fasces dignis civibus olim,
iussit bellum pacemque,
feras gentes domuit,
captos reges carcere clausit?

(vv.676–82)

Where is the strength of the Roman people, which often broke illustrious monarchs, gave laws to our undefeated country, and to worthy citizens once the symbols of power; who declared war and peace, tamed fierce peoples and locked in its dungeon captured kings?

This section might be interpreted as expressing the hope that some new emperor, perhaps Galba, could bring back the power and the honorable spirit of the people as they were displayed in the early days of the Republic, but any such hopes fostered by the chorus will be undercut by its pessimism at vv.877 ff.

Poppaea, again on stage, tells her nurse of her nightmare: she dreamed of a crowd of Roman women mourning amid the repeated and horrible sounds of funeral trumpets, while Agrippina shook the bloody torch of cremation before the bridal suite, where a moment ago the nuptial torches had been waved. Impelled by fear, Poppaea in her dream follows Agrippina only to fall into a great chasm that suddenly opens in the ground. She finds herself on her marriage bed, spread out as though on her bier. Toward her comes not Nero, but her first husband, Rufrius Crispinus, doomed to exile in 65 (Tac. *Ann.* 15.71) and enforced suicide in 66 (Tac. *Ann.* 16.17), along with their son, fated to be killed while very young by Nero (Suet. *Nero* 35). They are escorted by a crowd, presumably of Nero's other victims, particularly those who were to perish with Crispinus in the aftermath of the Pisonian conspiracy. Crispinus tries to resume his interrupted kisses, but Nero bursts in and savagely buries his sword in Crispinus' throat, another prediction perhaps of his own manner of suicide in 68. These two incidents in the dream are surely significant for the dating of the play, as is the absence from the dream sequence of Otho, Poppaea's second husband, who so complaisantly yielded her to Nero. The jealous disquiet that Nero felt about Otho, before he sent him out to govern Lusitania, is conveniently transferred to Poppaea's previous husband. The overt surface meaning of this anxiety dream is that the ill-fated marriage to Nero will end in all manner of tragedies, as divine vengeance requites his wicked deeds. This is, if anything, emphasized by the implausibly favorable interpretations offered by Poppaea's nurse. The implausibility is meant to be obvious, when the nurse declares that the location in hell is a symbol of a stable and long-lasting marriage and that Nero's sword in Crispinus' throat means that he will bring peace, not war.

Poppaea, naturally unconvinced, wants the ill-omened dream expiated by sacrifice. The chorus, although here supporters of Poppaea, can find little to speak of in her praise, except for her beauty, which with no little dramatic irony is linked to the beauty of Helen: [*vultus*] *qui moverunt horrida bella / Phrygiaeque solo regna dedere* (vv.775 f.). Poppaea too, as the fateful symbol of the turning point in Nero's reign, the year 62, presages destructive war and the downfall of a dynasty.

Once more the growing anger and lawless turbulence of the mob in its support of Octavia is brought to the audience's attention—this time in one of the shortest messenger speeches in literature. The minor disturbances in favor of Octavia in Campania are duly exaggerated into a mass revolt: assaults on the palace, the tearing down of Poppaea's statues, and general mayhem. Even now the incestuous character of Julio-Claudian marriages is emphasized in the statement of the lynch mob's aims:

> reddere penates Claudiae cives parant
> *torosque fratris* debitam partem imperi.
> (vv.789–90)

The citizens make ready to restore to the daughter of Claudius her home and *the bridal bed of her brother* as her rightful share of imperial power.

[68]

Nero enters in a rage, vowing bloody revenge on the mob and death to that wife and sister of his, the cause of all the unrest. He then utters his notorious threat to fire Rome:

> mox tecta flammis concidant urbis meis;
> ignes, ruinae noxium populum premant
> turpisque egestas, saeva cum luctu fames.
> (vv.831–33)

> Then let the city's roofs sink in my flames,
> Fires and falling ruins the mass oppress,
> In all its guilt, so too degrading want,
> The savag'ry of famine and the grief.

Of course this speech flies in the face of what we know of Nero's actual behavior in the aftermath of the fire, when he did everything he could to help the homeless (Tac. *Ann.* 15.39). Nero then accuses the people of being corrupted by his generosity; ungratefully they have rejected his famous *clementia* and cannot stomach the peace he has brought to Rome. (This may be an unwitting admission on the part of the author that Nero had been careful to keep his popularity with the masses.) Now the people must suffer to learn the lesson of complete obedience to imperial caprice. His speech culminates in two lines which may be construed both as flattery of a still powerful figure and also as dramatic irony:

> sed adesse cerno rara quem pietas virum
> fidesque castris nota praeposuit meis.
> (vv.844–45)

But I see at hand the man whose rare devotion, and whose well-known loyalty, has earned command of my garrisons.

The still unnamed praetorian prefect has restored order with a few executions. Nero, however, wants revenge for the attempted burning of his palace and for the mob's insolence in trying to break up his union with Poppaea. The punishment, namely the firing of Rome, will never be forgotten. But first Octavia, the cause of his anger, must die. The mob has already been castigated for its *incesta manus* (v. 859); again harping on the theme of incest, Nero specifically demands now the death of his *sister*. The prefect is depicted as hesitant, even playing the role of defending lawyer as Seneca had done earlier. His pleas are useless; Nero orders Octavia embarked for eventual execution (vv. 783 ff.).

The chorus at this point reverses its earlier admiration for the power of the people and reflects on the deadly changeability of popular favor (vv. 877 ff.). The populist heroes, the Gracchi and Livius Drusus, were all victims of the fickleness of the masses. The sentiments here are hard to reconcile with the theory that a main part of the propaganda embodied in the *Octavia* is for returning substantial power to the people. The masses need the strong guidance of men who are willing to take risks on their behalf without reckoning the consequences.

Octavia's last interchange with the chorus simply reinforces the image of Nero as a tyrant with Poppaea his queen (*tyrannus . . . regina* vv. 899–900). The same Ship of Death that carried Nero's *mother* now stands ready for his *sister*. The chorus, while blaming Fate and Fortune, recalls to Octavia, somewhat inappropriately for modern sensibilities, the sorrows of the Elder Agrippina, Livia, Julia, and Messalina.

The obvious purpose of this detailed list of domestic crimes and punishments is to drive home the play's general condemnation of the Julio-Claudian dynasty and its futile attempts, by familial murders and incestuous unions, to secure its continuing succession to the throne. The implication of the *Octavia* seems to be that any new start would be preferable for the governance of Rome.[78] The author has gone to the heart of the matter. The paranoia of the early successors to Augustus reached its peak in Nero. He shared his family's belief that no senator or *nobilis* could

78. This is a point well made by Cizek (1982) 51, who adds that the attempts in 68–69 to discredit Nero as a true Julio-Claudian were meant to whitewash the aspirants to imperial power, none of whom could lay claim to Augustan connections.

or would aspire to the throne without some sort of connection, by blood or marriage, to the Julio-Claudian line. This was the motive for the incestuous marriage of Agrippina and Claudius and for Nero's determination to eliminate systematically all potential rivals who had any such connections with the dynasty. These of course were terrifyingly numerous for a nervous emperor.[79]

The *Octavia* is a political document. Primarily "a diatribe against Nero," it risks dramatic implausibility and even tedium in cataloguing his crimes of cruelty, tyranny, vengeance, and sexual passion, however dispersed the narration is among the different actors in the drama. But it is also an attack on both of the last two Julio-Claudian incumbents of the imperial throne, and so by implication of the whole line in general. Even Augustus, whom Seneca had advocated as a model emperor for Nero's emulation in the *Apocolocyntosis*, does not come off unscathed. The praise appropriately reiterated by the character of Seneca in our play (vv.477 ff.) is ably rebutted by Nero himself (vv.504 ff.) with a lengthy list of Augustus' vengeful acts against his fellow citizens before he felt secure enough, all threats to his power eliminated and with the army solidly behind him, to sheathe his weary sword. The condemnation of the imperial house so far is not limited to its bloody behavior toward foreign enemies and Roman citizens who threatened the establishment of the Augustan autocracy, but also harps on the vicious internecine warfare and marital maneuvering amongst the members and branches of the family in the plotting for succession and the obviation of potential enemies. The leitmotifs tyranny and incest are as intertwined as they are in Seneca's *Thyestes*.

Is there a more specific and positive purpose in the *Octavia*? A recent critic finds that the "black" propaganda against Nero and

---

79. As Cizek says: "Les prétendants et parents de la maison impériale étaient en fait plus nombreux qu'on ne le pense. Les grandes familles aristocratiques, par l'enchevêtrement de leurs alliances, formaient une véritable caste: les Calpurnii Piso, les Silani, les Domitii, les Cornelii Sulla, les Annii, les Valerii Messala, et, bien sûr, les Julio-Claudiens, bien que rivaux étaient tous cousins" (1982) 51.

the Julio-Claudian dynasty is counterbalanced by laudatory allusions to a non–Julio-Claudian pretender to the purple, namely
Galba, because Galba's coinage has a strong anti-Neronian and
pro-populist slant. The slogans adduced are *Libertas P.R.*, *Victoria P.R.*, *Securitas P.R.*, and similar variations.[80] But the same
plank of an imperial program was used, although to a lesser
degree, by others such as Otho and Vitellius. Otho certainly
angled for popular support, claiming that he would rule *communi
omnium arbitrio* (Suet. *Otho* 7). Unlike Galba, he could and did
capitalize on the undoubted popularity of Nero, his opponents'
claims to the contrary: *ab infima plebe appellatus . . . nullum indi-
cium recusantis Nero* (*Otho* 7).

The author of the *Octavia* is presumably aware of the possibility that claimants of the purple would represent themselves as
champions of the people, but the argument that the *Octavia* is
pro-Galba per se on this basis is undercut by the gloomy reflections on the caprice of popular favor and the disasters that not
uncommonly befall the people's champions (vv. 877 ff.). The author of the *Octavia* is a cautious man. He deliberately obfuscates
the identity of the praetorian prefect, who must surely be Tigellinus, given Nero's compliments. It is reasonable to assume that
his anonymity, indeed his sympathetic speech on Octavia's behalf, is due to the fact that Tigellinus was still alive, protected
by Titus Vinius and Galba until his death.[81] The playwright,
however, was not yet prepared to put his money on the continuing success of Galba—wisely, in view of the fact that Galba,
capax imperii perhaps, did not succeed in establishing a dynasty
and the founder of the Flavian house seems in no way an issue
at this time. Hence the narrow limits we can establish for the
composition of the play: early in the brief reign of Galba.

As for its authorship, only speculation is possible. It would be

---

80. So Kragelund (1982) 41: Insofar as the coinage reflects the propaganda of the
rebels and the emperors Galba, Otho, Vitellius, and Vespasian, none of them can be
said to have advertised his concern for "Mankind," for the "Senate and People of
Rome," and, above all, for the "People of Rome" as strongly and variously as old
Galba.

81. Tac. *Hist.* 1.74; Suet. *Galba* 15.2.

tedious to rehearse the credentials of the various candidates. The writer is devoted personally to Seneca and his philosophy, is obviously a poet, and had detailed information about events at Nero's court in 62. So Annaeus Cornutus, himself an author of tragedies, remains the most plausible candidate and Lucilius Iunior, Seneca's young Roman friend, a reasonably attractive guess.

With the *Octavia*, Neronian literature comes to a dramatically appropriate end. The prince who is glorified in the *Apocolocyntosis* as the savior of Rome from the excesses of the past is now himself the wicked past and the new savior of Rome is still to come. *Plus ça change . . .* a new dynasty and a bald-headed Nero were still in the future.

The rebarbative attacks on the dead ruler in the *Octavia* were parting shots, but they were the first salvo in a continuing onslaught. The *damnatio memoriae* to which Nero, like most assassinated emperors, was to be subjected had now begun. Flavian, Trajanic, and Christian propaganda were to go to even further, more imaginative, lengths. This would outweigh the praise Nero received from Greek writers and overwhelm the favorable accounts of his reign that we know from Josephus were published and circulated. Trajan's repeatedly stressed admiration for the now recognized, if undatable, *Quinquennium Neronis* remains almost the only important tribute preserved in our later Latin sources.[82] To pass judgment on Nero as man or monarch is not to our purpose;[83] our aim is to put Nero in his proper place in literary history, along with the generation of writers he promoted, provoked, or prompted. The humorous epitaph that Hilaire Belloc wrote for himself comes immediately to mind: "His sins were scarlet, but his books were read."

---

82. Recorded by Sextus Aurelius Victor in his *Liber de Caesaribus* 5.2: *tamen tantus fuit, augenda urbe maxime, uti merito Traianus saepius testaretur procul differre cunctos principes Neronis quinquennio.*

83. For some temperate qualifications of the traditional view of the reign of Nero, which probably goes back to the Elder Pliny and Cluvius Rufus, see Levi (1949) 37; Warmington (1969) 170; Grant (1970) 206, (1975) 173; and Cizek (1982) 16.

Chapter II

Callimachean Critiques:
Nero and Persius

The importance of Callimachean theory and practice as seminal literary forces in the literature of Rome from Ennius down to the Augustan period has long been recognized. Yet so much has been written about "Alexandrianism," "Neotericism," "Callimacheanism," and "neo-Callimacheanism" in the pre-Augustan and Augustan periods of Latin literature that it is not an easy task, given the limits of this study, to define succinctly their characteristics. The attempt, however, must be made, because the evidence indicates that modified and mutated forms of these critical approaches continued to be the dominant poetic in Neronian literary circles, despite some dissident judges or practitioners such as the satirist Persius and the Greek epigrammatist Lucillius. Roman literary fashions and the critical terms they generated were strikingly more durable, or more recurrent, than is the case in modern literature. In discussions of Roman prose and oratory, for instance, the question of what is and what is not Atticism crops up in different forms for several generations.[1]

It is impossible to reconstruct exactly a coherent and fixed Callimachean theory, particularly as it evolved in Roman litera-

---

1. Cf. e.g. Quint. *Inst.* 10.12, 14–15; Petr. *Sat.* 1–2; in general, Dihle (1977) 162; and most recently, Sinclair (1984) 231.

ture and criticism. Friendship or hostility toward poetic contemporaries will tend to bias literary judgment, as may be seen
from several of Horace's epistles. The introduction into the tradition of innovative and original work may expand the original
principles, such as they were. For all that, whatever a writer's
attitude to Callimachus, his direct or mediated influence could
hardly be escaped, as Horace was well aware. There was a temptation for each generation of poets, almost each poet, to fashion
his own definition of Callimachean theory. As Ross puts it:

> Each generation of Latin poets, from Catullus and the neoterics
> on through Virgil and Gallus, through (the later) Virgil and Hor-
> ace, through Ovid and on even through the Silver Poets until Sta-
> tius, was to create a different image of Callimachus according to
> the needs of their own verse, an image which often had little re-
> semblance to the original.[2]

With these caveats in mind, one may tentatively describe some
of the characteristics and models associated with this poetic before attempting to define its continuing influence in Neronian
literary circles. Here then are some definitions, which may not
accord with the usage of other scholars but will serve as a guide
through the following discussion. "Callimacheanism" should be
defined as the poetic theory deducible from the fragments and
critical comments of Callimachus himself and the scholiasts on
Callimachus. "Neotericism" is best described as the practice of
that generation of Roman poets who were younger than Cicero,
but older than Propertius and the Augustans. Although Callimachus was familiar to Ennius, the satirist Lucilius, and Lucretius, his influence as a model, almost as a cult, begins with the
Neoterics, a term we owe to Cicero, who also dubbed them (or
some of them) *cantores Euphorionis*.[3] The obvious examples are
Catullus, Calvus, Cinna, Valerius Cato, and Ticidas. "Neo-
Callimacheanism" would then be the theory and practice of such

2. Ross (1975a) 142.
3. See Cic. *Att.* 7.2.1; *Orat.* 161; *Tusc.* 3.45.

poets as Gallus, Propertius, and Ovid who like the Neoterics admired Callimachus, but who adapted his principles and his practice for their own evolving aims and who were prepared to depart considerably from the canons of the master.[4] The neo-Callimacheanism that derived from the theories and practice of the Neoterics was reinforced by the influence of the émigré Parthenius,[5] friend and adviser of Cornelius Gallus, who begins the succession of Roman elegists, the inheritors of the Neoteric tradition. Vergil too belongs to this generation. His first productions, the *Eclogues* and the *Georgics*, were both neo-Callimachean in inspiration. Propertius was finally to proclaim himself the Roman Callimachus, as Vergil was clearly in line for the mantle of Homer, and Horace, for all his diversity, prided himself most on his lyric poetry.[6]

It may be asked in what ways did neo-Callimacheanism differ from Callimachus' theories. First, some of the verse practice followed a strictly Latin development in abandoning, for instance, the elision of final *s*, although other well-known characteristics of the Neoterics—the fondness for the double spondaic hexameter, Greek adjectives, polysyllabic pentameter endings—derive directly from Alexandrian models. But some of those importations were also to be dropped later by the neo-Callimacheans; the polysyllabic pentameter ending, for example, declines gradually in Propertius and is almost completely absent from the elegiac practice of Tibullus and Ovid. Similarly, the ambiguous disapproval of epic and opposition to the long continuous poem on a standard mythical (or historical) theme, an opposition voiced by Catullus as well as Callimachus, became relaxed or reinterpreted.[7] The work of Apollonius Rhodius, whatever the truth

4. Wimmel (1960) 50.
5. Clausen (1964) 181.
6. Prop. 4.1.64, 3.1.1 ff., 3.9.43 f., 4.6.3. f., 3.34.61 ff. (Vergil and Homer); Hor. *Carm.* 1.1.34, 1.26.11, 1.32.5; Hor. *Ep.* 2.2.99 (Horace and Alcaeus).
7. Cf. Pfeiffer (1953) *Epigram* 28, v.1 (ἐχθαίρω τὸ ποίημα τὸ κυκλίκον); Pfeiffer (1949) fr. 1 vv.21 ff. (Apollo's address to the poet near the opening of the *Aetia*.) Catullus' dislike of any lengthy poem or epic is apparent from *Carm.* 22.36 (*Annales Volusi*).

that underlies the story of his quarrel with Callimachus, had survived as an Alexandrian classic. Given this model, and frequent reminiscences acknowledge the gift, Vergil must have felt that Alexandrian polish and craftsmanship, even etiological interests, could be successfully deployed in the making of a substantial poem deriving its beginnings from the Trojan cycle but culminating in something totally Roman and new. Ovid, although disagreeing perhaps with Vergil about the choice of an apparently conventional epic subject, felt much the same, as his *carmen perpetuum*, the *Metamorphoses*, proves. Ovid may have believed that Callimachus' objections to lengthy poems were not purely aesthetic, but were partly due to his own lack of inspiration and fluency.[8] This may account for Ovid's somewhat derogatory judgment on his predecessor.

Particularly noteworthy among the Neoterics and the subsequent generation is the infusion of the personal note, the uniquely Roman autobiographical emphasis in both shorter poems (*nugae*) and elegies, although it should be observed that this same characteristic distinguishes Roman from Greek epistolography. But the most characteristic Callimachean innovation, what modern scholars now conveniently call the "epyllion," remained the hallmark of the Neoterics and their Augustan successors.

The epyllion was the short elaborated poem that eschewed conventional epic material and treatment. If a mythical topic were chosen from the epic cycle rather than from local or out-of-the-way sources and legends, it would be a minor facet or trivial detail of the familiar myth. Callimachus' *Hecale* represents the paradigm. The story chosen was Theseus' capture of the Bull of Marathon, but the poem focuses on the hospitality of the aged Hecale, Theseus' humble hostess. This was a comparatively long epyllion, but shorter examples are to be found in Theocritus 13 and 24. Catullus' extant *Peleus and Thetis* (64), Cinna's *Zmyrna*, Cato's *Dictynna*, and Gallus' *Grynean Grove* may be cited as the

---

8. Ovid on Callimachus, *Am.* 1.15.13 f.: *Battiades semper toto cantabitur orbe / quamvis ingenio non valet, arte valet.*

most familiar Roman examples. The approach was also suitable for elegiac treatment; Propertius' neat elegy (1.20) on the kidnapping of Hylas by the nymphs on the outbound voyage of the Argo presents an obvious instance.

It would be going too far to postulate schools, but a detectable web of influences is easy enough to trace. Callimacheanism affected the following poetic forms: didactic poetry, pastoral, epigram, hymn, elegy, and those shorter hexameter epyllia that stand in stark contrast to the epic poems on historical subjects such as the *Annales* of Volusius. The style is fundamentally learned, indeed recherché, and often deliberately cryptic. For subject matter its practitioners preferred recondite myths, ingenious catalogues, scientific information, etiology, scenes of town or country life, and, surprisingly often, general discussion of the art and appropriate themes of poetry. Callimachus had himself pioneered the *recusatio*, the poet's refusal to write on certain themes.[9] Callimachus' praise was reserved for Hesiod, Aratus, Theocritus, Heraclitus of Halicarnassus, and Euphorion; he doubtless would have approved of Lycophron and Nicander. His commonest critical terms were λεπτός ("smooth") and τορός ("delicate"), which came into the Latin critical vocabulary as *tenuis* (or *gracilis*), *levis*, and *teres*; ἀγρυπνίη and μαρτυρήσις led to the Roman concepts of *doctrina* and *doctus*.

The Neoterics and their successors also believed in judicious archaizing, a trait perhaps fostered by Callimachus' admiration of Hesiod and his own revival of arcane Greek words.[10] Consequently, Horace's dislike of neo-Callimacheanism, particularly as expressed in elegy, the most popular poetic form in his day, is in no way inconsistent with his objections to the admirers of archaic poetry, a different but clearly not alien group of critics. He was to be followed in this set of prejudices by Persius, who thus found him not only an excellent model but also an ally.[11]

<hr>

9. Wimmel (1960) 50.
10. See Tränkle (1960) passim; Vergil's use of archaisms in the *Aeneid* is commented on by Servius.
11. *Sat.* 1.34 f.; 76 ff.; 96 f.

Horace favored the principles we associate with classicism; he stood for public poetry, with meaning and message. The more esteemed genres, such as epic, drama, and lyric, he praises directly or by his own practice. Satire, like epistolography so congenial to the Roman genius for moralizing and self-revelation, he admits to its modest place in the hierarchy of literary forms, but he wages an intermittent war on the elegists and their Neoteric precursors. He omits any mention of their highly popular productions from the *Ars Poetica*.[12]

Between the death of Augustus and the accession of Nero, there is a dearth of original poets writing in Latin. True, Nero's grandfather Germanicus translated (and corrected) Aratus' *Phaenomena*, a work much admired by Callimachus, and Tiberius' enthusiasm for Parthenius and Rhianus indicates that Alexandrianism was not a spent force. Epigrams in Greek were written, collected, and read, all a part of the burgeoning philhellenism.[13] But it is not until the literary renaissance of the Neronian age that one may again investigate with profit the cresting critical fortunes of Callimachus in Rome and see also the intimations of his imminent decline as critic and poetic model. The nadir of his reputation is descried in Martial's well-known lines:

> non hic Centauros, non Gorgones Harpyiasque
>   invenies: hominem pagina nostra sapit.
> sed non vis, Mamurra, tuos cognoscere mores
>   nec te scire: legas *Aetia* Callimachi.
>
>   (10.4.9–12)

You won't find here Centaurs, Gorgons and Harpies: our writings smack of mankind. But you, Mamurra, don't want to understand

12. Cf. Hor. *Ep.* 2.2.91, 99–101; *Sat.* 1.10.17–19. For the *Ars Poetica*, see Brink (1963) 72, 167, and for hostility to elegy, Sullivan (1976) 12. Of course Horace was not consistently anti-Callimachean (cf. *Carm.* 3.1.1), but he perhaps resented the pedagogue's self-professed and popular Roman disciples.

13. For the dating of the *Garland of Philip*, see Cameron (1980) 43; it is reasonable to date the epigram of Antiphilus on Nero (*AP* 9.178) to 53, when the future emperor gave a speech on behalf of Rhodes, which would put the publication of the collection in the reign of Claudius or Nero.

your way of life or know yourself: you'd better read the *Aetia* of Callimachus.

Worse yet was to follow. The *Suda* informs us that Severianus in the late fourth century constantly derided Callimachus and, when he was particularly annoyed, which was often, he would spit on his copy of the poet.[14]

Another caveat is necessary here. It is very difficult, indeed impossible, to distinguish a reaction to Callimachus' own work from a reaction to the Roman development of Callimacheanism by the Neoterics, the later elegists, and the early works of Vergil, and those who followed these as models. There had been established, as it were, an Alexandrian corpus in Latin poetry, which in turn established for the generations immediately following the acceptable genres and a fashionable poetic style. The more ambitious or innovative writers had to break with this, if something new and valuable was to be achieved in Latin poetry. This is not a criticism of Callimachus himself or his earlier Roman imitators, such as Propertius, who had transformed to their own purposes his precepts and practice and had succeeded in providing Rome with enduring classics. It is to accept the fact that the progress of literature necessitates change and renovation, not mechanical imitation. However sublime the poetry of Dryden and Pope, the Romantic movement (or something like it) was necessary for English poetry to rescue it forcibly from the epigoni of Pope; just as Pound and other modernists had to break the Georgian mold. Persius' prologue and his first programmatic satire, taken along with all the other evidence, provides our proof that neo-Callimacheanism, in the broad sense, was the dominant poetic mode among Neronian poets and poetasters, but it was not to every taste.

A growing dislike and disapproval of much of what Callimachus stood for is easily documented. The learned and scholarly bent of the Alexandrian schoolmaster, whether deployed in his

14. Pfeiffer (1965) fr. 85.

poetry or even in his specifically literary criticism, offended some of his detractors. Lucian, somewhat later than the period under discussion, compares Callimachus, Euphorion, and Parthenius most unfavorably with Homer. By comparison with Homer's directness, he asks, "How many lines in these others do you think it would take to get the water to Tantalus' lips or to set Ixion's wheel turning?"[15] This sort of prolixity and excess was undoubtedly a feature of post-Augustan and Neronian poetry, as is evident from the first criticism we have of one notable Callimachean verse practice—ingenious periphrases for time. The criticism occurs in Seneca's *Apocolocyntosis*, where Seneca offers us nine parodic lines of poetry to describe the date and time of Claudius' death:

> iam Phoebus breviore via contraxerat ortum
> lucis et obscuri crescebant tempora somni,
> iamque suum victrix augebat Cynthia regnum
> et deformis hiemps gratos carpebat honores
> divitis Autumni iussoque senescere Baccho
> carpebat raras serus vindemitor uvas . . .
> iam medium curru Phoebus diviserat orbem
> et propior nocti fessas quatiebat habenas
> obliquo flexam deducens tramite lucem.
>
> (2)

> Phoebus had now abridged the light's ascension,
> Shortening his road, dark Sleep his time augmenting;
> Now Cynthia's triumphs amplify her realm.
> Foul Winter plucks the crown from wealthy Fall
> And Bacchus is bade wither on the vine,
> While the tardy vintner plucks the last few grapes . . .
> The chariot of Phoebus reached mid-orbit;
> Closer to night he shook his tired reins,
> Sending the curving light down paths oblique.

Between twelve noon and one o'clock, 13 October, as he then tells us in prose.

---

15. *De conscrib. hist.* 57 = Pfeiffer (1965) fr. 78.

English literature found similar parodies congenial and Abraham Cowley offers a convenient example in *The Country Mouse*:

> It was the time, when witty poets tell,
> *That* Phoebus *into* Thetis' bosom fell:
> *She blusht at first, and then put out the light,*
> *And drew the modest Curtains of the night.*
> Plainly, the troth to tell, the Sun was set,
> When to the Town our wearied Travellers get.[16]

Periphrases for time of course go back to Homer's rosy-fingered Dawn and continue to be found in epic, Apollonius Rhodius providing many obvious examples, but these periphrases became a very elaborated device in Callimachean poetry as well as in Theocritean pastoral.[17] Seneca criticizes the practice in his *Epistulae ad Lucilium*, 122.11–14 and cites some examples from Julius Montanus, an inferior poet writing in the age of Tiberius. The most egregious examples are

> incipit ardentes Phoebus producere flammas,
> spargere se rubicunda dies; iam tristis hirundo
> argutis reditura cibos inmittere nidis
> incipit et molli partitos ore ministrat.
>
> (122.12)

> Begins now Phoebus fling his fiery flames,
> The redd'ning day to spread; now swallow sad,
> Returning to shrill nests the food to cast
> Begins, and with soft mouth divides the shares.

> iam sua pastores stabulis armenta locarunt,
> iam dare sopitis nox pigra silentia terris
> incipit . . .
>
> (122.13)

---

16. Cowley (1663) 109.

17. Cf. e.g. Pfeiffer (1965) fr. 388.9–10 (Φωκάεων μέχρις κε μένη εἰν ἁλὶ μύδρος, ἄχρι τέκη Πάλλας κῆ γάμος ᾿Αρτέμιδι . . . for never); 202.69–70, 21.2–3, 260.55–56, 177.5–8, 238.19–21, 75.10–11 (a striking image of oxen anticipating the sacrificial knife); Call. *Hymn* 4.296–97; Theocr. *Id.* 13.25–26.

> Now shepherds settled down their flocks in folds,
> Now night to drowsy earth its lazy hush
> Begins to give . . .

The prevalence of such poetic periphrases in Neronian times (and earlier) can be confirmed from the verse practice of Lucius Junius Columella Moderatus in Book 10 of his *De Re Rustica*, which was published about 63. Columella, an earnest prose writer on agriculture and kindred subjects, should not be overlooked as a witness. For his friend Publius Silvinus he cast into verse only one book of his treatise on farming, Book 10, which takes horticulture as its theme. The inspiration is Vergil's *Georgics*, and it is a reasonable assumption from the evidence that Columella, typically a moralist in his prefaces, was no literary critic and no poetic revolutionary either. He followed his model, who had followed Hesiod, and he accepted the principles of didactic verse composition as he found them, that is to say, as they would be accepted by his literate contemporaries. Certain allusions in the poem reveal these presuppositions. He begins (vv. 2–5) with echoes of Vergil's fourth *Georgic*; he professes to be taking up a task abandoned by Vergil to others. Didactic poetry, a favorite Callimachean genre, needed no defense from him, and his awareness of this is expressed in his invocation of the Pierian Muses: "Pierides *tenui* deducite *carmine* Musae" (v. 40). After this request for a *slender poetic note* Callimachean or Vergilian touches abound. Besides periphrases for time and the seasons, Columella indulges in fairly obscure mythological descriptions of constellations; he inserts a digression on the origins of man; he versifies a geographical list of places where cabbages grow; and, finally, he introduces myths or αἴτια associated with such various plants as myrrh and hyacinth.[18] The habit of giving such lists and such detailed instructions in verse is an Alexandrian resumption of Hesiodic practice in the *Eoeae* and the *Erga* and it

---

18. Some examples: time and season, 41 ff., 52 ff., 77 ff., 155 ff., 189 ff., 311 ff., 400 ff., 418 ff.; constellations, 52 ff., 78 ff., 155 ff.; the origins of man, 58 ff.; cabbages, 126 ff.; myths, 172 ff.

[83]

was well established in Latin literature by Vergil's *Georgics* and Ovid's *Ars Amatoria*, *Medicamina*, and *Metamorphoses*. Columella freely admits his debt to Vergil and thus his adherence to Callimachean principles, based on that poet's admiration for Hesiod:

> hactenus hortorum cultus, Silvine, docebam,
> siderei vatis referens praecepta Maronis,
> qui primus veteres ausus recludere fontes
> Ascraeum cecinit Romana per oppida carmen.
>
> (433–36)

> Thus far I have been giving instruction, Silvinus, on the care of gardens, recalling the precepts of the heavenly bard, Vergil, who first dared to open up the old springs and sang his Ascraean poem through the Roman towns.

The significance of Columella's writing lies in his automatic assumption that his enterprise and his manner of undertaking it are perfectly proper and acceptable. He apologizes for the quality of his poetry, but not for its form, structure, or stylistic adornments. He provides therefore unselfconscious evidence for the standard poetic mode of the Neronian period. Calpurnius Siculus' practice supports the contention: periphrases for time are particularly common in his *Eclogue* 5, a sort of Shepherds' Almanac, quite similar to Columella's Gardener's Handbook, but they recur elsewhere in his work.

Seneca's strictures in the *Apocolocyntosis*, then, are well founded. Such verse practices had become a tired, and tiring, mannerism that was flourishing unchecked among pre-Neronian and Neronian poetasters. Seneca's criticism, however, is mild by comparison with the invectives launched elsewhere against Callimachus' learned ingenuity. In his near-contemporary *Garland* Philip of Thessalonica derides the followers of Callimachus for their acrid pedantry and obscure enquiries; he describes them as "Super-Callimachuses." The same charge is found in Antiphanes, who denounces the meddlesome tribes of grammarians, the dry and bitter "hounds of Callimachus," who ruin the poets they discuss. Similarly, those who write learned and convoluted poetry (obviously Callimachus and his followers) are attacked by Antipater of Thessalonica, who speaks disparagingly of "water drinkers," an allusion to the well-known Callimachean (and Pindaric) motif. This earlier dislike of philological learning continues to surface in the poetry of the Neronian epigrammatist, Lucillius, who would bar philology from his banquets, another corroboration of the growing animus against the Alexandrian polymaths. Further evidence is furnished by Lucillius' harsh reference to τοῖς ἀπ' Ἀριστάρχου γραμματολιϰριφίσιν, oblique grammarians from the school of Aristarchus, who expound the puzzles in Homer. That this is not just a reference to prosaic philological discussion but is also aimed at learned and discursive poetry is evident from the description ἀοιδομάχοις λογολέσϰαις and from another Lucillian epigram attacking a Roman writer for his boring elegies and threnodies.[19]

This unmistakable association of Callimachus with the scholarly tradition, with dry-as-dust learning, and thus with remoteness from life, was bound to affect the estimate of *both* aspects of Callimachus' creative activity. Unlike A. E. Housman, Callimachus displayed his erudition in both his art and his scholarship.

Why did Lucillius and others dislike Callimachus and, by implication, his contemporary epigoni? Part of the reason is that Callimachus was a very different kind of poet. Lucillius goes in for point, exaggeration, and paradox in his epigrams, not for elaborate language or learning; his practice had in turn a great effect on Martial, who has more or less defined *our* notion of an epigrammatist. The coldness toward Callimachus seen in Martial would partly derive from Lucillius, although the general tendencies of Roman literature in his time—the fondness for rhetorical point especially—obviously had something to do with it. In this reaction, any appreciation of the radicalism of Calli-

19. See *AP* 11.321, 347 (Philip); *AP* 11.322 (Antiphanes); *AP* 11.20 (Antipater); *AP* 11.140, 135 (Lucillius).

[85]

machus' poetic theory, which had so affected his early Roman imitators and indeed colors any appreciation of Callimachus' sophistication and novelty, was naturally lost. After all, parody of Alexandrian poetic modes had begun not long after the great age of Callimacheanism in Rome. The pseudo-Vergilian *Moretum* and *Culex*, for example, are parodies of this type, and they are not dissimilar in form from the contemporary parody of Vergil's first *Eclogue* in Numitorius' *Antibucolica*.[20]

This reaction to Callimachus as too learned and scholarly is comparatively limited and superficial. The Greek and Roman epigrammatists of the time wanted more directness, simplicity, and point, but the influence of Alexandrianism or neo-Callimacheanism was still broadly pervasive in the other poetic productions of the Neronian era.

Although the two genres so far discussed, didactic and pastoral, met with Callimachus' approval, they were not at the core of the Callimachean poetic as interpreted by Catullus' contemporaries and the later elegists. For our purposes, closer to the heart of the matter (at least in the Neronian context) is the ironic allusion in Petronius' *Satyricon* to one of Callimachus' best-known poems, the *Hecale*. The Circe episode, where the ironic allusion occurs, is amusingly down-to-earth, occasionally obscene, and mockingly romantic. The humorous sentimental effect is achieved by erotic allusions to the classics—to Lucretius, Vergil, and Ovid.[21] Then, in describing in exotic and elaborate detail the humble room and paltry furnishings of Oenothea, the priestess of Priapus, Petronius compares it to the poverty-stricken abode of Theseus' saintly hostess Hecale, as described by Callimachus:

> qualis in Actaea quondam fuit hospita terra
> digna sacris Hecale, quam Musa sequentibus annis
> Battiadae veteris miranda tradidit arte.
>
> (*Sat.* 135.8)

---

20. See Ross (1975b) 235; Morel (1975) 104.
21. Cp. e.g. *Sat.* 128.6 and Lucr. 4.962–1036, 131.7 and Ov. *AA* 3.662, 132.11 with the conflated quotations from Verg. *Aen.* 6.469 f., 9.436 and *Ecl.* 5.16.

It might have been Hecale on Attic soil long ago, that saintly hostess, whom the Muse of old Callimachus with his wond'rous art
described for the ages to come.[22]

The first line echoes the opening of the *Hecale*: 'Ακταίη τις ἔν-
αιεν Ἐρεχθέος ἐν ποτε γουνῷ, and the allusion *digna sacris* seems
a reference to the ending of Callimachus' poem, where Theseus
sets up a cult in Hecale's honor.[23]
This reference is not uncomplimentary and its aptness suggests that Petronius was familiar with the poem itself, although
it by no means follows that Petronius saw himself as a writer in
the Callimachean style. Petronius is rather alluding to a cur-
rently accepted classic for his own literary and comic purposes
and elsewhere shows himself, in taste, if not in practice, a literary traditionalist. Indeed, his critique of Lucan's *Pharsalia*, insofar as it was not dictated by political considerations, was simply
a pro-Vergilian attack on Lucan's elimination of divine machinery and his excessive reliance on historical facts, subtly dis-
torted, to convey his Republican vision of the Civil War. There
is no suggestion that old-fashioned epic per se is a questionable
poetic form, which might follow from an appreciation of Callimachus' importance. Petronius' use of Callimachus, therefore,
is simply confirmation that the *Hecale* was an accepted, or at
least not unfamiliar, classic in Nero's time.
To strengthen the hypothesis that neo-Callimacheanism, an
influence soon to be diminished in extant Latin literature, was
the dominant poetic mode in Neronian literary circles, our prize
witness must be Persius, but some documentation of Nero's own
literary tastes and those of his cronies is a necessary preliminary.
It was suggested earlier that the *Ilias Latina* was a contribution
to the poetic activity of Nero's literary circle and that its most
likely author was Silius Italicus. Silius, it will be remembered,

22. The actual text is corrupt: Battiadae veteris *Sambucus duce Iunio*: Baccineas
veteres *vel sim. codd.* miranda arte *Fuchs* mirando aero *codd.*
23. Pfeiffer (1965) *ad* fr. 230. It should be noted that the description of Oenothea's
dwelling and the whole episode contains also reminiscences of the Baucis and Philemon episode in Ovid's *Metamorphoses* (8.629–94).

[87]

was consul in 68, an energetic and loyal prosecutor of Nero's enemies, and thereafter an able governor of Asia, who perhaps resuscitated his earlier enthusiasm for poetry in order to live down his discredited record in Neronian times and avoid further political vicissitudes.[24] The poem itself, however, irrespective of its authorship, sheds some illumination on the literary predilections of its age.

The *Ilias Latina* is only 1,070 lines long, but it enjoyed considerable popularity in antiquity and the Middle Ages; after all, it outlasted both Lucan's *Iliacon* and Nero's *Troica*. As in Petronius' *Troiae Halosis*, the pace of the action accelerates and events are more scantily treated as the narrative moves along. The first 537 lines cover the first five books of the *Iliad* and the remaining nineteen books are summarized in 533 lines with drastic curtailments of the Homeric story. Many of the battle scenes disappear, along with such famous episodes as the Τειχοσκοπία and the Διὸς ἀπάτη. Alexandrian influence may be detected in the portrayal of Odysseus in his post-Homeric role as a swindler and the refusal of Hector to fight with Ajax because the Greek is the son of Hector's abducted aunt Hesione. Most notable perhaps is the Roman poet's treatment of Hector's funeral. Homer's somber and dignified description of the rites is passed over in favor of a short, pathetic scene in which Andromache attempts *suttee*, trying to throw herself and Astyanax on the burning pyre (1057 ff.).

There are other Alexandrian emphases and interests, more reminiscent of Apollonius Rhodius, Vergil, and even Ovid than

24. For his career and literary tastes, see Pliny *Ep.* 3.7, whose description of his work (*maiore cura quam ingenio*) is reminiscent of Ovid's characterization of Callimachus (note 8 above). Silius' genuine veneration for Vergil and the almost unavoidable influence of Lucan on the writing of historical epic on Roman themes posed a literary dilemma, which Silius solved by rejecting Lucan's abandonment of divine machinery, while embracing his devotion to Republican *virtus*. It must be acknowledged that the preemption of the founding of Rome and the destruction of the Republic by the two greatest Latin poets of the century left him but little choice of subject. Ennius, living too near the times, had only skimmed the poetic possibilities of the Punic Wars in *Annales* 8 and 9 and the historical significance of the conflict with Carthage had been retrospectively magnified by Vergil, Livy, and Horace.

of Homer. The archaic springs of epic action in the *Iliad*, knightly pride, outraged honor, and the self-respect of the warrior are replaced by the elegiac squabbling over lost paramours between two powerful, love-smitten heroes. The focus is on passion rather than on valor.[25]

If this fairly elaborate essay in the narrative epyllion is typical of the young poets around Nero, it will not be remarkable to find the emperor's own poetry predominantly Neoteric and so ultimately Callimachean in inspiration. Another convincing, because hostile, witness is Martial, who describes Nero's poems as *carmina docta*—*doctus* being a key word in Neoteric circles and one that kept its critical implications into the next century. Martial further testifies in this passage (8.70.7–8) that Nero had hailed Nerva as the Tibullus of his age, presumably on the basis of his elegies. And one of the few sure lines of Nero's that survives, thanks to Seneca, is *colla Cytheriacae splendent agitata columbae* (fr. 2, Morel [1975]). This line with its Greek adjective and chiastic deployment of nouns and modifiers, a variant (*ABaB*) of "the golden line," provides a further argument for the emperor's neo-Callimacheanism. (It would not be enough to confirm it, except for those who detect the same sonorousness in the verses quoted by Persius and examined later.)

Callimachus, moreover, had written a light court poem on the Lock of Berenice, deftly translated into Latin by Catullus and later to be parodied by Pope in *The Rape of the Lock*. An outré subject, we might think, had not Statius, another admirer of Callimachus, obligingly written a commissioned work, *Capilli Flavi Earini*, on the dedication of the curls of Domitian's favorite to the Temple of Aesculapius at Pergamum. Nero's effusion on Poppaea Sabina's amber hair fits appropriately into this context.[26]

25. This alone should cast doubt on Plessis's theory that the paraphrase came from the pen of a schoolmaster (see note 34, Chapter 1). The authoritative critical evaluation of the *Ilias Latina* is to be found in Clarke (1980) 20.

26. Plin. *NH* 37.3.12; cf. Call. fr. 110 (Pfeiffer 1965); Cat. 66; Stat. *Silv*. 3.4. Statius invokes Philitas, Callimachus, Propertius, Ovid, and Tibullus in his *Epithalamium* for Stella (*Silv*. 1.2.252–55). The Elder Papinius was an expert on Callima-

Callimachus has left us a collection of *Hymns*: Nero delivered and presumably composed a hymn to the sea divinities, Amphitrite and Poseidon, and a short song to Melicerta and Leucothea, the sea nymphs, both to inaugurate his soil breaking for the proposed Corinth canal.[27] He had written a poem on chariot racing in which he had criticized King Mithridates for introducing the ten-horse chariot race, although he himself entered that contest at Olympia (Suet. *Nero* 24). It is quite likely that this was an etiological poem, again a Callimachean genre. His humorous and erotic verses followed the tradition honored by Catullus and Tibullus, not to mention the Younger Pliny and a great many other Roman worthies.[28] We cannot determine the poetic form or style of Nero's thanksgiving poem on the collapse (without casualties) of a theatre in Naples after he had given a performance there, but his *probrosa carmina* against Afranius Quintianus and Clodius Pollio and his poetic attacks on Lucan and others[29] would not contradict the evidence for his Callimachean tendencies; Callimachus' prologue to the *Aetia* and the *Ibis* (attributed to Ovid) are similar examples of verse invective.

One aspect of Callimachean theory exemplified in the *Hecale* is the predilection for the obscurer aspects of epic myth. The *Hecale*, in dealing with one of Theseus' labors, as we noticed earlier, does not concentrate on the main story but elaborates instead on a minor feature of it, Theseus' encounter with Hecale, just as the loss of Hylas, not the recovery of the Golden Fleece, can be made the central topic of a poem based on the myth of the Argonauts. The Alexandrian aspect of Nero's own

---

chus (*Silv.* 5.3.156–57: *tu pandere doctus / carmina Battiadae latebrasque Lycophronis atri*). Papinius had served in the armies of Nero and, in view of the prizes he had won in various contests in Greece, he would have merited a place in Nero's entourage on his visit to Greece in 66.

27. Ps-Lucian, *Nero* 23; for the circumstances, see Wiseman (1978) 48; (1979) 505. Possible oblique allusions to the projected Corinth canal are more common in Neronian literature than has been noticed. To the reference in Seneca's *Medea* (35–36), on which see Calder (1976a) 28, add Pseudo-Seneca, *Hercules Oetaeus* 82 ff., Seneca, *Hercules Furens* 336, and Lucan, *Phars.* 1.100 ff.

28. Suet. *Nero* 42: *iocularia in defectionis duces carmina*; Mart. 9.26.10: *lascivum opus*; cf. Plin. *Ep.* 5.3.6.

29. Tac. *Ann.* 15.34, 15.49; Suet. *Dom.* 1.

verse can be similarly detected in at least one motif of his *Troica*. According to Servius (*ad Aen.* 5.370), Nero makes Paris not the uxorious weakling of the *Iliad* but the strongest champion of the Trojans. Clad in rustic disguise, he even defeats Hector at wrestling in the Trojan games. Nero may have got the idea from Euripides' *Alexandros*, but this unexpected and recherché story is very much in the spirit of Callimachus. Nero even refused to follow the Vergilian transfer of these games to the tomb of Hector and apparently was avoiding standard epic themes of the sort Callimachus had condemned. Again, the introduction of a little-known king of Troy, Cynthius, into the poem may be another sign of his Neoteric affiliations; Nero's "epic" might well be a Callimachean antiepic.[30] The scholiast on Lucan 3.261 quotes three lines which, if genuine, might very well belong to Book 1 of the *Troica*:

> quique pererratam subductus Persida Tigris
> deserit et longo terrarum tractus hiatu
> reddit quaesitas iam non quaerentibus undas.
> (fr. 1 Morel [1975])

And the river Tigris is led away and abandons Persia through which it once wandered and, drawn by the long fissure in the land, returns the waters once desired to people who no longer desire them.

The geographical detail here is typically Alexandrian.[31] And it is presumably this work that is so extravagantly and sarcastically praised in the first *Einsiedeln Eclogue* as superior to the epics of Homer and Vergil (vv. 39 ff.). If, however, Nero did actually recite passages from it describing the capture and firing of Troy during the disastrous conflagration of Rome in 64, the lines presumably came from near the end of the work. It is tempting to speculate that Nero chose Paris as his "hero" because he would reflect the paradoxes of Nero's own character with its combina-

30. For Cynthius, cf. Hyg. *Fab.* 91; 273.12. On the possible ambiguity of Callimachus' attitude to epic and the latent concept of "antiepic," see Klein (1974) 217.
31. See Ross (1969) 95.

tion of sensual living and careful training, its passion for the stage and the arts, and its equally Hellenic fondness for chariot racing and wrestling. The last might explain the depiction of Paris in the poem as a mighty wrestler.

The most decisive evidence, of course, for the Callimachean affiliation is the fact that Nero wrote a poem, performed on the lyre in 59 at the *Iuvenalia* and entitled *Attis* or *The Bacchantes*.[32] This leads us directly to Persius' first satire and the prologue to his collection.

The most devastating rejection of Callimacheanism in the poetry of the Neronian age, not surprisingly, takes a Callimachean form in Persius' choliambic prologue to his satires. The *recusatio*, the refusal to write certain sorts of poetry, was a prominent feature of the Callimachean heritage and the variety of its manifestations in Augustan literature is too familiar to summarize here.[33] Persius, in reacting against what he construed as a decadent Callimacheanism, a reaction he shared with Martial and Juvenal, took his stance in a fresh handling of the poet's "apology," the form in which Callimachus and his imitators had frequently expounded their literary principles. Here is Persius' compact introduction to his satires:

> nec fonte labra prolui caballino
> nec in bicipiti somniasse Parnaso
> memini, ut repente sic poeta prodirem.
> Heliconidasque pallidamque Pirenen
> illis remitto quorum imagines lambunt
> hederae sequaces; ipse semipaganus
> ad sacra vatum carmen adfero nostrum.
> quis expedivit psittaco suum "chaere"
> picamque docuit nostra verba conari?
> magister artis ingenique largitor
> venter, negatas artifex sequi voces.
> quod si dolosi spes refulserit nummi,

---

32. Dio 62.20: ἐκιθαρῴδησε τε Ἄττιν τινὰ ἢ Βάγχας.
33. See Wimmel (1960) passim.

corvos poetas et poetridas picas
cantare credas Pegaseium nectar.

(Prologus)

A paraphrase will bring out Persius' meaning best:

I don't recollect sloshing my lips in the nag's fountain on Helicon
[like Propertius, cf. 3.3.51–52] nor sleeping on two-headed Parnassus [like Ennius], following in the steps of Homer and Hesiod,
so that I suddenly turn out a poet like this. The Pierian Muses on
Helicon and Pegasus' fountain with its sickly water I leave to our
Roman aristocrats and court. I am little more than a plain, blunt
man, as I bring my poetic works to the altar of those who proclaim themselves bards [such as Propertius, cf. 4.6.1 ff.]. But,
speaking of imitators, who set up the parrot with his "Bonjour!"
and taught the magpie to try human speech? That master of arts,
that bestower of genius, the belly, ingenious at pursuing verbal
talents denied it. For if the hope of deceitful coin glitters, you'd
believe that crows were poets, magpies poetesses, and both were
producing songs full of the nectar of poetic inspiration.

The point Persius is making is that modern poets are in busi-
ness because it is a way to social and material advancement, to
patronage by the emperor or by the rich. The first satire will
make it clear that Persius is not of this number nor does he hope
to be. It is highly unlikely that Persius, even ironically, includes
himself in the number of those driven to artistic endeavors by
their greed. But before attacking the *motives* of contemporary
poetasters, he specifies the artistic forms they most frequently
employ: epic, in the reference to Parnassus, and elegy or similar
forms, in the allusion to Helicon. The more Callimachean forms
he pillories in *Satire* 1, and his own distaste for epic he makes
clear in the opening parody and critical reflections of *Satire* 5
(vv. 1 ff.). Callimachus, the poetic revolutionary, had made clear
his hostility to epic, and was followed in this by Roman imitators, such as Propertius. Now in turn Callimacheanism had become outmoded and lifeless as a way of writing poetry, even in
its falsely modest and self-deprecatory forms. The Neoterics,

[93]

particularly Catullus, had been proud of their trifles (*nugae*), but Persius attacks these too in *Satire* 5:

> non equidem hoc studeo, pullatis ut mihi nugis
> pagina turgescat dare pondus idonea fumo.
>
> (19–20)

This is not my aim: to have my page swell with pretentious trifles, writing that can give weight to smoke.

Despite their elaborate art, which produces a false impression of seriousness disguised as levity, contemporary productions of this sort are ultimately *trifling*, which is of course to turn back on the Neoterics their own mock-modesty as a weapon.

The whole of Persius' *Satire* 1 is to be interpreted as an attack on contemporary poetry, which Persius sees as reflecting contemporary morality, and both are bad. We may for the nonce concede to Persius, along with a great number of ancient and modern thinkers, that men and women are generally wicked in all periods. We may even concede the much more dubious proposition that bad writing reflects bad morals, despite Hilaire Belloc's quip that "his sins were scarlet, but his books were read."[34] With these concessions, *Satire* 1 and indeed the whole oeuvre exemplifies the proper art form that Persius proposes to practice in the place of the despised and decadent genres current in his day. He is advocating the non-Alexandrian genre of *satura*, which is totally native and Roman:[35] Persius' quotation from his predecessor Lucilius at the opening of his first satire ("o curas hominum, quantum est in rebus inane!") and the Horatian allusions in the fifth satire serve to confirm this. Satire could now stand on its own feet as an art form. Its apologies for its lowly lan-

---

34. Belloc, of course, is not the latest in the line of those who subscribe to the opposite romantic illusion that all great artists must be morally or physically flawed or contrive their own ruin through syphilis, drink, drugs, or burning the candle at both ends in some way or another.

35. Quint. *Inst.* 10.1.93: *satura quidem tota nostra est*. I interpret this disputed sentence as meaning not only is satire a specifically Roman genre, but also it is one in which Roman writers excel. For a defense of this view, see Sullivan (1972a) 233.

guage, like the apologies of the Neoterics and the elegists, fulfill the same function of disguising thinly and formally its serious claims; these in turn are supported by scathing attacks on traditional epic, tragedy, and also the favored Callimachean genres.

What is Persius attacking? Why does he wish to dethrone current literary modes, even if only a few cognoscenti will appreciate what he is doing? Focus for a moment on just one word in this first satire: *Appennino* (v.95), an example of the notorious Neoteric double spondee. The use of *Appenninus* is found in earlier authors,[36] but where is it found in Neronian literature? In Lucan 2.396, Petronius *BC* 279 (where the latter seems to be deliberately echoing Lucan), and, finally, in this hostile and satiric context. The Neoteric vocabulary was still being used by Roman poets, even in serious works such as epic, and the reiteration of the word in Lucan and Petronius authenticates the picture that Persius offers us of the literary situation around 60 and after. Contemporary poetic effusions were, to his jaundiced eyes, an *olla podrida* of neo-Callimachean trifling:

> . . . ecce inter pocula quaerunt
> Romulidae saturi quid dia poemata narrent.
> hic aliquis, cui circum umeros hyacynthina laena est,
> rancidulum quiddam balba de nare locutus
> Phyllidas, Hypsipylas, vatum et plorabile siquid,
> eliquat ac tenero subplantat verba palato.
>
> (1.30–35)

. . . Look, the bloated Roman milords over their glasses ask what deathless poetry has to say. Here someone with a hyacinth shawl round his shoulders lisps some rotten trifle through his nose: a Phyllis, a Hypsipyle, or some elegiac frettings and decants the words against his tender palate.

Persius is inveighing against the modish dilettantism of the court and other high circles, a literary dilettantism that is on a par with the prevalent snobbish practices of high living—one

---

36. In Cornelius Severus, *ap.* Morel (1975) 118; Hor. *Carm.* 16.29; Ov. *Met.* 2.226.

remembers Petronius' expensive fluorspar wine dipper and Otho's lavish unguents for the feet of his dinner guests. Persius is also specifying the poetic forms common at these after-dinner recitals. Although the reference to *Phyllidas* may be overdetermined by the appearance of *Phyllis* in pastoral poetry (e.g. in Calpurnius Siculus), the elegiac reference to *Phyllidas* and *Hypsipylas* probably derives from Ovid's elegiac *Heroides* (2 and 6). Persius is perhaps glancing at the lamenting heroine in general (Catullus' Ariadne, for example, and Ovid's *Ciris*). The satirist's animosity toward elegy (*vatum et plorabile siquid*) is in any case unmistakable.[37] Elegy was an Alexandrian and a Callimachean specialty, according to Quintilian (*Inst.* 10.1.58), and *vatis* was a description Propertius usurped proudly for himself.[38] Persius continues the attack on elegy later with his reference (v. 51) to the *elegidia*, the pathetic little elegies, which the *haut monde* dictates on a full stomach. The importance of the genre in Callimachean and neo-Callimachean poetics had been strongly reinforced in Latin literature by Gallus, Tibullus, Propertius, and Ovid, to name only the classics. Persius' hostility toward neo-Callimacheanism naturally commandeers such critically related watchwords as *mollis* and *tener*, ambiguous adjectives, easily milked for their underlying moral connotations. Such words had been used by Propertius and the others, in barely veiled defiance, to express adherence to Callimachean theory; the undertones of effeminacy and literary decadence remained for satiric exploitation. Persius objects that the same decadent and empty style is regarded as suitable for themes requiring the utmost poetic seriousness:

> sive opus in mores, in luxum, in prandia regum
> dicere, res *grandes* nostro dat Musa poetae.
> ecce modos heroas sensus adferre docemus
> *nugari solitos Graece.*
>
> (1.67–70)

37. The line has echoes of Horace's dismissal of elegy at *Carm.* 1.33.2–3 (*miserabiles elegi*) and 2.9.9 (*flebiles modi*).

38. Prop. 4.6; for its developing connotations see Newman (1967) passim.

Or if there's a demand for work on morals, luxury, or aristocratic gluttony, then the Muse gives our poet *weighty* subjects for his verses. Lo, now, *used only to Greek trifling*, we teach the use of heroic sentiments.

And Persius goes on to point out that the poets he refers to refuse even to write on traditional Roman themes.[39]

A slighting reference follows to the admirers of archaic Roman poets, such as Accius, Pacuvius, and the tragedians. Like one of his models, Horace, Persius objects to the persistent fashion for archaic writing, a taste not incompatible with the neo-Callimacheanism that is his main target. Horace had similar objections to his contemporary neo-Callimacheans and to the archaizers, with whom he associates them.[40] Persius' imaginary interlocutor at this point takes up the cudgels for modernism:

> 'sed numeris decor est et iunctura addita crudis.
> cludere sic versum didicit "Berecyntius Attis"
> et "qui caeruleum dirimebat Nerea delphin,"
> sic "costam longo subduximus Appennino."
> "Arma virum," nonne hoc spumosum et cortice pingui
> ut ramale vetus vegrandi subere coctum?'
>
> (1.92–97)

A paraphrase would run as follows:

> 'But don't you see that in modern poetry elegance and smoothness have been imposed upon our rude versification. We've learnt to finish a line with "Berecynthian Attis" and "the dolphin that cleaved the blue Nereus" and "we removed a rib from the long Apennines." "Arms and the Man," isn't this frothy and thick-skinned, like an old branch covered with insubstantial cork?'

And he continues with further modern examples of technique:

39. Cf. Verg. *Aen.* 6.179 ff. and Norden's edition ad loc.; Lucr. 3.390 ff.; Prop. 4.4.3 ff.; Hor. *AP* 16; Petr. *BC*; Sen. *Oed.* 530 ff.; Sil. 6.146 ff.; Juv. 1.7. Usually these descriptions are preceded by formulas such as *est locus.* . . .
40. Cf. Hor. *Sat.* 1.10.15 ff. and Brink (1963) 165.

'torva Mimalloneis inplerunt cornua bombis,
et raptum vitulo caput ablatura superbo
Bassaris et lyncem Maenas flexura corymbis
euhion ingeminat, reparabilis adsonat echo.'

(99–102)

'They filled their menacing horns with Mimallonian boomings;
and the Bassarid ready to carry away the head torn from a proud
calf and the Maenad ready to guide the lynx with reins redouble
their "Euhio!" An echo renews the sounds.'

The individual faults of such modernist poetry need not be
enlarged upon here, but lest it be thought that Persius was only
a voice crying in the literary wilderness, we should adduce further evidence from the contemporary writing in Greek. First
consider the epigrammatist Cerealius, who is plausibly dated to
the Neronian period.[41] He echoes precisely one thrust of Persius'
criticism. The unfamiliarity of the little piece makes it deserving
of quotation in full:

οὐ τὸ λέγειν παράσημα καὶ Ἀττικὰ ῥήματα πέντε,
    εὐζήλως ἐστὶν καὶ φρονίμως μελετᾶν.
οὐδὲ γὰρ εἰ "κάρκαιρε," καὶ εἰ "κοναβεῖ" τό τε "σίζει"
    καὶ "κελάρυζε" λέγεις, εὐθὺς Ὅμηρος ἔσῃ.
νοῦν ὑποκεῖσθαι δεῖ τοῖς γράμμασι, καὶ φράσιν αὐτῶν
    εἶναι κοινοτέραν, ὥστε νοεῖν ἃ λέγεις.

(*AP* 11.144)

To utter obscurities and five or so Attic words is not a well-directed
or sensible literary goal, not even if you say "quaketh" and
"clangeth" and "hisseth" and "gurgleth," will you be an instant
Homer. Meaning should be the foundation of writing and its lan-

---

41. For the date of Cerealius and the possible identification with Martial's friend
Julius Cerealis (Mart. 10.48; 11.52) or Pliny's friend, Velius Cerealius (*Ep.* 2.19;
4.21), see *RE* s.v. (Reitzenstein). One might add Palladas to the list of Neronian
epigrammatists on the basis of his similar criticism of the style of his day. His Had-
rianic dating is very problematic. Add also Antiphilus, Philip, and Antistius Sosianus; see Cameron (1980).

guage should be closer to common speech so that people may understand what you say.

This gives us a background for Persius' plea for the *verba togae* (5.14) and the rejection of archaism in Latin poetry also. Why archaizing was a constant temptation to both Greek and Roman poets after the Augustan age may be partly attributed to Roman traditionalism as well as to the perennial aesthetic preference for the good old days. These literary conservatives are the butt of Lucillius at *AP* 11.132, who complains how hard it is for a young poet to get a hearing. Often the evidence for this *cacoethes scribendi* is provided incidentally by these Greek epigrammatists when they are satirizing some other weakness of human nature. Particularly noticeable, in view of the contemporary interest in drama, stage recitals, and lyre performances, which ultimately stemmed from the court's cultural diversions, are the satirical comments on this *théâtromanie*. Typical targets are the singing of Demophilus, a tragic actor (Nicarchus, *AP* 11.186); the indigent tragedian Apollophanes (Lucillius, *AP* 11.189); Eutychides, the recently deceased lyric poet, who took with him to hell twelve lyres and twenty-five cases of music (Lucillius, *AP* 11.133); the large turnout of singing poets at the Isthmian and Pythian games (Cerealius, *AP* 11.129); the threat of being made the subject of a rotten drama by Melito (*drāma sapron* on Niobe, Lucillius, *AP* 11.246); and the evacuation of the town of Nauplion caused by Hegelochus, who put on such a bad performance in the singing part of Nauplius, that town's eponymous villain. Even Leonidas of Alexandria, who had written complimentary epigrams to Nero's mother Agrippina (cf. *AP* 6.329) and to the emperor himself (*AP* 6.321; 9.352), somewhat tactlessly complains of the fashion for lyre performances (*AP* 11.187).

The satirical epigrams, then, of Book 11 of the Palatine Anthology provide a good deal of evidence that Persius' views of the contemporary literary scene were shared to a large degree by Neronian epigrammatists. Lucillius directs several barbs at

[99]

bad or ignorant poets comparing them in their fatal effects to medical practitioners of the day. The symbolism of disease that runs through Persius' analysis of the contemporary situation is relevant here, as this is a major source of his imagery.[42] So Lucillius offers us the best confirmation of the literary and cultural curses of Persius' day: the poet Potamon (*AP* 11.131) is aptly so named; he and Heliodorus, the playboy of poetry (cf. Persius 1.70, *nugari solitos Graece*) and a *macrofluaretes*, a producer of long boring nonsense (*AP* 11.34), might both have stepped straight from Persius' first satire. The criticism of Roman *elegidia* there (1.51) is paralleled by Lucillius' own attack on the elegist Marcus at 11.135 and, more generally, at 11.136 where there is a critique of Callistratus' hexameters.

The general target of Persius' criticism is obvious. It is the tired Grecized versification that continued to be written long after the excitement of Neoteric poetry had become mere mannerism. If Propertius was the Augustan Donne, then these lines point to a Neronian Henry Vaughan or Abraham Cowley. But is it possible to be more specific about the victim of these satiric darts?

Commentators are sometimes willing to trust scholiasts on unimportant matters, but often reject their evidence when it seems too good to be true. The *Vita Persi* clearly states that Persius *did* attack Nero:

> lecto Lucili libro decimo vehementer saturas componere instituit cuius libri principium imitatus est, sibi primo, mox omnibus detrectaturus cum tanta recentium poetarum et oratorum insectatione, ut etiam Neronem illius temporis principem inculpaverit. (51–56 Clausen)

> After reading Book 10 of Lucilius he began furiously to compose satires and imitated the opening of Lucilius' tenth book. His aim was to criticize first himself, then everybody, along with such an assault on contemporary poets and orators that he even castigated Nero, the emperor at that time.

42. Bramble (1974) 35.

[100]

Similarly, the *scholia antiqua* (ed. Jahn) allege that there are quotations from Nero's verses between vv.93 and 102 of Persius' first satire. Nor does the scholiast tell us merely once of Persius' quoting Nero. He informs us that the poet inserts bombastic endings used by Nero and he then attributes the four quoted lines to the emperor.[43] It is true that the scholia add a further explanation, namely, that Persius invented the verses in this form to imitate other poets of the age and make his critical point more directly: that contemporary verse sounds impressive but means nothing.[44] But, as elsewhere in the scholia, of two explanations offered, the second is not necessarily the truer or the more convincing. The problem is how to extract what grains of truth there may be, however crushed, in the mélange that has come down to us posing as elucidation of the complex satires of Persius.

There are in fact several pieces of evidence, particular and general, to support the tradition reported by the scholiast and at least to weaken the thesis that Persius, perhaps like Horace and Juvenal, *never* attacked a prominent personality even covertly, thus precluding any specific criticism of Nero here. When one asks why this unlikely self-denial on the part of satirists, scholars point, first of all, to the obvious danger, since the older libel laws of the Republic had now been connected with the vaguer and more serious crime of *maiestas*.[45] Then it is often argued that the development of satire since the time of Lucilius had wisely precluded significant personal denigration, partly because of the sporadic Greek tradition of avoiding individual attacks and emphasizing general vices. The prevalent opinion is "Neither Horace nor Persius nor Juvenal ever attacked an eminent contemporary, either by name or by unmistakable innuendo."[46]

43. See v. 93: *et dicit his versus Neronis in haec nomina desinentes*; and vv.99–102: *hi sunt versus Neronis et huic sunt compositi.*

44. *ipse autem Persius finxit hos versus, velut alii dicunt, in aliorum imitationem, quorum scripta sonum grandem habent sensum nullum.*

45. See Smith (1951) 169; Bauman (1962) 246; Williams, *OCD*² s.v. *Libel, Laws of.*

46. Kenney (1962) 36; for similar views, most recently, Bramble (1974) 128.

What are the credentials of the scholia that run counter to this modern view? One would here point to certain nuggets of information which seem to belong to a source or sources of genuine information about the literature of the Neronian age.

For instance, Σ *ad* 1.121–23 correctly preserves the information that Nero wrote a *Troicon*, because it is confirmed by Servius *ad Aen.* 5.370. Persius in these lines claims that he would not exchange his humorous secret even for an *Iliad*. The scholiast glosses this with *hoc carmen meum . . . non tibi dabo si mihi Iliada Labeonis aut Neronis Troicon tradas. scripsit enim Nero Troicon.* Persius' reference to an *Iliad* is vague and the scholiast may be making only inferences and guesses here, as he does later, in commenting insipidly on v.128. The scholia, however, do support the view that Persius in his first satire went after Nero directly, as an example—a corrupting example—of decadent neo-Callimacheanism. A further trace of this interpretation may perhaps be found in the glosses on *Callirhoen* (v.135). Of the three explanations, the second is that Callirhoe was a nymph who consorted with Paris before his entanglement with Helen and subsequently bemoaned his infidelity. This might have been a minor and obscure motif in Nero's *Troicon*; his hero Paris is still a shepherd when he comes to Troy to defeat Hector at wrestling and be recognized. It is, of course, not unlikely that an ignorant commentator confused Callirhoe, daughter of the River Scamander and wife of Tros (Apollod. 3.12.1), with Oenone, daughter of the River Cebren and Paris' first "wife" (ibid. 3.12.6).

Juxtapose with all this Dio's evidence (62.20) that Nero gave at the *Ludi Iuvenales* a performance with his own lyre accompaniment of a composition which had some such title as *Attis* or *Bacchantes* (Ἄττιν τινὰ ἢ Βάγχας) and then consider the relevant lines of Persius:

summa delumbe saliva
hoc natat in labris, et in udo est, Maenas et Attis.
(1.104–5)

This enervated thing, this *Maenad* and *Attis*, swims on the lips, on top of the spittle and stays in the wet.

There is a proverbial connotation of *in labris* and *summis labris* with inexperience and a lack of deep knowledge.[47] Persius is insisting that compositions such as *Attis* (or *The Maenads*) are effeminate and superficial, all too easy to toss off and completely lacking in real poetic or moral expertise. He has earlier quoted (or composed) seven whole or part lines, most of which would appropriately belong to a poem on the subject of Attis. Not unexpectedly, Maenads and Bassarids figure prominently: *Berecyntius Attis* precedes *Bassaris et lyncem Maenas flexura corymbis*.

It is precisely at this point that opinions become divided as to whether the scholiast is right in claiming that these verses are really the emperor's own.[48] The probability that they are actually by Nero is higher than modern critics allow. As for the danger of such open quotations or allusions, are they any more dangerous than the contemptuous condemnation of a poem with a title curiously similar to that of a composition the emperor had performed at a thronged public performance less than three years before, and perhaps even more recently than that? A similar thrust at Nero may be detected in v. 128 (*et lusco qui possit dicere "lusce"*), since Nero had written a satire entitled *Luscio* against the ex-praetor Clodius Pollio (Suet. *Dom.* 1). The theme of Attis had been handled by Catullus, whether or not his galliambics are a translation of a Greek original, and it would therefore seem to be a typically Neoteric subject, because Attis is associated with Cybebe or Cybele, who is, in Catullus' phrase, *Dindymi domina*, and *Magna Mater*, the subject of a poem by Catullus' associate Caecilius.[49] She was a Dionysian figure, partly because of her

47. Cf. Cic. *ND* 1.8.20; *Cael.* 12.28; Sen. *Ep.* 10.3; Lact. *Inst.* 3.16.4.
48. O. Jahn and earlier editors of Persius believed they were genuine; Conington (1874) mentions the attribution without pronouncing one way or the other. The most recent commentator, Bramble (1974) 126, takes them as typical of contemporary poetry in general, accepting the scholiast's second explanation of the verse in conformity with the general thesis that specific and direct attacks were eschewed.
49. Cat. 63 (Attis); 35.14, 18 (Cybele).

syncretistic identification with Rhea; she was attended by Thraco-Phrygian Corybants and her car was drawn by lions, an avatar reminiscent of Dionysus in his lynx-drawn car, attended by throngs of Maenads, Bassarids, or Bacchantes.[50] Catullus himself sets Maenads in attendance on Cybebe in his Attis poem (63.23). It would seem that the two orgiastic cults had become fused, if not confused, in later mythology and poetry.

It is a reasonable inference, then, from the alternative titles given by Dio, that in Nero's retelling of the Attis legend a company or chorus of Bacchantes played a conspicuous part and that Persius is openly alluding to these in his choice of the more memorable (or notorious) lines to criticize, lines that are attributed to Nero by the scholiast. A belief in mere coincidence of subject becomes at this point strained. There are no other known examples in Neronian poetry of such Bacchic themes and it is quite likely that Nero looked back to Catullus as one of his chief models. The poem on Poppaea's hair, had it survived, might have provided further evidence, linking itself with Callimachus and Catullus through their common subject, the Lock of Berenice. It is therefore plausible to conclude that Persius selected one of Nero's best-known poems, delivered at a widely publicized festival, as his prime target and as the prime example of decadent neo-Callimachean verse practice.

It has to be remembered, of course, before we make Persius into a moral hero, that Persius' satires were not published before his death in 62; indeed it is not known at what date Caesius Bassus finally gave them to the public. If Persius intended them initially for a very small circle of friends, then he need have had few qualms about adopting the personal invective of his admired Lucillius. The theory that Persius is simply imitating the modernist style for parodic purposes is somewhat weak. "Parodier tout le monde, c'est parodier personne," as Collignon said

---

50. See Roscher (1890–1897) s.v. *Kybele (und der Dionysoskult)* and Vermaseren (1977).

in another context, and a contemporary poetaster obviously might deny the fidelity of the imitation.

Indeed, if these lines were not quotations, as in *sic arma virum* at v.96, why did not Persius indulge further this alleged gift for parody and give us something more substantial, or at least coherent, in ridiculing the modern style? Surely Persius' critical and satirical ends would be best served if he attacked the most prominent exponent of the type of poetry he denounces, particularly as Nero himself was mainly responsible for the inordinate writing activity to be seen in upper class circles at this period. Persius had earlier grumbled about this recent and inordinate wave of productivity, just as Seneca, a prominent culprit himself, complains a few years later: *litterarum intemperantia laboramus*.[51] The growth of literary circles other than Nero's would be a natural consequence of imperial encouragement and example; and the general picture of public recitals and after-dinner versifying presented in Persius' opening satire is probably little exaggerated. Whether or not the moralistic young poet was too idealistic to grasp their political significance or whether, like many Roman writers, he thought of politics in moral terms, he would have had to be blind indeed not to discern the source and center of this frenzied scribbling, reciting, and theatrical performing that involved so many of the prominent men of his day, whom he refers to contemptuously as decadent descendants of Romulus (*Romulidae*, v.31). If he wished to imitate his admired Lucilius, however small his audience must be (cf. vv.2–3), among the easiest marks would be Nero himself.

---

51. Pers. 1.13; Sen. *Ep.* 106.2. It is true that this is a familiar satiric *topos*, cf. Hor. *Ep.* 2.1.108 ff. and Juv. 1.1 ff., but satire must have some connection with reality. Augustus, a prose and verse writer himself, who attended poetry readings and even prose recitals (Suet. *Aug.* 89), was also a great patron of letters and (with Maecenas' help) must thereby have stimulated, if inadvertently, bad poets as well as such geniuses as Horace and Vergil. The justice of Juvenal's complaints about the swarm of contemporary writers is easily documented from Martial's epigrams and Pliny's Letters. Nerva and Hadrian, we know, were both poets and the connection between the reigning emperor's taste and literary predilections can hardly be coincidental in the days when a mass reading public had not come into existence.

The general skepticism about Persius' attack, by innuendo or direct quotation, on the emperor himself has been justified, as we have seen earlier, by the belief that it was extremely dangerous under a supposed tyrant such as Nero to indulge in such writing, even covertly. But the usually hostile Suetonius is also witness that Nero was unexpectedly tolerant of verbal attacks against him and his policies, at least in his earlier years as emperor.[52] There are very few cases of apparent suppression of free speech that we can point to: Antistius Sosianus was in fact praetor when in 62 he recited, or circulated, his calumnious poems against his imperial master at a crowded dinner party. Whatever the precise nature of the charge of *maiestas* laid by Cossutianus Capito, the case ended up as a confrontation between Nero and Thrasea Paetus. The details are suspicious: Nero is accused of contriving a show trial to display his clemency and is then given credit for suggesting that the senate could acquit his victim if it so wished.[53]

Another notorious case is the exile of L. Annaeus Cornutus around 65, supposedly for criticizing Nero's project for a poem on the foundation of Rome.[54] This has all the earmarks of a useful anecdote for Tacitus to illustrate Nero's sensitivity to criticism, a sensitivity Suetonius has explicitly denied. More likely explanations of his banishment are his close connection with the now suspect Thrasea Paetus and with the Annaean family and the growing association of some Stoic circles with anti-Neronian opposition and even plots.

52. Suet. *Nero* 39. Pliny's anecdote (*Ep.* 5.5.5–6) about Nero's ghost patiently reading over the charges leveled at him by C. Fannius in his catalogue of Neronian victims is worth mentioning here. For a general survey of this type of literature, see Marx (1937).

53. Tac. *Ann.* 14.48: *Antistius praetor, quem in tribunatu plebis licenter egisse memoravi, probrosa adversus principem carmina factitavit vulgavitque celebri convivio dum apud Ostorium Scapulam epulatur. exim a Cossutiano Capitone, qui nuper senatorium ordinem precibus Tigellini soceri sui receperat, maiestatis delatus est. tum primum revocata ea lex.* See Rogers (1953) 711 and (1964) 91; Bradley (1973) 172.

54. Dio 62.29.3. It should be noted, moreover, that the suggestion that Nero's historical epic on Rome should properly run to 400 books was not the emperor's own, but the proposal of sycophants. This passage suggests that the *Troicon* was now completed and Nero was looking for another ambitious subject.

In effect, the picture of the intimidation and harassment of critical writers under Nero should be radically revised. To read back into Persius' work the cautious attitudes of a Juvenal, who had lived under Domitian, is mistaken, even though the satirist and others linked the two closely.[55] Persius' model was the outspoken Lucilius and, although conditions were indeed different and more inhibiting, the case for the complete emasculation of the satirist at this time, particularly one who had no great desire for an audience other than his close friends and mentors, is weak.

It was not Lucan's *famosum carmen* or even the flagrant anti-Caesarism of the *Pharsalia* that led to his suicide, but his proven implication in the Pisonian conspiracy. Nero's supposed ban on his publication, whatever form that took in the very different literary conditions of the day, can hardly be taken seriously. The prohibition on practice in the law courts was easier to enforce. Obviously, falling into disfavor with the new emperor would not make one's private recitals popular with those still enjoying that favor or hoping to gain it. Lucan was therefore more a victim of a conspiracy of silence, or, at least, a diminished potential audience. Writers and journals in our day can suffer a similar fate and the result may be just as demoralizing as any legal censorship.[56] The ban on overt publication must have been largely ineffectual, since Petronius in his *Bellum Civile* shows knowledge of *Pharsalia* 10 as well as the first three books, which had been made available by 62.

Persius did give at least one recital, we are told; it was the occasion when Lucan applauded the superior seriousness of his poetic friend, but the *Life* does not make it clear that he was

---

55. Juvenal describes Domitian as *calvus Nero* (4.38) and it is not impossible that the antisenatorial attitudes of Domitian are attributed to Nero from the beginning rather than after 62; these were naturally reinforced by the Pisonian conspiracy and led to the consequent bloody purges.

56. *Private Eye*, a British satirical magazine, for example, is simply not stocked by the powerful W. H. Smith chain of newsagents; this hardly differs from the legal ban by the Republic of Ireland on the importation of *Playboy*. In the 1950s, McCarthyism had the same stifling effect on the writing of film scripts in the United States. It would be otiose to introduce parallels from more authoritarian or totalitarian countries or the now ineffectual *Index Librorum Prohibitorum* of the Catholic church.

reciting *any* of his satires, let alone the first. In sum, Nero was, for Persius, the most important neo-Callimachean and the most appropriate victim of his unveiled, but perhaps also unpublished, attack. To *invent* such lines would blunt his point, as the sophisticated reader could object to the caricature. Persius would have every motive to quote specific examples, just as he had quoted Lucilius at the beginning of the first satire. In any case, whether Persius is attacking Nero head-on or just parodying the *type* of poetry to be heard in aristocratic circles such as Nero's, he was clearly a resolute opponent of the epigoni of the Augustan Callimacheans. Horace's dislike and scorn of the Roman Callimachus, Propertius, was revived with even greater fervor in Persius, who added thereto a moral dimension of his own.

How is this connected with the imperial politics of the Neronian age? The issue, and the connection, is morality, which in ancient aesthetic theory was closely linked to and reflected in the character of a man's writing: in a very important sense, *le style est l'homme même!* Few would have espoused this principle more fiercely than Persius. The genesis of the theory that literature and morality are closely involved with each other, whether in society as a whole or in the relationship between an individual's character and the writing he or she produces goes back very far indeed. It was perhaps most cogently articulated, in its broader applications, by Aristophanes in the *Frogs* and Plato in the *Republic*, but for Neronian times Persius' contemporary Seneca offers a more relevant exposition of the view—a view strongly opposed, it will be remembered, by Catullus, Ovid, Pliny, and Martial, among others,[57] who all insist that, however immoral their writings may appear, their actual lives are impeccable.

Seneca expresses most succinctly the Stoic views on style and the man that would be held by Persius. In *Epistle* 114 (especially 1–3, 11–12), he argues that certain ages are characterized by the development of a corrupt style of oratory; at one time it is fulsome bombast, at another effeminate singsong rhetoric (*expli-*

---

57. See Bramble (1974) 23 for a collection of references to both viewpoints.

catio . . . infracta et in morem cantici ducta). One age favors auda-
cious exaggeration; another favors short cryptic utterances that
mean more than they say. Again, there was even a time when
metaphor was grossly abused. The answer lies in the Greek
proverb "men's speech mirrors their lives" (*talis hominibus fuit
oratio qualis vita*). Oratorical style is similarly a reflection of men's
behavior. If moral standards have slipped into degeneracy, then
style degenerates. Extravagant speech, if regarded as normal by
a community, is a sign of a generally extravagant life-style. The
intellect and the personality of a man share the same characteristics. A sound personality, stable and serious, goes along with
a temperate and sober mind. If the personality is corrupted, so
too is the intellect. If even the body is affected by the personality,
a depressed person moving slowly, an angry one quickly, how
much more so will the intellect be affected by anger, depression,
effeminacy, and similar qualities?

Seneca concludes from this logic that wherever a corrupt style
of speech is prevalent, morals must be in decline. Extravagance
in entertainment and clothing indicates an ailing society—Persius' reference to the purple cloak of a decadent aristocrat at 1.32
comes to mind here. Licentious speech also indicates the degeneracy of the minds that indulge in it. This applies to both high
and low in society.

Such sentiments provide a gloss on Persius' first satire, but
the poet's presentation of the intimate connection between life
and literature is more oblique and poetic. The interrelation of
sexual immorality, gluttony, and literary decadence is brought
out in a sequence of packed and savage images.[58] Consequently,
since Persius included in his work satire on the qualifications
necessary for a ruler, it would require little intelligence or sensitivity on Nero's part to construe correctly the literary, moral,
and personal implications for himself of Persius' work. It is this
possibility that makes Persius' attack fundamentally political. It
is the way in which modern abstract art is subject in the Soviet

58. For further analysis, Bramble (1974) 16.

Union to political restrictions, not simply to art criticism. For Persius and Nero this connection between art and the state would not seem as very strange as it does to modern bourgeois critics who espouse the doctrines of art for art's sake. An attack on Nero's art, or the art favored in court circles, was an attack on Nero's character and morals, and therefore upon his fitness to be emperor.

What finally, one asks, was the style and substance of the poetry that Persius offered to replace this decadent Callimachean trifling? And what entitles Persius to rank as a classic in the true sense, even if his reputation has varied through the ages in direct proportion to the critical comprehension extended by his readers?

Reckford, in his study of some of Persius' metaphors, offers some interesting remarks:

> The study of Persius' themes by themselves inevitably proves sterile. *Loci communes* may be dug up like carrots: what a wonderful mind Persius must have had to tell us that self-knowledge is good and flattery bad! . . . Persius characteristically thinks in concrete images, not abstract terms: thus the undesirability of flattery may be a commonplace, but the asses' ears are not. To regard his metaphors as poetic embellishment leads to an unrewarding peeling away of onionskins: those who find nothing within need blame only themselves.[59]

But this is only half of the critical story. It is true that Persius' objections to the poetry of his contemporaries is that it is tired, thoughtless, empty, and bombastic, concentrating on sound rather than imagery and the thoughtful use of language. An analogy in English literature would be the reaction of the Imagists and Modernists against Victorian and Georgian poetry. Persius was setting himself up in competition with Lucilius and Horace as a practitioner of what turned out to be one of the most vital and long-lived of Latin literary genres. (Between the birth of Lucil-

---

59. Reckford (1962) 283. A similar view is to be found in Dessen's study of the poet (1968). For a discussion of other critical viewpoints, see Sullivan (1972b) 48 and the references there.

ius and the death of Juvenal about three hundred years elapsed: erotic elegy ran its course in little over half a century.)

Persius' difficulty, even "crabbedness," is not, as some critics would have it, the result of forgetfulness, deliberate or unintentional obscurity, or the simple inability to make his verses as clear as Horace's, but rather his reasoned choice of a unique metaphorical style. This style, properly understood, and with the natural difficulties of its being in Latin rather than English discounted, should be congenial to a generation familiar with the Metaphysical poets, or at least with Donne—indeed Samuel Johnson's description of Metaphysical poetry is not inappropriate to apply to Persius: "the most heterogeneous ideas are yoked by violence together." Yet a stress on his metaphors should not hide the careful allusiveness, the subtle literary echoes of Horace, Lucretius, Lucilius, Ennius, and others, some of whom we may not recognize since the originals are no longer extant. These are set against the background of the *verba togae*, the ordinary educated Roman speech, which, in different ways and within different limits, was accepted by Lucilius and Horace as the standard medium, or rather basis, of *satura*. Persius, however, instead of accepting the smooth, polished version of the *sermo pedestris* that Horace generally employed in his *Sermones* and *Epistulae*, harked back to the freer, rougher, and more anomalous diction of Lucilius; he tried to present a contemporary equivalent of Lucilius' "improvisations" in a careful amalgam of archaisms, vulgarisms, literary allusions, the clipped affectation of real dialogue, and the homely, or sometimes vivid, language of the household and the harbor. Persius' art is, largely, a matter of language, not just a matter of abstruse philosophical content. Through this handling of language he creates a refined mode of irony which shows itself in certain delicate linguistic ways, in a sensitivity to how language is used in other contexts, and in a deployment of these other uses for its own humorous and satiric aims, in order to produce an effect directly contrary to their effect in the usual contexts. So magniloquence, as with the quotations from Nero's poetry, can be made to criticize

[111]

magniloquence, vulgarity to criticize vulgarity, and poeticisms to criticize poeticizing.

If it were merely a matter of imagery and metaphor the modern reader would have less of a struggle with Persius' language. It is his striving to make every word count, to achieve precisely the right tone, down-to-earth, archaic, pompous, or ironic, that makes his style so delicate and difficult a thing to analyze. The denseness of his verse, that is, the average number of words to the line, is significantly higher than that of most classical authors, a Lucilian characteristic also.[60] This is part of his antirhetorical critique and explains why he is so strongly opposed to the "music" of poetry, which he sees as essentially enervating and immoral, although the modern reader may not wish to follow him in this view. Such an attitude to writing accounts for his difficult sentence structure and the complexity of his language, which deliberately avoids any cheap sound effects or rhetorical figures except for parodic purposes.

From his criticism of the poetry of the court Persius' positive aims become more readily comprehensible: literary allusion (most notably to Horace); the avoidance of worn and commonplace language by deliberate archaisms, vulgarisms, or unexpected qualifiers (*iunctura*, as it were); the avoidance of hackneyed mythical themes and ornament except for satirical comment on them; and, last but not least, a highly inventive and individual style of imagery and metaphor, which is pointed up by his mockery of the traditional poetic devices.

Once modern readers can feel their way into some such reading of Persius' satires, into an appreciation of his mastery, not only of the genre but also of the Latin language, then they will be able to put aside the misleading conventional pictures of the earnest young poet or the Stoic moralist, for which, it must be acknowledged, Persius is partially responsible by his too-overt

60. Persius *Sat.* 6 and *Sat.* 1, for example, have 7.11 and 7.05 words, respectively, in the average line; Lucilius has 7.11, whereas Ovid and Vergil have 6.43 and 6.11, respectively.

linkage of art and morality in his attack on Nero's verse in particular and court poetry in general.

Thus far we may follow Reckford in his vindication of the
purely aesthetic or literary aspects of the poet's work. But one
might present just such a picture of a learned and well-read poet
in many different ages and still not account for the durability
and status of a writer who compares not unfavorably with Horace and Juvenal in the tradition of Roman satire. Although the
slogan "art for art's sake" embodies in itself an evaluation, it
leaves us uneasy if we let it stand as the final judgment on a poet
who thought of, or at least presents, himself as a moralist *toute
simple* who stands firmly opposed to that doctrine as exemplified in the musical and technical trivialities of *la poétique Néron-
ienne*. Yet we cannot accept his valuation of his oeuvre any more
than we can apply external Platonic criteria of value and adjudge
Persius as morally, if derivatively, useful and therefore good.
Neither Persius' professed intentions nor his possible improve-
ment of the morality of mankind would lift him out of the ruck
of the well-intentioned moralizers who embodied their salutory
purposes in verses that do not properly do the job their authors
intended them to do. And here Persius does excel. Conventional
and derivative though his Stoic morality may be, it is absorbed
fully and expressed convincingly in his unique language and imagery. There is never a question to be raised about the adequacy
of his medium for his purposes. It had not been done, and therefore had not been better done, before, although it or something
like it has been done differently since, and one might think here
of Boileau or Swift.

Hence Persius has survived as a *serious* poet in all the senses of
that word in a way that the poetry he attacked has not. One
brings away from him an acute sense of having encountered a
poet who is struggling, and struggling successfully, with matters of grave import to us all, and so manages to transcend the
immediate occasion of his poetry. (In the last analysis, it does
not really matter whether he quotes Nero or not in the first

satire.) For the human themes he treats are still relevant and Persius engages with them through a unique and successful style. That is why he remained a classic and a model for the serious satirists of the seventeenth and eighteenth centuries, Donne, Dryden, and Pope.[61]

61. For "seriousness" as an important criterion for classical status, see the subtle discussion in "The Definition of Literature" by Robson (1982) 1–19.

CHAPTER III

The Stoic Opposition?
Seneca and Lucan

Over a hundred years ago Gaston Boissier proposed the theory that the opposition to the emperors in the first century A.D. was predominantly led by Stoics, who were morally opposed to the principate rather than embracing a coherent political philosophy.[1] This was an exaggeration. The opposition to any Julio-Claudian emperor consisted predominantly of blue-blooded or plebeian senators who were vulnerable to imperial authority and mistrust and who therefore deplored the erosion of their erstwhile power and privilege. Natural ambition and some form of military support explains the rest.[2] Only a few dreamed of restoring Republican *libertas*, which was not, of course, what a modern reader would mean by liberty. *Libertas* essentially meant the "freedom" of the exploiting classes to promote their own interests and evade the dictates of any central authority other than the senate and its carefully elected (or selected) officers. As a romantic and unrealistic slogan invoked by the senatorial or

1. See Boissier (1913) 102: "Ils détestaient leurs vices et non leur pouvoir. . . . L'opposition qu'ils faisaient aux Césars n'était donc pas tout à fait politique dans son principe, mais plutôt morale"; more detailed and up to date is MacMullen (1967); see also Becker (1950), Sattler (1960), Wistrand (1962) 189, and Vogel-Weidemann (1979).
2. For the constant harassment of the Julio-Claudian emperors by plots and ideological or personal opposition, see the concise summary by McAlindon (1956) 113.

equestrian classes, the term had nothing to do with the *libertas* involved in the emancipation of a slave or the unimpregnable *libertas* of the Stoic *sapiens*.[3] The principate similarly had no other purely *political* goal but its own self-preservation, and that self-preservation, as Nero knew well, was dependent on a nonrevolutionary population, whether slave or proletarian; on the acquiescence, voluntary or forced, of the senatorial and equestrian classes; and above all on the support of the armed forces, in particular, the support in emergencies of the Praetorian Guard. The Praetorian Guard combined the functions of storm troops, an imperial bodyguard, a civil defense unit, and a secret police. The number of centurions from this body who figure prominently in imperial history is noticeable, although the *praefecti* in the Himmleresque figures of Aelius Sejanus, Ofonius Tigellinus, and Nymphidius Sabinus generally occupy most of the historian's attention. The senate, on the other hand, by officially delegating its former powers, could legitimate an accession to the purple or it could conspire against an unpopular emperor, but, as a body, it had no battalions of its own to command.

Augustus, profiting from the bad example of Julius Caesar's high-handedness, had made the apparent, occasionally real, cooperation of princeps and senate a cornerstone of his policy. Claudius, because of his interest in efficient government and his reinforcement of an already powerful civil service, predominantly composed of freedmen, had shown up the impracticality, or undesirability, of this aim, although the unreality of serious cooperation had been already foreshadowed in the reigns of Tiberius and Caligula. Claudius was a realist in this. Those senators who had the ambition and ability for government were, with some exceptions, still fundamentally pessimistic Republicans with no incentive to make the imperial system work as it should, or too snobbish or cowardly to put their shoulders to the wheel. Most of the rest, apart from the emperor's cronies

3. A more temperate view of *libertas* may be found in Wirszubski (1950); cf. Momigliano's remarks on this in (1951) 146.

and friends, lacked the character and talents required. It must be added in their defense that opportunities for the exercise of power had changed since the days of the Republic; administrative abilities rather than the gift of decisiveness were called for. There was the additional problem that the more able and ambitious could pose a threat to the reigning emperor. In fact, Nero did violate Augustus' general principle in giving important military commands to senatorial figures such as Corbulo and Galba.

Seneca, while voicing his other grievances in the *Apocolocyntosis* deplored most vehemently the tendency of Claudius' regime to centralization and absolutism, as well as the political purges that this entailed.[4] He hoped that, with his aid, a youthful and presumably malleable Nero would revert to what he naively conceived as Augustus' true intentions. Hence Nero's declaration, formulated by his tutor, that he would observe the principles of the Augustan settlement.[5] Seneca was eventually to discover that the innate tendencies of the principate, and Nero's own character, could not reverse the direction in which power flowed. The antisenatorial bias inherent in the principate could not be glossed over even by Augustus, let alone the flamboyant and insecure Nero. Unfortunately and inevitably, as each reign progressed, the logic of the principate and the supineness of most senators ended the honeymoon and the true nature of the Roman autocracy reemerged. The best the senatorial order, in its more realistic moods, could hope for was a more complaisant ruler than the current emperor. The rallying cry of *libertas* still had some value for the more discontented, or fearful, senators, and in literature and philosophy the concept was symbolized in the figure of the Younger Cato, who had been, fortuitously, a

---

4. The cost, 35 senators and 221 knights (Sen. *Apoc.* 14), seems grim, but it is low by comparison with some of Claudius' predecessors and with modern totalitarian regimes in Nazi Germany, Franco's Spain, the USSR under Stalin, Chile under Pinochet, Somoza's Nicaragua, present-day Haiti, and numerous other states. Moreover, the numbers have to be seen in relation to the far greater number of *trials* of senators and equestrians.

5. Suet. *Nero* 10; Tac. *Ann.* 13.4; cf. Dio 59.6.1, 8; Plin. *Pan.* 62.2; Plut. *Galba* 15.1.

notable Stoic. Cato was therefore venerated as the last hero of the Roman Republic, the champion of Republican *Libertas* both against Caesar, and, had there been real need, Pompey also. His obstinacy, his heavy drinking, his avarice, and his lack of emotional rapport with his wives, were all overlooked.[6]

The symbolism of Cato the Younger becomes extremely important in the ideological and literary debates that thrived in Neronian salons and contemporary publications.[7] Lucan's imposing portrait in the *Pharsalia* is paralleled in Seneca, although Seneca carefully uses him as the ideal Roman Stoic, not as the great champion of Republican liberty.[8] It is a pity that we have lost the various near-contemporary pamphlets that alternatively built up and tried to destroy Cato's reputation: the laudatory pamphlets by Cicero, Brutus, Fadius Gallus, and Munatius Rufus which confronted the hostile productions of Julius Ceasar, Aulus Hirtius, and, eventually, the aging Augustus.[9] But the generally favorable verdict of the Augustan period is enshrined in Vergil's *Aeneid* and Horace's *Odes* as well as later writers who depended on them.[10] This stiff-necked Stoic, the conservative bastion of the Republican oligarchy, is hardly sympathetic to modern tastes, except perhaps in his weakness for the bottle and his marital troubles, but he became a symbol around which ro-

6. For Cato's problems, see e.g. Plut. *Cato Min.* , *passim*; Cic. *Att.* 1.18.7; Mart. 2.89; Gelzer (1963) 257. Cicero's *Pro Murena* provides a good sketch of him as a politically intransigent nuisance.

7. For a somewhat perfunctory survey, see Pecchiura (1965) 47. Cato's great-grandfather, Cato the Censor, became, not coincidentally, another symbolic figure in Roman literature, along with his descendant, the pair often representing, in modern terms, Mrs. Grundy and Anthony Comstock types, (cf., e.g. Petr. *Sat.* 132.15; Mart. 1. *praef.*; 9.28.3, 9.39.15, 10.19.21, 11.2.1, 11.15.1, 12.6.8). The two Catos, being outstanding examples of civic virtue, tended to be fused or grouped together in the plural as *Catones*. The symbols of Cassius and Brutus, the liberators and tyrannicides, were more dangerous to use.

8. Cf. Sen. *Ep.* 11.10; 95.70 f.; *Const. Sap.* 2.2; *De Ira* 2.32; *Ad Marc.* 20.6; *De Prov.* 2.9; Pecchiura (1965) 59 ff.; Griffin (1976) 191; on Lucan's portrait of Cato in the *Pharsalia*, see Ahl (1976) ch. 7 and the references there.

9. See Pecchiura (1965) 25; Bardon (1956) 276.

10. Verg. *Aen.* 8.670; Hor. *Carm.* 1.2.35; 2.1.21 f.; cf. Sen. *Tranq.* 7.5; *Const. Sap.* 2.3; *Ben.* 5.17; *Ep.* 95.69; 104.29; Pers. *Sat.* 3.44 f.; Plin. *Ep.* 4.27.

mantic Republican feelings could crystallize. Because a number of crypto-Republicans were also Stoics, it would be interesting to know the real thrust of Thrasea Paetus' *Life of Cato* (probably the main source for Plutarch's extant biography), as Paetus became Nero's most undaunted critic. Did the work express Republicanism as well as the traditional Stoic admiration for Cato? Biography, like historiography, drama, and declamation, was always a convenient mode of direct or oblique criticism of the established order.[11] Serious philosophers of the Porch, such as Annaeus Cornutus, may thus have taken on the Republican tinge of their patrons and aristocratic friends and found themselves in trouble through guilt by association.

Even for those, like Seneca, who entertained no serious hope of restoring the Republic, who accepted the *necessity* of the principate, Cato and other Republican champions could function as symbols for a more powerful and independent senate, more active magistracies, and greater freedom of speech. Both Seneca and Lucan are supremely political writers. Seneca espouses the pragmatic view that better emperors, perhaps better institutions, were all one could expect, as a Stoic *sapiens* was unlikely to ascend the throne, even if he were willing. Seneca's nephew Lucan enshrines, in his poetry at least, the youthful and idealistic view that the Republic could, and should, be restored, although the conspiracy he joined had no such aims. To put it bluntly, Seneca accepted the principate, hoping it would be tempered with mercy, compassion, and moderation. Lucan, the young idealist, identifying himself more and more with the senatorial class and smarting from the insults of Nero, whatever form they took, projected in the *Pharsalia* a return to the oligarchic role of the upper classes during the Republican period, even if this meant accepting another emperor. Disillusion with Nero was swift among some senatorial groups after the initial honeymoon. Certainly by 62, the pivotal year, and perhaps some time before,

11. See MacMullen (1967) 35.

the emperor's excesses, whether artistic or domestic, had alienated all but his closest cronies or new-found friends, the *deteriores* of Tacitus' account.

Lucan, a dupe of the myth of Catonism, made himself a representative of the so-called Stoic faction, even though it was more of a political than a philosophical alliance; and he expressed their ideals in more and more perfervid language as the *Pharsalia* progressed. Yet Stoic philosophy, unlike Cynicism, was compatible with monarchy and autocracy, and its stress on individual liberty and individual virtue did not naturally lead to political revolution, for all the growing connection between that sect and the anti-Caesarian activists. Stoicism as a political philosophy was by no means monolithic. We can detect even in Seneca a split between those who considered political involvement necessary and those who considered it unnecessary. Lucan was at pains to justify Cato's participation in a civil war which, in hindsight and in view of its consequences, was unholy and wrong. Ideally, the wise man should be ruler. Failing that, one could reasonably stay aloof from politics, but there were many positions, as Seneca's life and writings show, between these two extremes.

With Seneca the Disraelian partnership of art and politics begins early. Even a brief inspection of the works written during his term of exile on Corsica (41–49) confirms from the beginning the political nature of many of his writings. The charge against Seneca, true or false, was adultery with one of Caligula's sisters. The likely reason was Messalina's view of him as a possible threat to her political ascendancy through his association with a hostile court clique of former friends of Sejanus.

Seneca was as unhappy on Corsica as was Ovid at Tomi and he turned to literature as Ovid did, not so much as a psychological outlet but as a possible way of securing his recall. Like Ovid, he tried to defend himself against both the overt and covert grounds for his banishment. His poetry was used to express his misery and discomfort; his prose to express his innocence and harmlessness; his patient hopes of clemency; and his gratitude to Claudius that worse had not befallen him. His justified complaints of the rocky barrenness and hot summers of Corsica alternate with neat Ovidian protests against exile itself:

> Corsica terribilis, cum primum incanduit aestas,
>   saevior, ostendit cum ferus ora Canis:
> parce relegatis; hoc est, iam parce solutis!
>   vivorum cineri sit tua terra levis!
>
>   (*Anth.* 236. 5–8);

> barbara praeruptis inclusa est Corsica saxis,
>   horrida, desertis undique vasta locis.
> non poma autumnus, segetes non educat aestas
>   canaque Palladio munere bruma caret.
> imbriferum nullo ver est laetabile fetu
>   nullaque in infausto nascitur herba solo.
> non panis, non haustus aquae, non ultimus ignis;
>   hic sola haec duo sunt: exul et exilium.
>
>   (*Anth.* 237)

Corsica, horrible when the summer first burns, is more brutal, when the Dog Star shows its face: pardon the exiles, that is, pardon those who have paid already! Let your soil be light on the ashes—of the living!

Barbarous Corsica is enclosed by steep crags, horrid, desolate, with wilderness in every direction. Autumn brings no fruit, summer no crops and hoary winter is without Pallas' gift [of olives]. The rainy spring is gladdened by no growth and no grass grows on the accursed soil. No bread, no fresh waters, lastly, no fire; only two things are here: the exiled and his exile.

These plaintive poems and some other epigrams that are possibly Seneca's in the Voss Codex Q.86 were surely meant only for private circulation initially, but the carefully crafted prose works were obviously intended for wider dissemination.

The *Consolatio ad Marciam*, written about the year 40, is a curiously belated treatise to send to a mother whose tears for her son, three years dead, should long since have dried, even if she remained apparently in mourning. There is a strong political coloration to the work, as one might expect in a disquisition to a woman whose father, A. Cremutius Cordus, in 25 had fallen victim, along with his writings, to the persecution of the now infamous Sejanus. Advice on how best to handle grief is given through examples drawn from the history of the Julian house; Octavia's desolation over her son Marcellus is unfavorably contrasted with Livia's dignified behavior after the loss of Drusus and Julia Augusta's similar unselfish propriety. This last Seneca attributes in part to the comfort given by Areus, the philosopher companion of her dead husband, and, as a philosopher himself, he duly reiterates Areus' exhortations. Further instances from recent Roman history are then adduced and it is in the course of such discussion that Seneca manages skillfully to grind his own particular axe. The introduction of Sejanus (15.3) may seem gratuitous, but it is presumably meant to alert the reader to certain hidden purposes of the writer's own. Sejanus turns up again not long after (22.4) as archvillain in the minutely, even painfully, described forced suicide of Marcia's father. This is the second time Marcia's earlier, distressing bereavement is invoked, as though to console her for her latest loss. This tactlessness has been best explained by the theory that Seneca had been previously associated with the friends of Sejanus and, in a changed and now dangerous political climate, was trying to dissociate himself from those ties by attacking Sejanus in a tract composed for the daughter of one of Sejanus' bitterest critics.[12]

Even the *Consolatio ad Helviam*, written in the first year of his

12. Proposed by Stewart (1953) 82. My own investigation may throw some doubt on his conclusion that "the spirit of opportunism which is so often present and sometimes so offensive in his writings tends to disappear as a controlling factor in the later works" (85). But it should be added in Seneca's defense that opportunism of one kind or another is a frequent factor in the creation of literary works and it is not necessarily a detriment either to the status of the author or the writings. Griffin (1976) 16, 22 loyally defends Seneca against such charges of literary opportunism by the often invoked but somewhat unconvincing argument of the ancient writer's heavy reliance on models in general. Stewart's thesis on the *Ad Marciam* is weakly dismissed on the grounds that there is no *independent* evidence of a date after 39. Griffin has other objections to detecting specific political purposes and allusions in the *Ad Helviam* and *De Vita Beata* (op. cit. 19, 21). For similar considerations involving the *Ad Helviam*, see the following discussion and Ferrill (1966) 253.

exile, supposedly to console his mother for his departure, contains detectable political elements. Several passages expatiate on chastity and sexual virtue: adultery and such crimes, claims Seneca, are alien to his family. The obvious motive for these gratuitous, perhaps even tasteless, remarks was to clear his own name of the charge for which he had been exiled to Corsica: the affair with Germanicus' daughter, Julia Livilla. Nor is this all. Despite the evidence of the epigrams, which may after all have been written at any time during his enforced sojourn on Corsica, Seneca professes himself happy and active (*laetum et alacrem velut optimis rebus*, 20.1); he accepts his lot with rational stoicism (5.2); and, significantly, he disclaims any further interest in money, offices, or influence (*pecuniam honores gratiam*, 5.4). This last indicates that he perceives himself as having possessed these before his downfall, but also that he has now seen through their attractions. Who could have a better case for recall then a disabused philosopher?

Seneca's next venture in this genre, however, is even less palatable to his uncritical admirers, even though understandable in the circumstances. The *Consolatio ad Polybium*, written about 43 to the powerful freedman of Claudius, allows for no mistake about motive—small wonder that Seneca later tried to suppress the piece.[13] The only purpose of the pamphlet, like many of Ovid's *Epistulae ex Ponto*, was to secure his return from exile. Polybius had just lost a brother and Seneca gained an opportunity; the philosophical sentiments are conventional enough, although expressed in Seneca's now practiced and scintillating style. Nevertheless the gross flattery of Polybius himself and of the emperor Claudius go beyond even the generous conventions of Roman eulogy. For example:

> nam si quicquam tristitia profecturi sumus, non recuso quicquid lacrimarum fortunae meae superfuit tuae fundere; inveniam eti-

---

13. Polybius was Claudius' secretary *a studiis* (Suet. *Claud.* 28) and by this time may have been promoted to the secretaryship *a libellis* (*Cons. Polyb.* 6.5). For Seneca's attempt to suppress the work, see Dio 61.10.

amnunc per hos exhaustos iam fletibus domesticis oculos quod affluat, si modo id tibi futurum bono est. (2.1)

For if we are likely to achieve anything by sorrowing, I do not refuse to shed whatever tears are left over from my own fate for yours. For I shall find something even now to let flow from these eyes, already drained by my personal griefs, if only it would be of some good to you.

The praises of Polybius that follow are sycophantic in the extreme. He is praised for his lack of materialism, although he was, of course, very rich (2.3); for his personal amiability (2.4); for his good reputation (2.5); for his scholarship (6.3); for his love of letters (2.6, 3.4); for his literary talents and fame (2.6);[14] for his unwillingness to abuse his power (3.2); for his blameless life (3.4); for Claudius' affection for him (6.2); and, finally, for his unremitting industry on his master's behalf (6.4).

The adulation of Claudius is equally prominent and exaggerated, and Seneca's references to the emperor's clemency pointedly allude to his own plight:

ut multos flentes audire possis, ut preces periclitantium et ad misericordiam mitissimi Caesaris pervenire cupientium, lacrimae tibi tuae adsiccandae sunt. (6.5)

So that you can listen to a weeping multitude, and hear the pleas of those who are in danger and who desire to obtain mercy from most gentle Caesar, you must dry your own tears.

haec, utcumque potui, longo iam situ obsoleto et hebetato animo composui. quae si aut parum respondere ingenio tuo aut parum mederi dolori videbuntur, cogita quam non possit is alienae vacare consolationi quem sua mala occupatum tenet, et quam non facile latine ei homini verba succurrant quem barbarorum inconditus et barbaris quoque humanioribus gravis fremitus circumsonat. (18.9)

14. Polybius had translated Homer into Latin prose and Vergil into Greek prose (*Cons. Polyb.* 8.2; 11.5).

I have composed these thoughts as best I could with a spirit grown old and dulled by long decay. If they seem to correspond too little to your own character or offer too inadequate a remedy for your distress, bear in mind how a man preoccupied with his own troubles finds it impossible to secure the leisure to console others and how Latin words do not come easily to a man about whose ears there rings the uncouth racket of barbarians, painful even to the more civilized barbarians.

Claudius is praised for his manly bearing of the burdens of Empire. He is compared to Atlas holding the sky on his shoulders (7.1). His vigilance, his industry, his tirelessness, his self-sacrifice (7.2–3) are praised in turn by the future author of the *Apocolocyntosis*. Seneca recommends a history of Claudius' reign as a subject for Polybius' literary talents (8.2). He alludes approvingly (and with little justification) to Claudius' policy of safeguarding the Empire by good works rather than armed forces;[15] he speaks of "the greatness and splendor of his divinity"; his kindness and gracious favor to his friends (12.4). His prayers for Claudius' safety are almost embarrassing, as this brief selection shows:

> di illum deaeque terris diu commodent. acta hic divi Augusti aequet, annos vincat. . . .
> abstine ab hoc manus tuas, Fortuna, nec in isto potentiam tuam nisi ea parte qua prodes ostenderis. patere illum generi humano iam diu aegro et adfecto mederi, patere quidquid prioris principis furor concussit in suum locum restituere ac reponere. sidus hoc, quod praecipitato in profundum et demerso in tenebras orbi refulsit, semper luceat. hic Germaniam pacet, Britanniam aperiat, et paternos triumphos ducat et novos; quorum me quoque spectatorem futurum, quae ex virtutibus eius primum optinet locum, promittit clementia. . . .
> interim magnum miseriarum mearum solacium est videre misericordiam eius totum orbem pervagantem; quae cum ex hoc ipso angulo in quo ego defixus sum complures multorum iam anno-

---

15. The work may have been written just a little before military operations were begun in Britain in 43; *Longo . . . situ* (18.9) is doubtless an exaggeration.

rum ruina obrutos effoderit et in lucem reduxerit, non vereor ne me unum transeat. . . . o felicem clementiam tuam, Caesar, quae efficit ut quietiorem sub te agant vitam exules quam nuper sub Gaio egere principes! (5–13.4)

May the gods and goddesses lend him long to earth! May he rival the accomplishments and surpass the years of the deified Augustus! . . .

Keep your hands off him, Fortune, and in his care show your power only where you are beneficial. Let him cure the human race, long sick and afflicted; let him restore and return to its place whatever the madness of the emperor before him had toppled. May this star that has shed its light upon a world plunged into the abyss and sunk in darkness shine forever. May he pacify Germany, open up Britain, and celebrate his father's triumphs and fresh ones of his own. His mercy, which heads the list of his virtues, raises in me hopes that I too shall be an onlooker at them. . . .

Meanwhile, the great consolation of my own miseries is to see his compassion roaming through the whole world; and since, even from this distant corner in which I am immobilized, his mercy has unearthed many who were buried under a fall from many years ago, and has brought them back to the light of day, I have no fears that I am the only one it will pass over. . . . O how blessed is your mercy, Caesar, which allows exiles to live a more tranquil life under your rule than did prominent men recently under the rule of Gaius!

On his return from exile, however, Seneca almost immediately added a third book to his *De Ira*, which had been largely composed on Corsica.[16] Here again the opportunistic nature of some of Seneca's philosophical and political writings is clear. Protected by the power of Agrippina, he indulges in more or less overt criticisms of the emperor who had exiled him. Claudius was affected with a bad temper; he even went so far as to issue a reassuring edict about its effect on his policies (Suet. *Claud.* 38). There he distinguished between *ira* and *iracundia*, a distinc-

---

16. The lateness of Book 3 has now been demonstrated on stylistic grounds by Nicolova-Burova (1975) 1.

tion also made in Seneca's treatise (1.4). The motivations behind the pamphlet are further underlined by Seneca's referring to exile, his own fate, as an example of imperial cruelty combined with cowardice.[17]

A similar attack can be detected in the *De Brevitate Vitae*, probably written in 49 (although 55 is another possible date).[18] This time the darts seem to be directed against Claudius' antiquarianism and his pedantically argued extension of the *pomerium*.[19] Now there are many signs in Seneca's writings of his awareness of how precarious his tenure of office would be as tutor and counselor to Nero. A particularly significant passage occurs, again in the last book of the *De Ira*, where Seneca speaks of the great evil of anger when backed by supreme power. The examples given are naturally historical; Seneca's reflections, however, echo his feelings about his recent exile and his present situation. He comments on the restraint of the victims involved in these regal or imperial traps:

> necessaria ista est doloris refrenatio, utique hoc sortitis vitae genus et ad regiam adhibitis mensam: sic estur apud illos, sic bibitur, sic respondetur; funeribus suis adridendum est. an tanti sit vita videbimus; alia ista quaestio est. non consolabimur tam triste ergastulum, non adhortabimur ferre imperia carnificum: ostendemus in omni servitute apertam libertati viam. (3.15.3)

This repression of anguish is essential, especially in those whose lot brings them this sort of life and who are invited to the table of kings. This is the way one eats with them, drinks with them, answers them; one must laugh at the deaths in one's family. Whether life is worth that much, we shall see: that is another question. We shall not sympathize with those in such a miserable prison; we shall not encourage them to bear with the dictates of their butch-

---

17. Cf. 3.43.3–4; Momigliano (1975) 245.
18. See Griffin (1976) 401, and the references there.
19. See Syme (1958) 514. Tacitus clearly shared Seneca's contempt for such things. Seneca may also have been annoying Claudius by implying that Paullinus, a friend who held the politically sensitive post of *praefectus annonae*, should resign; see Momigliano (1975) 246.

ers: we shall show them that in every kind of slavery the highway
to freedom is open.

Prophetically, Seneca advises suicide and describes rhetori-
cally the various modes of self-destruction available, as he had
done earlier in the *Consolatio ad Marciam* (20.2–3). His last example is tragically ironic, when we consider his own end sixteen
years later:

> quaeris quod sit ad libertatem via? quaelibet in corpore tuo vena!
> (3.15.4)

> You ask what is the highroad to freedom? Any vein in your body!

A further set of comments is easily construable as oblique criticism of Claudius; here Seneca holds forth on the expediency
for rulers of controlling their anger:

> sed cum utilis sit servientibus adfectuum suorum et huius praeci-
> pue rabidi atque effreni continentia, utilior est regibus: perierunt
> omnia ubi quantum ira suadet fortuna permittit, nec diu potest
> quae multorum malo exercetur potentia stare; periclitatur enim
> ubi eos qui separatim gemunt communis metus iunxit. plerosque
> itaque modo singuli mactaverunt, modo universi, cum illos con-
> ferre in unum iras publicus dolor coegisset. (3.16.2)

> But although it is expedient for those of inferior status to exercise
> control over their emotions and particularly over this mad un-
> bridled passion, it is more expedient for sovereigns: everything is
> finished, when fortune permits whatever anger prompts, and no
> power can last long which is exercised to the detriment of many;
> for it is endangered when a shared apprehension has united those
> who groan separately. As a result, most rulers have been assassi-
> nated, sometimes by individual action, sometimes by concerted
> action, when common suffering has forced men to combine their
> individual resentments into one.

Seneca proceeds to further examples of regal anger and brutality, giving specific Roman instances. He makes it clear that

the danger of this behavior lies closer to home. Caligula was, as always, an acceptable example to trot out, and Seneca even apologizes for what may seem a digression in his treatise (3.19.1). Nevertheless he expounds on the theme at some length and contrasts instances of hideous cruelty (not strictly his subject, as he well knows) with some counterexamples of merciful rulers. He even praises Philip of Macedon for a trait that he shared with Nero, extreme tolerance of insults (Suet. *Nero* 39). This, states Seneca, is of great help in shoring up a throne.[20] To drive home the positive side of his disquisition, Seneca cites the divine Augustus as an example of a ruler who was *not* governed by anger and tells the story of his relations with the abusive historian Timagenes (3.23.3–8). The flattery of Nero implicit in all of this does not disguise the veiled prediction of assassination, if these warnings and examples are not taken to heart.

In yet another digression Seneca argues that envy gives rise to the most destructive anger of all and he describes the plot to assassinate Julius Caesar. Here he has high praise for the real founder of the Julio-Claudian dynasty, claiming, for example, that no man had ever made a more generous use of victory.[21] Caesar's fatal problem was that he could not satisfy *all* the expectations he aroused in his friends. Is this passage also advice to his young pupil, the pupil who was to develop into the generous, indeed profligate, Nero of history?[22] The possibility is increased when he lists instances of likely complaints:

> tanta tamen inportunitas hominum est ut, quamvis multum acceperint, iniuriae loco sit plus accipere potuisse. "dedit mihi praeturam, sed consulatum speraveram; dedit duodecim fasces, sed non fecit ordinarium consulem; a me numerari voluit annum, sed deest mihi ad sacerdotium; cooptatus in collegium sum, sed cur in unum? consummavit dignitatem meam, sed patrimonio nihil

---

20. 3.23.2: *contumeliarum patientia, ingens instrumentum ad tutelam regni.*

21. Caesar claimed nothing from it except the ability to be liberal: *neque enim quisquam liberalius victoria usus est, ex qua nihil sibi vindicavit nisi dispensandi potestatem* (3.30.4).

22. For Nero's generosity, see Suet. *Nero* 10–13, 30, but one should remember that there were various sorts of return in the form of presents and bequests.

contulit; et dedit mihi quae debebat alicui dare, de suo nihil pro-
tulit." (3.31.1–2)

So great however is the presumptuousness of men that although
they have received a lot, the fact that they could have got more
serves as an injustice. "He gave me a praetorship, but I'd hoped
for the consulate. He gave me the twelve fasces, but didn't make
me a consul of the year; he was willing that the year should be
dated by my consulship, but I still don't have a priesthood. I have
been elected to a priestly college, but why just one? He elevated
me to my proper dignity, but he did nothing for my financial
situation; he gave me what duty demanded he give somebody, but
he didn't add anything on his own account."

The message here is meant for the disgruntled elements of the
senatorial class, whose discontent with Nero, after the lengthy
honeymoon, was to grow into extreme hostility. An equally
critical remark is directed at those senators who look back long-
ingly at the liberty of Republican days:

respondisse tibi servum indignaris libertumque et uxorem et
clientem; deinde idem de re publica libertatem sublatam quereris
quam domi sustulisti. (3.35.1)

You are indignant because your slave, your freedman, your wife,
your client have given you a back-answer; then you complain that
the state has been robbed of the liberty of which you have robbed
your home.

A dominant stress, however, in this book of the *De Ira* is on
the qualities, notably clemency or mercy, that the ideal emperor
should possess.[23] Seneca was to return to this theme almost as
soon as Nero came to power, in the *De Clementia*. His sneers
against Claudius for lacking these desirable qualities were to become far more overt in the *Apocolocyntosis* and the *De Beneficiis*.[24]

23. Nero did in fact try to exercise this quality ostentatiously in such cases as
Antistius Sosianus (Tac. *Ann.* 14.49).
24. Cf. e.g. *Apoc.* 10–11; *Ben.* 1.15.1–6.

The *De Clementia* was written in late 55 or early 56[25] and was addressed to Nero. It makes clear, as always, that Seneca, unlike Lucan and others, accepted the realities of the principate.[26] He accepted its absolute power, its immunity to every danger except assassination plots, the insurgency of the legions or, more remotely, a popular or slave uprising. He gives a description of Nero's position as he would have Nero describe it: he is the regent of the gods on earth;[27] the arbiter of life and death to the peoples of the world; arbiter of position and one's lot in life: supreme commander of armies, whom only his peacefulness restrains from destroying whole nations; the giver and withholder of freedom and majesty among states.

The supposed question Seneca sets himself is how this supreme power is to be guided. Here enters once more the outrageous flattery to which readers of Neronian literature have to become accustomed. Seneca puts into Nero's mouth a protestation that, with all this power, he exercises it with an even temper, unprovoked by human obstinacy and devoid of vainglory. He exercises it above all with mercy (*clementia*) and so can, at any time, look the gods in the face.

This type of pamphlet, "Advice to a Ruler," is of course familiar from many national literatures, Machiavelli's *Il Principe* being perhaps the most distinguished and notorious. The genre is literature as an instrument of indirect government, although there are few instances of the success of such writing and Seneca's treatise certainly provides no exception to the rule.

The basic message conveyed is that Nero has inherited a trust, the state, and he must be able to boast that his principles have faithfully guarded this trust. He may congratulate himself on a

25. As the reference to Nero's eighteenth birthday at 1.8.9 shows.

26. Note the criticism of aristocrats who bewail their lost Republican liberty cited above (*De Ira* 3.35.1) and the frequent and open uses of the word *rex*, a detested title under the Republic, although it came to lose some of its pejorative connotations under the Empire.

27. So far as we can see, Nero did not officially adopt the theory Seneca outlined of divine election, although the hostile author of the *Octavia* makes such a theory Nero's justification of his behavior. For his supposed absolutism and tyrannical behavior, see Fears (1977) 325; for the possible motives, see Cizek (1982) 141.

rare quality, innocence of wrong (*innocentia*, 1.1.5), and Rome is
duly and warmly grateful for its happiness and prosperity. Nero
is credited with bringing the Roman people security, justice, and
above all, *libertas* (1.1.8–9). This is, of course, another note of
imperial propaganda, which is equally prominent in Pliny the
Younger's praise of Trajan. Seneca, however, insists that Nero is
most admired for his clemency. A philosophical disquisition on
this quality follows, the details of which do not concern us, as
our purpose is to divine the occasion and the motives of this
open letter to a ruler. A hint is soon given:

> nec innocentiae tantum clementia succurrit, sed saepe *virtuti*,
> quoniam quidem condicione temporum incidunt quaedam quae
> possint laudata puniri. (1.2.1)

> Clemency not only comes to the rescue of innocence, but often
> also of *righteousness*, since, because of the state of the times, certain
> acts take place which, although praised, are subject to punish-
> ment.

Seneca is presumably speaking here, as in the *De Ira*, of the
behavior of the dogged champions of Republican (or senatorial)
liberty such as Thrasea Paetus, whose high-mindedness—and
high-handedness—were admired in contemporary circles. Such
austere moralizing could bring down upon them severe penalties, should the emperor so choose, and Thrasea did eventually
commit suicide on Nero's orders. Seneca's hope is that the exercise of clemency will convert potential or actual enemies of
the regime into its staunchest defenders. He is advocating, as
earlier, a conciliatory attitude toward the senatorial class; this
will in turn produce compensating advantages:

> illius demum magnitudo stabilis fundataque est quem omnes tam
> supra se esse quam pro se sciunt. (1.3.3)

> A stable and well-founded greatness belongs then to him whom
> all know to be as much for them as he is over them.

They will sacrifice themselves for such a ruler's safety and be vigilant in his interest:

> obicere se pro illo mucronibus insidiantium paratissimi et substernere corpora sua, si per stragem illi humanum iter ad salutem struendum sit; somnum eius nocturnis excubiis muniunt, latera obiecti circumfusique defendunt, incurrentibus periculis se opponunt. (1.3.3)

> They are supremely ready to put themselves in the way of the daggers of assassins for him and throw their bodies down to make a human path through slaughter to safety for him; they protect his sleep with their nocturnal watches; fronting and surrounding him, they protect his flanks; they face onrushing perils.

Seneca, in this argument to Nero's self-interest, is playing on the fears of assassination or deposition which were rightly entertained by almost all emperors, and by none so much as by Nero, as can be seen from the aftermath of the Pisonian conspiracy. Seneca, however, is also appealing to the senatorial order. The good emperor, he says, perhaps not without a trace of irony, is the bond of the commonwealth;[28] in protecting him, men protect their own safety. Without the emperor there would ensue the destruction of Roman peace and the ruination of Rome. Such dangers can be averted as long as citizens know how to submit to imperial control.[29] If this submission is abandoned, then the empire will fall apart. Seneca's plea for the status quo and the imperial centralization of power is even buttressed by a reference to Julius Caesar, who, in acting the emperor, so clothed himself in the powers of state that neither could be withdrawn without the destruction of both. Seneca's anticipation of civil war consequent on the forcible removal of the emperor was amply warranted by the internecine struggles that followed Nero's suicide in 68–69, the Year of the Four Emperors. If Nero then is the

---

28. 1.4.1: *ille est enim vinculum per quod res publica cohaeret.*
29. 1.4.2: *tam diu ab isto periculo aberit hic populus quam diu sciet ferre frenos.*

soul of the state and the state is the emperor's body,[30] mercy is prompted by self-interest.

That the tract is aimed at both Nero and the senatorial class is further indicated by remarks that exploit the hopes and fears of each. Seneca suggests, on the one hand, that the emperor, with divine partiality, should favor one class over another,[31] but he argues also that under a cruel and stormy regime even he who causes all the terror will have his own burden of fear to shoulder (1.7.3). This salutary warning to Nero is enlarged upon:

> animadversiones magnarum potestarum terrent latius quam nocent, non sine causa; non enim quantum fecerit, sed quantum facturus sit, cogitatur in eo qui omnia potest . . . regibus certior est ex mansuetudine securitas, quia frequens vindicta paucorum odium opprimit, omnium irritat. (1.8.5–6)

> Punishments inflicted by great powers terrify more widely than they do harm, and not without reason; for when the doer is omnipotent, men think not of how much he has done, but of how much he is likely to do . . . a more assured sense of security comes to rulers through temperateness, because repeated repression, while it eliminates the hatred of a few, stimulates the hatred of all.

On behalf of the senatorial class, Seneca goes so far as to advocate mercy even in the event of plots against the emperor, an almost certain eventuality, as both of them well knew. Nero, whether because of wisdom or cowardice, never took this advice. The suggestion is made in the form of a long story about Augustus' treatment of the conspirator C. Cinna, whom Augustus had spared although he was the latest in a long series of plotters against his life (1.9). Seneca concludes:

30. 1.5.1: *tu animus reipublicae tuae es, illa corpus tuum.*

31. 1.5.7: *deorum itaque sibi animum adserens princeps alios ex civibus suis, quia utiles bonique sunt, libens videat, alios in numerum relinquat; quosdam esse gaudeat, quosdam patiatur.*

haec eum clementia ad salutem securitatemque perduxit; haec gratum ac favorabilem reddidit, quamvis nondum subactis populi Romani cervicibus manum imposuisset. (1.10.2)

It was this clemency that brought him safety and peace of mind; this made him accepted and popular, although the necks of the Roman people were not yet bowed when he laid his hand on them.

Seneca mentions again Augustus' tolerance of personal insults and lampoons (1.10.3), but his main point is more general:

clementia ergo non tantum honestiores sed tutiores praestat ornamentumque imperiorum est simul et certissima salus. . . . salvum regem clementia in aperto praestabit. unum est inexpugnabile munimentum amor civium. (1.11.4; 19.6)

Clemency therefore not only makes rulers more honored but also more secure; it is simultaneously the glory of empires and their most certain salvation. . . . Clemency will ensure a king's safety on an open plain. The one impregnable defense is the devotion of one's fellow citizens.

Seneca's constant use of the symbolic figure of Augustus to drive his points home has wider significance. The *Apocolocyntosis* and Nero's first speech to the senate after his accession, supposedly written by Seneca, make it clear that Augustus was still a potent propaganda symbol in some quarters. Augustus had tried hard to veil his absolute power beneath an appearance of constitutionality. He had taken more care than most emperors, or than Julius Caesar for that matter, to conciliate the senate, to make it feel that it was still part of the order of things, although one would be reluctant to argue that through this alone he had enjoyed the longest reign of all the Julio-Claudian rulers.

In the first few years of his rule, Nero had seemed to take Seneca's advice. He paid attention to aristocratic susceptibilities in legislation and in the awarding of consulships; Tacitus tells us (*Ann.* 14.28) that he honored the senate's prerogatives by giving them legal parity with himself in the matter of financial deposits for appeals; and he gave three consolation prizes when the candidates for the praetorship were more numerous than the posts available.[32]

Various important factors, however, combined to deflect him from his early policies. Among these must be counted the political interference of Agrippina before her fall from power, Nero's own evolving ideas about the nature of the principate, the intransigence of certain senatorial factions and the disgust aroused in the upper classes by Nero's own wayward personal and public behavior. All of these proved too much for Seneca's politics of reason and realism. He helped topple Agrippina, but found himself victim in turn of court politics.

Seneca's pen, however, was not simply at the service of the state even in his palmy days. He had to think also of himself. For example, when Afranius Burrus died, then prefect of the Praetorian Guard and along with Seneca Nero's most influential adviser,[33] the aging philosopher felt that his own power was slipping from him and therefore attempted retirement from the court. This was the time when, as Tacitus sees it, Nero was lending his ear to inferior advisers, among whom we must include Ofonius Tigellinus (the new prefect of the Praetorian Guard), and after his consulship in 62, T. Petronius Niger (author of the *Satyricon*), as well as the future emperors Otho and Vitellius.[34] It was now that Seneca wrote the *De Otio*.

This is a sad little book, being a self-justificatory dissertation on the appropriateness of Seneca's decision, whether forced upon him or not, to withdraw from public affairs. It is addressed to his old friend Annaeus Serenus, Nero's devoted *praefectus vig-*

32. For the general character of Neronian legislation and its tendency at first to follow senatorial preferences, see Crook (1970) 357; and for the distribution of offices, Ginsburg (1981) 51.

33. See Gillis (1963) 5 and the useful bibliography there.

34. Tac. *Ann.* 14.52: *inclinabat ad deteriores*; see Syme (1958) 387 on additional candidates for this dubious distinction. Baldwin (1970) 187 and (1981) 134 reminds us, however, that Seneca was not entirely a spent force after this date, which fits with my hypothesis that Seneca continued to try to make himself felt and to exercise influence through his writings in retirement.

ilum, whose death in 63 greatly upset Seneca (*Ep.* 63.14–16). Because Serenus was also pursuing a public career and would know the politics of the court well, Seneca obviously regarded him a suitable addressee of this treatise and of the dialogue, *De Tranquillitate Animi*. He speaks of the right of a man who has earned his retirement and whose life is almost over (2.2) to turn to philosophy, cosmology, and similar interests, which would be quite different from those in which he has spent his working life. There is a subdued pessimism in his remarks on political matters: there is no state, he says, that the wise man could tolerate, or that would tolerate the wise man (8.3), not Athens, not Carthage, and, we are left to assume, not Rome either. This surely reflects his disappointment with the present situation at the court and his own loss of influence.

Yet Seneca's pen had been deployed in his own interest far more vigorously in an earlier period when he had come under attack. Tacitus informs us that in 58, P. Suillius Rufus, an old enemy of Seneca's from the days of Caligula and Claudius, was brought to trial and condemned.[35] In his vigorous defense Suillius voiced criticism that many of Seneca's opponents, perhaps even his close acquaintances, must have shared. He claimed that Seneca hated Claudius' friends, because that ruler had very properly exiled him; Suillius himself had been serving on Germanicus' staff whereas Seneca had been committing adultery in Germanicus' house. What branch of learning or philosophical school, asked Suillius, brought Seneca 300 million sesterces in his four years of friendship with the emperor? Suillius further accused Seneca of shameless legacy hunting and of exacting exorbitant interest rates on his loans to Italy and the provinces.[36] It was a typical attack on Seneca as the hypocrite who preaches

---

35. Tac. *Ann.* 13.42–43; also Dio 61.10.

36. On the evidence for Seneca's wealth and a defense of its accumulation, see Tac. *Ann.* 13.42; Dio 61.10.3; *PIR*[2] A617; and Motto (1966) 254. *Captatio* was a common practice and so a frequent object of satire in the early Empire (cf. Hor. *Sat.* 2.5; Pers. 5.73 ff.). It is perhaps significant that Petronius, whose *Satyricon* I shall argue had political motives (see Chapter IV), uses *captatio* as a major theme in his work. Schmid (1951) provides a full list of references on the literary use of the topic.

Stoic doctrine and indifference to wealth, while displaying a rapacious and worldly temperament. Suillius, it is true, was on trial when he made these accusations, and it is not improbable that Seneca had prompted the case. Seneca's answer to these charges was his treatise *De Vita Beata*, which is datable to this period.[37] The work is addressed ostensibly to his brother Gallio and a personal note intrudes from the start:

> omnem operam dedi ut me multitudini educerem et aliqua dote notabilem facerem: quid aliud quam telis me opposui et malevolentiae quod morderet ostendi? vides istos qui eloquentiam laudant, qui opes sequuntur, qui gratiae adulantur, qui potentiam extollunt? omnes aut sunt hostes aut, quod in aequo est, esse possunt. (2.3–4)

> I have done my best to bring myself out of the crowd and make myself known by some native endowment: what have I done but expose myself to the barbs and show malevolence where to bite? You see those creatures who applaud my eloquence, run after my money, court my favor, praise my power? They are all my enemies or, much the same thing, can become so.

It is not to our purpose to examine here the Stoic doctrines of happiness that Seneca brilliantly propounds: essentially, that virtue is the foundation of happiness, not pleasure or worldly goods. But Seneca is acutely aware of his vulnerability; he imagines an opponent criticizing him and others of the Stoic persuasion with needling questions:

> "quare ergo tu fortius loqueris quam vivis? quare et superiori verba summittis et pecuniam necessarium tibi instrumentum existimas et damno moveris et lacrimas audita coniugis aut amici morte demittis et respicis famam et malignis sermonibus tangeris? quare cultius rus tibi est quam naturalis usus desiderat? cur non ad praes-

37. See Waltz (1909) 391 n.3; Kamp (1930) 13; Lana (1955) 233; Giancotti (1957) 105; but see also Griffin (1976) 19, 306, who is dubious about dating and prefers to see the dialogue as addressing general criticisms of wealth, and not rising to a particular occasion.

criptum tuum cenas? cur tibi nitidior supellex est? cur apud te vinum aetate tua vetustius bibitur? cur aurum disponitur? cur arbores nihil praeter umbram daturae conseruntur? quare uxor tua locupletis domus censum auribus gerit? quare paedagogium pretiosa veste succingitur? quare ars est apud te ministrare nec temere et ut libet conlocatur argentum sed perite struitur et est aliquis scindendi obsonii magister?" (17.1–2)

"So why do you talk more bravely than you live? Why do you guard your words to a superior and why do you regard money as a necessary instrument of life and feel upset by pecuniary loss? And why do you shed tears at the news of the death of your wife or a friend and why do you show regard for your good name and sensitivity to malicious gossip? Why do you farm more land than your natural needs require? Why don't you dine in accordance with your own advice? Why do you have elegant furniture? Why is the wine drunk in your home older than you are? Why is all that gold on display? Why are your trees planted only to provide shade? Why does your wife wear the income of a rich family on her ears? Why is your retinue of young slaves dressed in expensive livery? Why is it an art to serve at your table and why is the silver not put out carelessly or anyway you please, but laid out expertly, and why is there a master carver to slice your meat?"

The charges Seneca imagines launched against himself are exhaustive and perhaps even exaggerated (for example, his foreign estates, his hordes of servants [17.2], the gold and silver plate). Particularly notable, however, is the fact that he defends his acceptance of legacies (23.2), and, very obliquely, his sex life (27.5): both were the subjects of charges made by Suillius. Seneca's defense is that he is *not yet* the Stoic sage, but, in any case, wealth for a Stoic is a matter of "indifference." He would watch it vanish with the utmost equanimity, unlike his detractors, but he prefers to be rich because of the opportunities that wealth provides for the exercise of virtues such as generosity.[38] The Stoic uses money without extravagance or miserliness (20.4). Seneca

38. Seneca, like Piso, was in fact regarded as an exemplary patron, cf. e.g. Mart. 12.36.8.

points out that similar charges have been laid against many great philosophers of the past. Even Cato the Younger, the enduring symbol of Stoic and Republican propaganda, is cited as an immensely wealthy man.

That the discussion is more personal than usual in Seneca's frequently personal philosophical writings seems indicated by the contemptuous terms he uses for his supposedly "imaginary" critics. Seneca often introduces fictitious adversaries into his writings and they generally serve no other purpose than to provide convenient men of straw. But adversaries in this dialogue take on a life of their own. Only in the later *Epistulae Morales* does Seneca display such bitterness. He speaks angrily of their malice (*malevolentia*, 17.3) and his own moral superiority (17.4); he calls them spiteful excrescences, the enemies of all the best men (*malignissima capita et optimo cuique inimicissima*, 18.1). He compares them to little dogs (19.2) and in a bravura passage he says:

> nec malignitas me ista multo veneno tincta deterrebit ab optimis; ne virus quidem istud, quo alios spargitis, quo vos necatis, me inpediet quominus perseverem laudare vitam, non quam ago sed quam agendam scio. (18.2)

> And that spite of yours, tainted with poison, will not deter me from what is best, not even that virulence, which you splash over others, and by which you are killing yourselves, will prevent me persisting in the praise, not of the life I lead, but of the life I know ought to be led.

And again, in an apparent burst of passion, he continues:

> vos quidem, quod virtutem cultoremque eius odistis, nihil novi facitis. . . . gemite et infelicem linguam bonorum exercete convicio, hiate, commordete: citius multo frangetis dentes quam imprimitis. (20.6)

> As for you, in the fact that you hate virtue and him who practices it, you reveal nothing new. . . . Groan away and exercise your

damned tongue in abusing good men, open your jaws and bite:
You will break your teeth far quicker than you will leave their
mark.

His detractors are envious; it is they who are the real slaves of
money, not Seneca (22.5). He cites as a proof of his uprightness
the very fact that he is disliked in some disreputable quarters
(24.4). Even Socrates is invoked in his defense (27.1), as though
the two were in similar situations or had similar incomes.

The treatise breaks off just as Seneca is making another coun-
terattack, full of veiled threats, a rhetorical eruption even more
vigorous and prolonged than his earlier efforts:

> vobis autem vacat aliena scrutari mala et sententias ferre de quo-
> quam? "quare hic philosophus laxius habitat? quare hic lautius
> cenat?" . . . obicite Platoni quod petierit pecuniam, Aristoteli quod
> acceperit, Democrito quod neglexerit, Epicuro quod consump-
> serit; mihi ipsi Alcibiaden et Phaedrum obiectate, o vos visu max-
> ime felices, cum primum vobis imitari vitia nostra contigerit. . . .
> at ego ex alto prospiciens video quae tempestates aut immineant
> vobis paulo tardius rupturae nimbum suum aut iam vicinae vos ac
> vestra rapturae propius accesserint. (27.4–28)

> As for you, however, have you time free to scrutinize other men's
> faults and pass judgment on anybody? "Why does this philospher
> live so comfortably? Why does this one dine so elegantly?" . . .
> Blame Plato because he went after money, blame Aristotle be-
> cause he took it, blame Democritus because he ignored it, blame
> Epicurus because he spent it; as for me, fling Alcibiades and Phae-
> drus in my face, although you'll look most fortunate when first
> you happen to copy my vices. . . . But, from my vantage point,
> I see storms threatening you that a little later will bring a cloud-
> burst, or storms, near enough already, that have come even closer
> to sweep you away and everything connected with you.

It is not difficult to detect in this last passage a reference to the
embattled Suillius, who was in fact condemned and exiled to the
Balearic islands (Tac. Ann. 13.43). Seneca's important treatise,
De Tranquillitate Animi, apparently belongs to the same histori-

cal context and is surely to be dated between 60 and 62.[39] This too is an *apologia* for Seneca's political activity and worldly power and seems to reflect his growing unease about his position at court, his influence in the emperor's councils, and perhaps even his worries about Nero's growing hostility.

After the later *De Otio*, however, Seneca, now in semiretirement, continued to produce philosophical or scientific books. The lengthy and encyclopedic *Naturales Quaestiones* belong to this period and between 63 and 64 he wrote, perhaps intermittently because they were published in serial batches, the *Epistulae Morales ad Lucilium*. These are for the modern reader by far the most interesting of Seneca's surviving works because of their literary liveliness, vivid style, and personal observation. Although political considerations had occasionally shown themselves in his more formal treatises—witness his otherwise gratuitous quotation and praise of a line of Nero's poetry in the *Naturales Quaestiones*—the *Epistulae* offered a more flexible form in which to express his views not only on abstract questions of moral philosophy, but also on some of his current preoccupations.[40] Ostensibly they are an exposition of various aspects of Stoic philosophy, interlaced with anecdotes and descriptions of Seneca's own day-to-day experiences. But they could take account obliquely of court politics. A radical change of tone in the later letters toward Epicureanism and Epicureans in society demonstrates the increasing bitterness and anxiety that Seneca was feeling about some of his supplanters, a feeling that may have driven him ultimately to some form of remote involvement in the Pisonian conspiracy of 65, and possible misprision of treason. One may even discern a rejection of his earlier moderating role in Neronian governance.

In the light of these letters any concept of an almost monolithic Stoic opposition would have to be discarded: they reveal

39. Skeptical arguments to the contrary are offered by Momigliano (1975) 252 and Griffin (1976) 316, 321.

40. The form may have been inspired by the recent publication around 63 of Cicero's *Letters to Atticus*: see Shackleton Bailey (1965) 61.

clearly how Stoicism, almost as much as Epicureanism, was as compatible with quietism and a neglect of public affairs, as it was with active participation in political and military life. From a Stoic perspective, Seneca discusses in laudatory terms the mixed constitution enjoyed by Sparta and then by Rome, as well as the government of the just monarch. Ethically, it was a creed more flexible than we might assume from its stereotypes such as Cato, Musonius Rufus, and Thrasea Paetus. Even Seneca admitted that an unjust ruler could be properly removed by force. While he utilized Stoic arguments to try to implant in Nero the principles of clemency, justice, and wisdom, he offered similar arguments to reconcile the more stubborn members of the senatorial aristocracy to the acceptance of an all-powerful princeps.[41]

Seneca's nephew Lucan was a less pragmatic Stoic, a revolutionary in several senses, and an interesting contrast, even foil, to his uncle, who had first introduced him to court life and imperial politics. The adaptability of Stoic doctrines makes more comprehensible the behavior of the poet and the thrust of his subversive epic, the *Pharsalia*.[42] Whatever Lucan's personal attitudes were toward the principate and court which his uncle and, for a time, he himself had faithfully served, there is no doubt that the *Pharsalia* is written from the standpoint of an emotional Republican. His Stoicism, although important, is secondary as a shaping force in the artistic development of the *Pharsalia*. The core of Republican ideology is presumably that, from Julius Caesar on, the de facto heads of the Roman state held their power *illegally*, whatever their pretensions and constitutional disguises, and that power must be restored to the *senatus populusque Romanus*, which in effect meant the senate, of which Lucan, following his premature augurate and quaestorship, was naturally a member. *Libertas senatoria* is the heart of the matter.

One of the factors that gave, as we have seen, a spurious plau-

---

41. For discussion of this complex question, see Griffin (1976) 202, 360.

42. I use the title for convenience and to distinguish the work from Petronius' *Bellum Civile*. For a detailed examination of the question, see Ahl (1976) 326.

sibility to the notion of a Stoic "opposition" was the ideological symbol of the Younger Cato, who preferred to commit suicide at Utica rather than witness the predictable extinction of Republican liberty. Through this last act his faults were all forgotten by the supporters of the Republic, though not, presumably, by the defenders of the principate. Cato had become a heavy part of the baggage of the senatorial "liberal imagination." He even became a standard subject in Roman rhetorical training.[43] When bitter disillusion with Nero's political and personal behavior grew within the senatorial ranks, it was natural that writers should turn once more to this potent symbol. It was Nero's most prominent critic, Thrasea Paetus, consul in 56, who wrote a life of Cato, with whom he supposedly identified himself, at least in the manner of his death. Later the Younger Helvidius Priscus, connected by family ties, was to write Thrasea's biography, doubtless perpetuating the hard-line Stoic tradition.

Seneca also found in Cato the nearest possible embodiment of the Stoic *sapiens* with his indomitable courage, indifference to worldly possessions and personal misfortunes, and his championship of the cause of freedom against both Caesar and Pompey.[44] Interest in the political implications of Cato's life and death seems to increase in the later works, such as the *De Beneficiis*. It is particularly evident in the *Epistulae Morales*, where the image of the proud "loner" would offset the writer's loss of influence with the prince he had once proclaimed the inaugurator of a new Golden Age. But it was left to his nephew Lucan to paint the most ideological picture of that flawed Stoic saint and express through him the aspirations and nostalgic longings of a minority of the senatorial class for a Republic that could never be restored.

A balanced evaluation of Lucan's epic is not our concern here, but rather its political implications and its place in the arena of Neronian literary infighting. Lucan's epic is not designed like

---

43. Cf. Sen. *Controv.* 6.4, 9.6.7, 10.1.8, 10.3.5; *Suas.* 6, 7; Pers. 3.44; Sen. *Ep.* 3.3.6.

44. See Pecchiura (1965) 59; Griffin (1976) 182.

Milton's "to justify God's ways to man," although a misreading of the deliberately grotesque and fulsome flattery of Nero in Book 1.33–66 might lead to such a conclusion. The passage has caused some trouble to critics, but it may be suggested that this very *detachable* section had more than just a conventional purpose: it is there to hide something, even to protect the poet. Had Lucan lived to finish and publish his epic, had the Pisonian conspiracy succeeded in toppling Nero, the modern reader might have known nothing of his flattery of the emperor except through some gossip writer hostile to Lucan. In these few lines Lucan claims that if civil war was the only way fate and the gods could bring forth Nero to rule Rome, then the city has no regrets. The crimes and the illegality involved were amply justified by their outcome:

> iam nihil, o superi, querimur; scelera ipsa
> nefasque hac mercede placent.
> (1.37–38)

Unlike Vergil, who alludes to Augustus and his family in a number of places throughout the *Aeneid*, Lucan does not mention Nero again after 1.33–66, nor is his ancestor Domitius Ahenobarbus as favorably treated as a thirst for adulation might dictate—he is absent, for instance, from the description of the siege of Massilia. This last would seem a flatterer's opportunity deliberately thrown away, as Nero placed considerable emphasis on his Ahenobarban connections.[45] The epic taken as a whole embodies the opposite conclusion to that stated in the fulsome address to Nero. *Nothing* could justify the Civil War and its results, least of all the house of the Julio-Claudians (*Caesareae domus series*), of which Nero was but the latest example. Either to subvert his eulogy further and convey a hint of the insincerity of his flattery to the sophisticated, or to exaggerate his feigned devotion to his friend the emperor, Lucan indulges in an absurd piece of hyperbole: on his deification and ascent to heaven, Nero is to take his place in the exact center of the heavens where he

45. See the *Acta Arvalia* for 2 December 57.

can view Rome directly from above without obstructing clouds, and where he will not by his weight disturb the equilibrium of the universe.[46]

References to Nero's posthumous deification and ascent to heaven are the common coin of Neronian sycophants, as we know from Seneca's *Apocolocyntosis* and Calpurnius Siculus. Lucan may have been within the acceptable limits of poetic adulation, which as we know from Martial and Statius were broad, in suggesting that Nero should be allowed to choose whether to take Jupiter's scepter or drive the fiery chariot of Phoebus or become whatever deity he wishes (1.42–52). Lucan is barely veiling his pessimism, however, when he prays that on Nero's translation the human race will stop fighting and will love each other, and that universal peace will at last allow the iron gates of the Temple of Janus to be closed.

Certainly the epic that follows reflects Lucan's profound lack of faith in destiny and the nature of most men. He even disregards the standard Stoic doctrine of the ultimate, if sometimes hidden, benevolence of providence. Whether the praise of Nero found in Book 1 is conventional or ambiguous flattery, a political insurance policy, or a stroke of disguised impudence, it is of little weight against the evidence of the whole poem from Book 1 onward. Naturally, Lucan's anti-Caesarism, which may already have disturbed Nero and may have been at least partly responsible for the ban on Lucan's publication, grew progressively stronger as the poet's own circumstances worsened.[47] Still, the message is there from the beginning, even if more cautiously expressed.

The horror of the Civil War, however tempting a subject, was hardly safe poetic material in the early principate. Despite some claims to the contrary,[48] there is little evidence of poetry devoted

46. For the arguments and literature on the question of the poem's intentions, see Ahl (1976) 35, and for the invocation of Nero and Lucan's inconsistent treatment of Domitius, ibid. 47.

47. See Ahl (1976) 41; he cites Book 7 as the most savage book in this respect, especially vv. 432–59 and 638–46.

48. See e.g. Smith (1975) 215.

to this painful topic between the Augustan and Neronian periods. Ovid's contemporary Rabirius wrote a moving epic piece on the death of Antony after Actium, but he founded no tradition of such writing. Only in the Neronian age do Civil War themes come back in vogue, to be treated by Lucan, Petronius, and the unidentified author of the *De Bello Actiaco*,[49] and even then the latter two seem parasitic on the former. After all, Augustus, the first princeps, had tried to give the impression early on that he had been responsible for bringing Rome internal peace.[50] Horace, Vergil, and Propertius had all treated the topic at a time when the issue was, if delicate, at least contemporary. *Libertas* and the evils of post-Augustan autocracy were touchy subjects, unless carefully located in the never-never land of Greek mythology, as in Statius' *Thebais* and Seneca's tragedies. Nevertheless, Lucan, from the very beginning of his epic, expresses through his characters sentiments he will express directly in later books. Nigidius Figulus prophesies:

> ". . . multosque exhibit in annos
> hic furor. et superos quid prodest poscere finem?
> cum domino pax ista venit. duc, Roma, malorum
> continuam seriem clademque in tempora multa
> extrahe civili tantum iam libera bello."
>
> (*Phars.* 1.668–72)

> ". . . and this madness will continue for many a year. And what benefit is it to ask the gods above for an end to it? With that peace there comes a master. Rome, drag out a continuous series of misfortunes, prolong the disaster for a long time to come, since now you are free only while there is civil war."

References in this book to such symbolic figures as Sulla and Marius (vv. 581, 583) emphasize their roles as destroyers of constitutional liberty rather than great military saviors.

---

49. *Herc. Pap.* 817 ed. Garuti (1958); for an interpretation, Benario (1983) 1656; cf. also Bardon (1956) 73, 136.

50. Cf. *Res Gestae Divi Augusti*, Brunt (1967) 34: *postquam civilia bella extinxeram.*

From the start, then, Lucan's *Pharsalia* had an ideological basis, as had Vergil's *Aeneid*. Lucan's primary aim no doubt was to
write a great poem, but literature and politics can make close
and not incompatible bedfellows. Lucan's epigrammatic and
rhetorical style, his epic innovations, are at the service also of a
mission that became more and more real for him as discontent
with Nero grew in the social and literary circles he frequented.
The *Pharsalia* is a lament for the losses of the great Civil War.
The last, most important casualty, in Lucan's view, had been
Republican liberty; the next most tragic loss was Cato, the embodiment of all Republican and Stoic virtues. Correspondingly,
the epic is an attack first on Caesar the destroyer and then on
Caesarism or, more specifically, on the Julio-Claudian dynasty
(4.823), one of the larger themes of the *Octavia*. Lucan writes as
a dedicated Republican,[51] a stance far removed from that of the
more pragmatic Seneca, who accepted the concept of a *rex iustus*
and had indeed striven to produce one in Nero.[52]

The prose and poetry of the age of Nero is full of highly emo-
tive political symbols, some lingering on from the late Republic.
We have seen ways in which the invocation of Augustus could
be used at the opening of a new reign. Vitellius was later to find
the invocation of Nero similarly advantageous (Suet. *Vitell.* 11).
Rex (and *regnum*) had pejorative overtones from ancient times,
apart from the context of the patronage system, but as a descrip-
tive title it became more and more acceptable for use in favorable contrast to *tyrannus*.[53] Seneca, accepting reality, had tried to
defuse this bomb in the *De Clementia*. *Libertas* as a philosophical
and literary concept, or rather a set of concepts, had had to
undergo some changes of connotation to survive the altered
conditions after the reigns of Julius and Augustus Caesar. Stoic
philosophy provided considerable help in blurring its original

---

51. This is not to say that in the Pisonian conspiracy he stood firmly with those
who felt it possible to restore the Republic; he might have gone along with Piso's
candidacy for the principate as the only practical way of removing the last of the
Julio-Claudian rulers.

52. See Kopp (1969) 139.

53. See Cizek (1982) 73 ("Le Roi et le Tyranne").

political meaning and even its social implications. Seneca has taken advantage of this in his literary propaganda. For the Stoics only the wise man is free; so the possibility of freedom under a *rex iustus* (or indeed *iniustus*) became another of their ably argued paradoxes. So when Persius writes of *libertas* in the context of manumitting slaves (5.73 ff.), he cleaves strictly to the prevalent Stoic definition: only in wisdom is there true freedom. But when Lucan talks of *libertas*, he means *libertas Romana* or, even more specifically, *libertas senatoria*.[54] It is this *libertas* for which Cato the Younger was fighting, even though Lucan would have had to agree that Cato, of all men, had already attained *libertas* in the Stoic sense, the sense in which Persius and Seneca often used it.

Other symbolic figures in the epic present fewer complications. From ancient or comparatively modern history, come either heroic figures such as Regulus and Brutus; hated representatives of unconstitutional government such as Marius, Cinna, and Sulla; or terrifying external enemies such as the Gauls, the Parthians, Hannibal, and Jugurtha. These symbols usually evoked uncomplicated responses in those who defended the principate and those who were secretly against it. More difficult for Lucan to use would have been the politicized materials derived from Roman religion and mythology. All gods, goddesses, and lesser divinities had their provinces and powers: inspirers of poetry or war, protectors of gardens or Rome, deliverers from the pangs of childbirth or from love. Where a traditional deity did not clearly reign, abstract divinities such as *Salus*, *Fides*, and *Concordia* could be called upon. In the propaganda battles that raged during and long after the Civil War, it was important to enlist on one's side as many of these religious symbols as possible: in battle cries, inscriptions, regimental names; on coins or monuments; and naturally, in the partisan literature of the time. The Julian clan went further than most; it claimed direct descent from Venus through Aeneas and his son Iulus. Consequently, the ancestor

54. See Wirszubski (1950) 125, 137.

of the Julian house is also the founder of Rome, and Vergil's *Aeneid* solemnly celebrates the claim.[55] But neither Julius Caesar nor Augustus was content with such a distinguished heavenly connection. Augustus in particular, sensitive to public opinion after the fate of his adoptive father, tried to organize his religious champions systematically: Jupiter, Apollo, Venus, Mercury, Vesta, Juno, and Mars are prominent among his Olympian backers, some in different avatars. *Pax*, *Fortuna*, *Honos*, and *Virtus* are among his more disembodied supporters, also in varying guises.[56] On the other hand, the crucial word Lucan chose was *libertas*, which then became the key image in his revolutionary and complex poem[57] as well as the standard around which the conspirators could rally. To quote a modern judgment: "Lucan's *Pharsalia*, alone among ancient epics, is not just a mirror of political power; it is an exercise in political power."[58]

It is unfair to point to one single theme in a multiplex epic, but an impartial evaluation of Lucan's great poem does not concern us here, only its political aspect. And politically the battle of Pharsalia is the spatial and temporal pivot of the work. It was after this battle that Roman *libertas* and the Republic itself came to an end. Julius Caesar, the founder of the Julio-Claudian dynasty, destroyed it, according to Lucan, because of his ambition and self-aggrandizement. Pompey, that *magni nominis umbra*, whose own motives and future intentions were also suspect to Lucan, was at least identifiable with the Republican system and the senate, even though he could not defend either the state or himself against the awesome energy and preternatural abilities of Caesar. Only Cato, with whose suicide at Utica the *Pharsalia* would probably have ended, was to emerge from the catastrophe of the Civil War with a luster undimmed in death. He would

---

55. For the Republic and early principate, see Taylor (1949) 76, and for Lucan's dilemma, Ahl (1976) 68.

56. Cf. e.g. *Res Gestae Divi Augusti* 11, 19 (ed. cit. 22, 26).

57. See Mooney (1927), s.vv. *liber, libertas*.

58. Ahl (1982) 925.

remain the perfect embodiment of *libertas* in both the political and Stoic senses.

It is inappropriate, perhaps, to describe Cato as the *hero* of the poem in a formal way: Pompey and Caesar get equal attention and it is hardly helpful to speak of three protagonists, or to suggest that the real hero is virtue or liberty or that the real antihero is Caesar, who thereby plays the scene-stealing role inadvertently given to Satan in Milton's *Paradise Lost*. Lucan's *Pharsalia* is too complex a work of art for this.

Historical epic, as far as we can see from Lucan and Silius Italicus, developed its own artistic traditions, differing from standard mythological epic, which could limit its heroes to one or two. Jason is the hero, whatever his weaknesses, of Apollonius Rhodius' *Argonautica*. Achilles is meant to be the hero of the *Iliad*, whatever our sympathies for Hector. Aeneas is the hero of the Aeneid, however unsatisfactory he appears to modern tastes and however sympathetically the villains or victims, Turnus or Dido, are presented. Even in the more fraught and ambiguous Theban cycle, Eteocles is the unsympathetic hero; Polynices his wicked, yet more appealing, antagonist. With historical epic, a genre that even Callimachus did not entirely despise, one main hero is not always picked out so easily unless the poem takes as its subject a small war waged by one general, which is not the case with either the *Pharsalia* or the *Punica*.

Not the least of Lucan's dramatic virtues is his ability to focus our attention on three major characters in turn: Pompey, Caesar, and Cato. Yet it is clear who at the end emerges as the "moral hero." In Cato, Lucan had most of the ideological implications he needed, and where necessary he could call on lesser historical figures such as Regulus. He therefore dispenses almost entirely with the commonest source of epic symbolism and the most flexible means of expressing an author's values, mythology.[59] The few references to gods are insignificant and little is to be

59. Cf. Ahl (1976) 68.

understood from these except that, as active powers for good or ill, the gods are unimportant or quiescent in the civil wars. *Fortuna* and *Fatum* are as close as Lucan comes to the traditional agents of the divine at work in mortal affairs.

For this revolution in the writing of epic, Lucan had some precedents. Didactic poets of epic scope had not always used two planes of action, one human and one divine. So Hesiod's *Works and Days*, Lucretius' *De Rerum Natura*, Vergil's *Georgics*, and other admired poems of some length were possible precedents. Lucan's Stoic views on religion, as well as his artistic views on the poetic viability of epic deities, may have helped him to his momentous and revolutionary decision, a decision destined unfortunately to be both criticized and disregarded. Statius, Valerius Flaccus, Silius Italicus all return to the older Homeric and Vergilian tradition. The tribute of imitation is not always a guarantee of success.

Lucan, it has often been suggested, set out to correct or to impugn Vergil's vision of Roman history. To do this, he had to contend with the almost total enlistment on the side of the Caesars of the most powerful deities. Against them he could muster only such Republican and Stoic abstracts as *virtus, pietas, libertas,* and such Republican heroes as Regulus and Cato. Divine machinery, moreover, can do little to help in eliciting sympathy for the vanquished, who *had* to be defeated because the gods or the fates desired this result for their larger purposes. The morality or rightness of the losers' cause cannot therefore be rigorously examined nor their motivation, psychological or moral, too closely scrutinized, because as the agents of the divine will they cannot be held ultimately responsible. Lucan, accordingly, chooses morality or immorality, ambition or altruism, dedication to freedom or the acceptance of slavery, to determine his characters' action rather than messengers from Olympus or heaven-sent dreams. How events fall out remains the decision of Fortune or Destiny; but the responsibility for how men behave is their own.

[152]

CHAPTER IV

Court Politics
and Petronius

The ways in which literature in the Neronian period could be used for flattery and personal advancement, to advocate a new aesthetics, or to advance moderate or extreme political causes should now be clear. A closer examination of the methods and techniques employed by different writers to further their own aims and careers by denigrating their opponents may prove morbidly fascinating to some and distasteful to those who believe that classical writers have somehow a superior sensibility to those of later ages. But there is some general truth in Norman Douglas's remark in *South Wind* that "nobody writes for humanity, for civilization; they write for their country, their sect; to amuse their friends or annoy their enemies." Attacks on personalities, on rival critical theories or specific literary modes, on unacceptable political or religious attitudes, have been common in all periods. Only the approach and the ground rules differ. Censorship, prosecution, libel suits, even physical attacks sometimes, are the Establishment's response to the threat posed by satire, parody, or invective.[1]

1. For example, Dr. Johnson records in his life of the poet the story, which is at least *ben trovato*, that John Dryden was beaten up by Lord Rochester's bully boys in December 1679 for supposedly being the author of an *Essay on Satire*. Popish writings were not licensed by the Stationer's Office in the later sixteenth and early sev-

Nero, it was noted earlier, professed to be indifferent to lampoons and verbal or written attacks on himself.[2] There were perhaps two minor instances of legal proceedings taken against notorious public insults,[3] but it was not until 62, when Nero was tiring of his conciliatory attitude to the senate, that he allowed the revival of the *lex maiestatis*, abolished by Claudius in 51, for defamation of the emperor.[4]

This is rather a poor haul for those who would look for the systematic penalization of provocative literature before 65, particularly as a great many pamphlets were passed around and graffiti in Latin and Greek chalked on walls are duly recorded in our sources. The usual themes of these were Nero's artistic obsessions, his growing power over the state, his extravagant buildings, and of course the elimination of his mother in 59.[5] Ten years later we discover that poems against Nero were circulating freely in Spain and Gaul. Despite requests from Nero, his procurators did not press the governors actively to suppress them, perhaps adopting Nero's own former indifference to such unimportant libels or not wishing to display excessive zeal in a cause they considered lost.

Libelous poems, then, were a feature of Neronian literary life.

---

enteenth centuries, although pirated copies were produced by the Stationer's officials. The censorship and book burnings of authoritarian and totalitarian regimes need no documentation. D'Israeli's *Quarrels of Authors* (1814) still provides absorbing reading.

2. Suet. *Nero* 39.1–2. He may have been somewhat unpredicatable here. He tolerated excessive candor from Burrus (Dio 62.13.1–2); Seneca boasted of his frankness toward him (Tac. *Ann.* 15.60); Petronius and Otho insulted him without losing his friendship (Plut. *Mor.* 60 d–e; *Galb.* 2.19.3); but the familiarities of Vestinus he resented extremely and eventually avenged (Tac. *Ann.* 15.68).

3. Isodorus the Cynic shouted that Nero was good at singing about the misfortunes of Nauplius, but not at taking care of his own property; Datus the Atellan actor made a witty and unmistakable allusion on the stage to the deaths of Claudius and Agrippina (Suet. *Nero* 39.3). Both were prosecuted and banished from Italy; the other case of the philosopher L. Annaeus Cornutus who was banished allegedly for criticizing Nero's literary plans (Dio 62.29.2) is better explained by his connection with dangerous political elements, which surfaced in the Pisonian conspiracy.

4. For Antistius Sosianus, see Bauman (1974) 143. His case and that of Fabricius Veiento were discussed in Chapter 2.

5. Suet. *Nero* 39; Dio 62.1.1. Fabricius' *Codicilli* (Tac. *Ann.* 14.5) and Seneca's last dictated message to the world (*Ann.* 15.63) both apparently enjoyed a fair circulation at the time they were written.

Nero's own squib against Afranius Quintianus, the future conspirator, was possibly less virulent than Lucan's poetic assault on
the emperor and his more prominent friends, where the material
was more promising and the writer more gifted.[6] Perhaps Curiatius Maternus was exaggerating the influence of his tragedy
Cato in undermining the malicious Vatinius, the cobbler turned
court jester (Tac. *Dial.* 11), but he gives some idea of the vagar-
ies of reputation and influence in Neronian circles and the influence writing might have on a highly literate ruler. The power of
words, indeed the power of letters in general, can rarely have
been seen to better effect than in Nero's court.

After the Pisonian conspiracy, when Nero's fears were justly
inflamed, all kinds of allegations were brought against all manner of people. In the literary sphere alone, Curtius Montanus
was accused in 66 of writing libelous verses, although again it is
more likely that his friendship with Thrasea Paetus and his possible involvement in treasonous circles prompted the case. Certainly the accusation of writing defamatory verse was not taken
seriously by his supporters and he was spared for his father's
sake, although debarred from political activity.[7]

Since accusations of writing defamatory or subversive literature could not apparently result in legal penalties or at least prosecution by delators, the forging of such literature may have become a practice in the later years of Nero's rule. Forgeries, for
example, were uttered in Lucan's name and his seal was used by
the emperor himself to swell the treasury by confiscations. Petronius was careful to break his signet ring before his death, so
that it could not be put to similar uses. Against this background,
two phenomena may be expected: on the one hand, the use of
literature to pay off private and political scores in the way Seneca
had revenged himself on Claudius in the *Apocolocyntosis* and on
Suillius and other critics in the *De Vita Beata*; on the other, a
reasonable discretion in the way such attacks were mounted. The

6. Tac. *Ann.* 15.49; Suet. *Vit. Lucan.* 5–6.
7. Tac. *Ann.* 16.28 (*detestanda carmina factitantem*), 29, 33.

naming of names is an infrequent characteristic of ancient literary polemic, witness Callimachus and his Telchines, Horace and Propertius, Ovid and "Ibis," and Martial and Statius. One must look for subtler methods of denigration, which though opaque to us and perhaps deniable in a law court, would be plain enough to intimates and contemporaries.

With this in mind, we may now reexamine the latter half of Nero's reign. Burrus was dead and had been replaced by the doomed Faenius Rufus and the dissolute Tigellinus, whose political agility and powerful friends allowed him to survive, though not for long, Nero's death. Seneca, although he had not been allowed to retire formally in 62, had withdrawn on grounds of ill health or philosophical pursuits from Nero's political and social activities. His enemies' charge that, since Nero had taken an interest in literature, Seneca had increased his own literary productions may have remained valid, however (Tac. *Ann.* 14.52, 57). Indeed much of Seneca's most interesting prose can be attributed to the period after 62 and it seems also reasonable to date some of the tragedies, given their political content and Nero's strong interest in dramatic performances, to any period after 59 or even the year of Seneca's reluctant retirement.[8] Apart from Nero's interest in the stage, there was, after all, a distinguished tradition for Seneca to follow. Ovid's *Medea* and Varius' *Thyestes* had been widely praised (Tac. *Dial.* 12), and Pomponius Secundus, on the basis of his *praetextae* such as the *Aeneas*, had been given the palm among Seneca's contemporaries by Quintilian (*Inst.* 10.1.98).

The use of mythological characters and themes to reflect on and interpret present-day realities has a long history, from Aeschylus' *Eumenides* down to Shelley's *Prometheus Unbound*, Coc-

---

8. E.g. *De Providentia, De Tranquillitate Animi, Naturales Quaestiones,* the *Epistulae Morales,* and perhaps some of the four books of poems with which he was credited in our later sources. Because Nero had such a fondness for the drama and for acting himself, the accepted view that Seneca's tragedies were not meant to be performed in some fashion seems a priori unlikely and has been contested by Fortey and Glucker (1975) 699. The small outdoor stage in the House of the Vettii in Pompeii gives some idea of how economically a dramatic recital could be staged.

teau's *Orphée*, and Giraudoux's *La guerre de Troie n'aura pas lieu*, to mention but a few. It could be dangerous, as Aemilius Scaurus had discovered in the reign of Tiberius, when his dramatic writing had contributed to his downfall.[9] Seneca's dramas also constantly confront the nature of kingship and tyranny, along with such themes as regal clemency; the adaptability and insecurity of courtiers; the dangers of public life; the inevitable corruption, instability, and evanescence of power; the treachery that surrounds it; the resentment bred by arbitrary rule; and the constant possibility of assassination.[10] As in his prose treatises, the

9. Mamercus Aemilius Scaurus had been accused by Sutorius Macro, the praetorian prefect, of *maiestas* partly on the grounds of writing a tragedy whose plot and certain lines could be taken as an attack on Tiberius (Tac. *Ann.* 6.29). The drama was *Atreus* (Dio 58.24.4). Significantly, Curiatius Maternus said he would use the same tragic theme for political criticism (*si qua omisit Cato, sequenti recitatione Thyestes dicet*, Tac. *Dial.* 3.3). It should be noted also that Seneca's *Thyestes*, which, according to Fitch (1981) 292, belongs to the latest group of his plays, seems to contain the severest criticism of Nero. Certainly the reflections in it on the tyrant's disdain of popular respect are echoed in similar remarks in the *Octavia* (cp. *Thy.* 206–18 and *Oct.* 453–60; 572–84). The mythic material provided by the Pelopidae and Atreidae seems to figure prominently in Neronian dramaturgy. The gruesome concatenation of incestuous sexual connections, the sacrifice of children, the brutal murder of relatives and kin by marriage for the sake of success or succession, all vividly exemplified in the relations between Thyestes, Atreus, Agamemnon, and Orestes, and, on the distaff side, between Procne, Philomela, Clytemnestra, and Electra could be paralleled somehow by an imaginative symbolist in the history of the Julio-Claudian emperors. Juvenal dubbed Domitian not only *calvus Nero* but also *Atrides* (*Sat.* 4.38, 65). This was not lost on the author of the *Octavia*, as we have seen, nor indeed on Seneca himself. Scaurus' prosecution, however, led to his suicide, but there seem to have been graver charges against him than treasonous libel. For an interesting discussion of the changing use of mythological themes in tragedy from nationalist celebration to protest and political criticism, see Zorzetti (1980) 93. For the use of mythological drama as a sort of code for critics of the imperial regime or a particular emperor, see MacMullen (1966) 36. A detailed study of the use of drama and also epic in the first century of the principate for political discussion and criticism is clearly needed. Although the dangers varied from one reign to the next, mythological examination of broad political issues was regarded as tolerably safe, e.g. by Curiatius Maternus and Statius, perhaps because apparent allusions would be deniable as due to coincidence or the literary tradition. Two Senecan cryptologists who perhaps carry their code breaking to extremes with Seneca's *Oedipus* are Pathmanathan (1967/8) and Bishop (1978).

10. Typical passages are found in *Hercules Furens* 84–85 (interpretable as advice to Nero); 159–201 (the dangers of public life and excessive wealth); 250–53 (the might that is wrongly dubbed right); 312–17, 325–28 (the fear and pessimism of power); 337–45, 352–53 (the use of military strength to retain power and ignore unpopularity—*ars prima regni est posse et invidiam pati*); 735–47 (the necessity of regal clemency to avoid the subjects' vengeance); and in *Phoen.* 152–54 (the dangers of anger in a

main thrust of the advice, or later perhaps the resentment, seems directed at Nero, but there are implicit warnings to the senatorial order and pleas for their cooperation in governance.

It is strange that these tragedies have caused such puzzlement to literary historians,[11] who have generally attributed them all to the period of Seneca's exile, when he was writing the *Consolationes ad Helviam* and *ad Polybium* and such short poems as are preserved in the *Anthologia Latina*, complaining of his place of exile, Corsica. but Seneca, as was argued earlier, rarely wrote without a purpose. The tragedies, with their many references to tyranny and its dangers, would hardly help persuade Claudius to recall him. That was left to Claudius' new wife, the imperious Agrippina, who supposedly did so in the best interests of her son Nero. Better then to see at least some of the tragedies as one of many responses to the activity of Nero's poetic workshops for amateurs. Seneca wished to retain his reputation as the leading man of letters of his day; he wished also to reinforce more subtly the lessons he had been inculcating in the *De Ira* and the *De Clementia*. If it be argued that Seneca in his latter years was producing a remarkable amount of work, one has only to look at the production and work habits of the Elder Pliny, as described by his nephew (*Ep.* 3.5). Seneca, whatever the criticisms launched at him, was no sluggard.

But nagging and manipulative moralists became tedious. To

---

ruler); 598–601 (the insatiability of power); 624–25 (kingship based on justice); 654–64 (the pains and rewards of autocracy). For similar advice and reflections, cf. *Med.* 185–86, 189, 221–24, 242–43, 252–56; *Phaedr.* 139, 204–17, 427–30, 486–500, 517–19, 980–88, 1123–43; *Troad.* 1–7, 250, 265–91, 335; *Ag.* 730–33; *Thy.* 176–84, 339–403 (part of this passage was a great favorite of Elizabethan courtiers such as Sir Thomas Wyatt, *stet quicumque volens / aulae culmine lubrico*, vv.391 ff.), 404–90 (the whole scene with Thyestes, Tantalus, and Pleisthenes seems to reinforce the message of the *De Clementia* and foreshadows material in Juvenal's tenth satire), 549–622; *Oed.* 82–85, 242–45, 509–29, 632–706 (on the pretense of quiescence in aspirants to a throne; the reluctance of all to accept second place; the inevitability of imperial suspicion, because arbitrary rule breeds resentment). Although the play is by an admirer of Seneca's, not the philosopher himself, one may add similar passages from *Hercules Oetaeus*: 5–7 (on tyrants); 228–30 (the pliability of courtiers); 604–99 (the nature of kingship); 1867–71 (Hercules as Stoic hero and destroyer of tyrants).

11. For the most accessible recent discussions, see Herington (1965) and Calder (1976b).

[158]

replace Seneca as the *arbiter litterarum* closest to Nero were such obvious candidates as Nerva (Mart. 9.26; 8.70) and, above all, T. Petronius Niger, perhaps a little before his suffect consulship in 62. Tacitus has given us a sketchy account of Petronius' career. After being governor of Bithynia, a prosperous but trouble-prone senatorial province, which the Younger Pliny was later to manage, Petronius entered the small circle of Nero's intimates. Not, to be sure, the most intimate circle, of which Tigellinus was a member, for Petronius had to obtain the details of Nero's less elegant and more licentious amusements from one of the imperial partners in vice, Silia, a consular's wife. Now if Petronius was not master of these revels, a role presumably preempted by the *magistra libidinum Neronis*, Calvia Crispinilla, if he was simply Nero's *arbiter elegantiae*, it is a reasonable assumption that over and above his civilized taste, lavish expenditures, and an eccentric but fashionable style of living, Petronius had ingratiated himself by his wit and cultural interests. Suetonius tells us that Nero distributed friendship and hostility according to the lavishness of men's praises for his vocal performances (*Nero* 25), and doubtless this habit extended into his more intimate relationships. The role of a court critic of taste, in matters both sybaritic and aesthetic, would be precisely the part Petronius could play from what is known of his life and writings.

Nero's literary and artistic interests had not waned since those early days when he had gathered around him a group of aspiring poets. Quite the contrary: to Tacitus' obvious disgust, he now wanted wider and more enthusiastic audiences (*Ann.* 14.16; 15.33). Even the fire of Rome could not entirely divert his mind from more serious things, such as his own verses on the capture of Troy, which may have been the conclusion of his *Troica*. It is hard to imagine that the emperor would spend one night discussing his collection of myrrhine ware over dinner with Petronius; the next, discussing some friend's verses or reading his own; and the next, for relaxation, closeted with Calvia Crispinilla, Silia, Tigellinus, Sporus, and other disreputable orgiasts of that type. No literary-minded emperor fails to include a considerable number of artistic friends among his courtiers and closest advisers. This might make some sense of the surprising anecdote relating that at an emergency meeting, summoned on the occasion of the revolt of Julius Vindex in Gaul (spring 68), Nero spent much of the time demonstrating a new type of water-organ (Suet. *Nero* 41). Even if this was a display of bravado in the face of pressing danger, as it was part of the imperial tradition to play down the significance of revolts in public, the choice of topic is suggestive and reminiscent of Juvenal's account of Domitian's war cabinet settling down to discuss recipes for mullet (*Sat.* 4.119 ff.).

To retain Nero's favor and his own power and influence, Petronius employed a number of tactics. There was, first, his disingenuous frankness; he chided Nero, one of the biggest spenders in Rome's history, with miserliness, a joke Nero would naturally enjoy, unlike the more cutting jests of Vestinus (Tac. *Ann.* 15.69). Petronius spared no expense in indulging his own taste for material luxury; Pliny records the price, 300,000 sesterces, of his myrrhine wine dipper (*trulla*) made of aromatized fluorspar or bluejohn, which imparted a delicate flavoring to the wines served from it. Such aspects of Petronius' character led eventually to his downfall; Tigellinus, also an experienced voluptuary, as witness the feast he gave for Nero (Tac. *Ann.* 15.37), grew jealous of Petronius' influence over the emperor and implicated him in the Pisonian conspiracy, because of his friendship with the sleepy, dissolute Flavius Scaevinus, who was largely responsible for the betrayal of the plot.[12] If Tacitus is correct in his high estimation of Petronius' status at court, Petronius must have had talents that would be more important to Nero the artist; he presumably posed, like Nerva, as an accomplished critic and writer. It would then be appropriate that he should exercise his skills in this area by amusing Nero and the court circle with

---

12. Plin. *NH.* 37.8.20; Plut. *Mor.* 60 d–e; Tac. *Ann.* 16.17–20 (note especially his night-owl habits). The similarity of his character to that of his friend, Flavius Scaevinus, is not generally noted; cf. Tac. *Ann.* 15.49 (*vita somno languida*), 54, 70, for Scaevinus' final banquet and then his unexpectedly stoical death.

serial readings of the *Satyricon* and perhaps some of the poetry attributed to him in the *Anthologia Latina*.

The *Satyricon* is a strange work unless it is firmly set in the ambience of Nero's court. The allusions and parodies woven into it make no sense otherwise. Like Petronius himself, it is a complex and often baffling phenomenon. Petronius was at home in Nero's court until the very end, and the combination in his humorous saga of funny, obscene, and vulgar elements with elevated literary criticism and parody would obviously appeal to an emperor who himself combined disreputable sexual tastes, a passion for wrestling and chariot racing, a fondness for rowdy night wanderings in the lower quarters of the town, with an unprecedented enthusiasm for lyre playing, dramatic acting, and poetic composition. This combination of culture, decadence, and a taste for low life is a frequent pattern in certain historical periods.[13] In consolidating his position and, to put it bluntly, pleasing his master, Petronius had two obvious targets for his critical and parodic talents: Lucan and Seneca, who had both by this time (between 62 and 64) fallen out of favor. No doubt their family relationship caused them reciprocal harm. Both were important targets: one was the most brilliant poet of the age, envied by Nero for his talents and distrusted for the political sentiments of his epic, the other a long-established literary and philosophical luminary, who had survived and written steadily through the reigns of three emperors. Their presence on the cultural and intellectual stage can alone explain certain features of the *Satyricon*.

One should first consider Lucan, who had by now published Books 1–3 of the *Pharsalia* and had then been forbidden by Nero

13. The late nineteenth and early twentieth centuries in England and France provide similar examples and descriptions in the works of Verlaine, Rimbaud, Baudelaire, Huysmans, Villiers de L'Isle-Adam, Oscar Wilde, Ernest Dowson, Aubrey Beardsley, Frank Harris, Roger Casement, Baron Corvo, and others. The classic documents are Huysmans's *À Rebours* and Wilde's *The Portrait of Dorian Gray*, see Praz (1951) 289. The notorious "private" life of the popular Prince of Wales, later King Edward VII, involving actresses and music hall artistes such as Lily Langtry, also reflects the spirit of the times. The court of Charles II after the Restoration provides another parallel. For Nero's *levitas popularis*, see Yavetz (1969) 120.

to disseminate his work through public recitations or overt pub-lication: *famam carminum eius premebat Nero prohibueratque osten-tare, vanus adsimulatione* (Tac. *Ann.* 15.49). Private copies, like our modern *samizdat*, would be impossible to suppress, as we know from the circulation of Fabricius Veiento's *Codicilli*. Lu-can's deviation from the traditions of epic, not to mention his anti-Caesarism, had left him open to hostile critics. It is easy therefore to appreciate the thrust of the attack on the *Pharsalia* by Nero's *arbiter elegantiae* in chapters 118–24 of the *Satyricon*, the so-called *Bellum Civile*,[14] and the critical preface that intro-duces it. The allusions and imitations of Lucan, which are meant to be recognized by the knowledgeable audience, rely mainly on Books 1–3. These, according to Vacca, were published more or less in their present form and before Nero's ban. The satirist's task was thus made simpler, particularly if his taste would not allow him to become tedious to himself or boring to his audi-ence. As Lucan was no longer *persona grata* with Nero, Petronius would not have had to make any great claims for the poetic quality of his attack on this discredited former friend—an im-portant point, because Petronius seems to have been an inter-mittently careless or hasty writer. He protects his aesthetic standing here by a critique of Lucan's approach, before offering an unpretentious, if exemplary, reworking of Lucan's material. This is presented as the work of the inveterate poetaster Eumol-pus, who himself concedes that his "attack" (*impetus*) on the theme has not yet been finally revised. The same comment, unfortu-nately for different reasons, could be made of the *Pharsalia*. Eu-molpus' succinct criticism must surely be directed at Lucan:[15]

14. There is no ancient authority for this conventional title or for the title *carmen de bello civili*. It seems to be based simply on *Sat.* 118.6 (*ecce belli civilis ingens opus quisquis attigerit*) and the contents of the poem. In the context a title would have been unlikely, since it is referred to with the words *impetus, . . . nondum recepit ultimam manum* (ibid.). As with the *Pharsalia*, I have used the title for convenience.

15. The whole question is still, of course, debated, and the exact relationship if any between the *Bellum Civile* and the *Pharsalia* has been much canvassed. The fun-damental discussion with a summary of the previous literature and a collection of parallels is Rose (1971) 61, 87; the main objections to the thesis were made by George (1974) 119, who was followed by Smith in his edition of the *Cena* (1975) 214. See

multos iuvenes carmen decepit. nam ut quisque versum pedibus
instruxit sensumque teneriorem verborum ambitu intexuit, pu-
tavit se continuo in Heliconem venisse. sic forensibus ministeriis
exercitati frequenter ad carminis tranquillitatem tamquam ad por-
tum refugerunt, credentes facilius poema extrui posse quam con-
troversiam sententiolis vibrantibus pictam. . . . praeterea curan-
dum est ne sententiae emineant extra corpus orationis, sed intexto
vestibus colore niteant. Homerus testis et lyrici Romanusque Ver-
gilius et Horatii curiosa felicitas. . . . ecce belli civilis ingens opus
quisquis attigerit nisi plenus litteris, sub onere labetur. non enim
res gestae versibus comprehendendae sunt, quod longe melius
historici faciunt, sed per ambages deorumque ministeria et fabu-
losum sententiarum torrentem praecipitandus est liber spiritus, ut
potius furentis animi vaticinatio appareat quam religiosae orationis sub testibus fides: tamquam, si placet, hic impetus, etiam si
nondum recepit ultimam manum. (*Sat.* 118)

Poetry has deceived many a young man. As soon as each of them
had made his lines scan and wrapped up his ideas in elegant periphrases, he thinks he's immediately arrived on Helicon. Tired by
their law practice they often fly to the calm waters of poetry as
though it were a port in a storm, believing it must be easier to
construct an epic poem than a speech that glows with scintillating
epigrams. . . . One must be careful that witty lines are not made
to stand out from the body of the narrative, but add their color
and brilliance to the texture of the poem. Witness Homer and the
lyric poets, Roman Vergil, and Horace's careful felicity. . . . Above
all, whoever attempts the great theme of the Civil War without
being full of the great writers, will fail under the task. For it is not
historical fact that has to be handled in the poem—historians do
this far better. No, the unfettered inspiration must be sent soaring
through riddles and divine interventions and a fabulous torrent of

---

also Grimal (1982) 118 for the implausible idea that the *Pharsalia* owes what debt
there is to the *Bellum Civile*. Martin (1975) 206 wishes to date the *Satyricon* to the
late Flavian era, c. A.D. 90. He argues that the *Bellum Civile* has a closer parodic
relationship to Silius Italicus' *Punica*. But both works are better seen as similar Vergilian reactions to the *Pharsalia*. For a longer discussion of my own views, briefly
summarized here, see Sullivan (1982) 170. The objections to the thesis of a close
derivative relationship, whatever its nature, between the two Latin poems boil down,
as usual, to invoking an unspecified mass of unknown material on which each author
may have separately drawn. For a recent discussion, see Hutchinson (1982) 46.

gnomic expressions, so that it gives the appearance of prophetic ravings rather than the accuracy of a solemn speech before witnesses.

Petronius is not saying anything original. Epic poetry is not easy, and writing epic is certainly no easier than producing a scintillating and epigrammatic speech for the law court. But perhaps there is a jab at Lucan's youth here. It is known that he pleaded in the law courts, otherwise Nero in 64 would not have specifically debarred him from this activity among others.[16] Further shafts may be detected in the suggested requirements for the would-be epic poet: Lucan shows a great, perhaps tendentious, familiarity with Vergil, but compared to Vergil's allusive familiarity with his Greek and Republican predecessors, Lucan might well be attacked as jejune and *parum doctus* in this respect. Again, it hard to deny Lucan's fondness (and talent) for epigrammatic lines that stand out from the texture of the narrative. It is also true that Lucan's language is not invariably elevated. He is capable of flat and pedestrian passages, and this may not have been unintentional.[17] His aim, after all, was to write a truly historical epic that would be reasonably accurate, even if poetically selective and ideologically biased. He wished to counterbalance or undercut the Vergilian glorification of the founders of Rome, the mythical ancestors of the *gens Iulia* and their descendants, with his own vision and his own version of Republican history. The events of the Civil War and its prelude with the actors involved on each side were to be used to explain the destruction of that original Rome after its long deterioration. The poetic history would also present the rise of an even worse order set up by the degenerate posterity of Rome's mythical founders.

This whole aim is the basis of Eumolpus' most fundamental criticism: poets should not deal in historical fact, that is the task

16. The chronology of Lucan's life and the publication of his writings and the ban upon them is too complex to discuss here. The best discussions of the problem are Rose (1966) 379 and Ahl (1976) 333.

17. The best analysis of these faults in Lucan's work is still that of Heitland (1887) lxxii.

of the historian. Extensive reading and inspiration, operating along the traditional epic lines, an aura of mystery, divine interventions and superhuman wonders, these are the requirements for a successful historical epic.

Eumolpus' criticism, whether intellectually sound or not, fits no *oeuvre* so aptly as Lucan's *Pharsalia*. And Eumolpus, in his rough sketch for the opening of a historical epic on the Civil War along traditional lines, leaves the reader in little doubt about his target. The verbal parallels with Lucan and the coincidence of themes make the relationship undeniable, unless we postulate some common sources or framework.[18] Petronius' poem is patently inferior to the *Pharsalia*, however Eumolpus excuses it. It is hardly possible then to be content with the explanation that Petronius is merely reworking some of Lucan's material and language into a more conventional and acceptable epic mode simply by adding the divine machinery and making the verse more Vergilian. Is Eumolpus sardonically showing Lucan how to do better? This may be part of the answer, but there also seems to be a political aim over and above derogatory evaluation of Lucan's talents as a poet. It was long ago suggested that Petronius' subsidiary aim, again in deference to Nero, was to defend Julius Caesar against Lucan's Republican bias.[19] In the light of our investigations of Neronian court politics, this becomes a more plausible theory. Petronius was certainly criticizing Lucan in a number of ways, but in this specimen of how to write an epic on the Civil War, Eumolpus, his *persona* for this purpose, deliberately makes Caesar the focus and hero of the fragment. And just as Lucan, for all the Republican slant of his poem, for all his basic sympathies with Cato, cannot deny Caesar his extraordi-

---

18. See the list in Rose (1971) 61, 87. Briefly, the common themes are: Caesar's speeches; general causes of the conflict, the decadence of the state; panic at Rome and Pompey's flight; the omens of civil war. Against those such as George (1974) 119, who would object (see note 15 above) that the resemblances may be poetic commonplaces of the period, it is enough to point out that one would then expect the diffusion of resemblances to be roughly equal throughout the ten books, whereas most of the resemblances to the *Pharsalia* in the *Bellum Civile* are dependent on Books 1–3.

19. Kindt (1892) 355.

nary energy and success in war,[20] so Eumolpus shows superficial deference to Republican sentiments and heroes without losing sight of his political purpose. Nor does he deny (why should he?) the serious, if by now traditional, charges Lucan brings against the corruption of Republican Rome. As a consequence, his rhetorical analysis of the causes of the Civil War is roughly the same as Lucan's; where the two analyses differ is on the question of whether Caesar was a symptom or a cure.

Petronius first describes Rome's decadence and luxury as conqueror and exploiter of the world. This is a standard diagnosis of the moral state of the late Republic and may be paralleled in Livy and Tactius; most writers, except for Velleius Paterculus, extend the analysis to the principate also. Even Silius Italicus in the *Punica* cannot resist diatribes on Roman luxury. Lucan's briefer analysis is much the same as Petronius' (cp. *Phars.* 1.158–62 with *BC* 1–60). Both Neronian authors connect this degeneration with the corruption and breakdown of political processes. There is, however, one detail in the Petronian account worth mentioning, because it concerns Cato, a prominent figure difficult to omit from an account of the Civil War. He is one of Lucan's three main characters, yet Petronius passes him over with the briefest of allusions. Lucan had talked about general political corruption and high offices stolen by bribery: *hinc rapti fasces pretio* (*Phars.* 1.178); Petronius, in a reminiscence of this phrase, specifically applies it to the case of Cato, the champion of the Republican freedom:

> pellitur a populo victus Cato; tristior ille est
> qui vicit fascesque pudet rapuisse Catoni.
>
> (*BC* 45–6)

Cato is defeated and rejected by the people; the electoral winner is the more disconsolate and is ashamed to have stolen the symbols of office from Cato.

20. Ahl (1976) 190.

This is the only allusion to Cato in the poem and he is treated respectfully but curtly. The attack confines itself to the venality of the popular assemblies (*BC* 39 ff.), which had little, and then no, power at all under the principate.[21] Nevertheless Petronius has managed to rework in brief compass the famous Lucanian themes of *victrix causa deis placuit sed victa Catoni* and *vincere peius erat (Phars.* 7.706).[22]

Petronius next sketches the rival contenders, Crassus, Pompey, and Caesar; this passage corresponds to Lucan's discussion of their characters and their destined roles in the historical events (cp. *BC* 61–66 with *Phars.* 1.98–157). Here occurs the first example of the partisan bias that distinguishes the two works. Lucan describes Caesar as a thunderbolt, but this possibly flattering analogy is preceded by a barbed description of his unscrupulousness and savagery:

> sed non in Caesare tantum
> nomen erat nec fama ducis, sed nescia virtus
> stare loco solusque pudor non vincere bello.
> acer et indomitus quo spes quoque ira vocasset,
> ferre manum et numquam temerando parcere ferro,
> successus urguere suos, instare favori
> numinis, inpellens quidquid sibi summa petenti
> obstaret gaudensque viam fecisse ruina.
>
> (*Phars.* 1.143–50)

But Caesar had on his side not only the name and fame of a general but also the courage that did not know how to stay where it was, his only shame to lose a war. Eager and unbeaten in leading troops to wherever hope and anger summoned, he never shrank from bloodying his sword. He was quick to follow up his suc-

---

21. For the deterioration of official popular representation under the principate and Augustan abolition of popular elections to the praetorship and consulship, see Rostovtzeff (1957) 79, and for its implications, see *CAH* 10.180. The people henceforth made their desires known in more informal ways, at the games and circuses or by popular demonstrations, on which see Cameron (1976) 157. Rhetoric about the restoration of power to the people, as in Galba's propaganda on his coins, was just that, as the political events of 69 showed all too clearly.

22. Cp. *Phars.* 1.176–80 with *BC* 39–50. See also Sen. *Ep.* 14.13; Tac. *Hist.* 1.50: it was clearly a standard theme.

cesses and take advantage of heaven's favor, pushing back whatever was in the way of his progress to the top, rejoicing to make
a path through destruction.

Petronius, on the contrary, says simply.

Iulius *ingratam* perfudit sanguine Romam.
(*BC* 64)

Julius bathed *ungrateful* Rome with his blood.

The partisan overtones, including the use of "Julius" instead of
Lucan's usual "Caesar," are obvious.

Petronius at this point introduces the supernatural element,
almost invariably eschewed by Lucan, except for the necroman-
tic scene at the end of Book 6. In the Phlegraean fields near
Naples Dis (Pluto) addresses Fortuna and, complaining of the
overweaning power and monstrous growth of Rome, asks her
for vengeance—for permission to glut his bloodlust with the
casualties of Civil War. Fortuna agrees with his request, regret-
ting her former generosity to Rome, and promises massive
slaughter, even enumerating the battlegrounds where it will take
place: Philippi, Pharsalia, Spain, Libya, Egypt, and Actium. Lucan has a somewhat different list of battlefields (cp. *BC* 67–121
with *Phars.* 1.38–43).

Now Fortuna, and to a much lesser extent Pluto, play a part
in the *Pharsalia* also, but Petronius, who, if an Epicurean in the
Roman fashion, was not a systematic philosopher, felt artistically free to make Fortuna a capricious and malicious goddess,
tearing down what she has built up through sheer desire for
change. She does not even have the quasi-moral objections to
Rome's current state that are voiced by Dis. She certainly has
nothing in common with the neutral τύχη of Epicurus. Lucan's
view of Fortune and Destiny was, like that of many amateur
Stoics, confused but, having dispensed with a personified goddess of Fortune, he has to be more opportunistic. Sometimes he
speaks briefly of the gods, as in the famous phrase, *victrix causa*

deis placuit sed victa Catoni; sometimes he invokes a vaguely personalized *Fortuna*, which, with no moral justification, favors one side or the other almost to the point of caprice; sometimes he alludes to the working of a destiny whose reasons are obscure.[23] The important point for him was to contrast with all these forces the strength of individual moral virtue, a thoroughly Stoic dichotomy. Such virtue was, in his eyes, exemplified almost to perfection in Cato.

Petronius continues with a list of divine omens foretelling the Civil War. It parallels Lucan's similar, if longer, catalogue, which included episodes of the Tuscan extispices, the astrologer Nigidius Figulus, and the crazed, prophetic Roman matron. Petronius does not prolong his list in this way, but moves abruptly from the supernatural into his epic action:

> exuit omnes
> quippe moras Caesar, vindictaeque actus amore
> Gallica proiecit, civilia sustulit arma.
>
> (*BC* 141–43)

Then Caesar threw off all delay and, driven by a passion for revenge, abandoned the Gallic wars and began the Civil War.

Lucan does much the same. Immediately after describing the social and political corruption of Rome, he presents Caesar in lightning action:

> iam gelidas Caesar cursu superaverat Alpes,
> ingentesque animo motus bellumque futurum
> ceperat.
>
> (*Phars.* 1.183–85)

By now Caesar had raced across the icy Alps and was aware in his heart of the mighty moves afoot and the coming war.

Placing Caesar at the Rubicon, Lucan confronts him with a vision of his fatherland, forbidding him and his army to proceed

---

23. On the whole question, see Friedrich (1938) 391; Ahl (1976) 297.

any further, if they have any respect for law. Caesar's reply is a justification of his actions and an appeal to Jupiter and the gods of the Julian house, so intimately connected with Rome's foundation, to favor his enterprise. He blames the opposition for making him Rome's enemy: *ille erit ille nocens, qui me tibi fecerit hostem* (*Phars.* 1.203).

Petronius, seeing an opportunity missed by Lucan, sets Caesar in the Alps, significantly in a place sacred to Hercules who was normally appropriated as a patron deity of Pompey. From there Caesar utters his appeal to Jupiter and Italy in full view of his native land. His argument is roughly the same as Lucan's: he was forced into this war and his opponents are the criminals. Petronius stresses, as Lucan does not, Caesar's great military deserts (cp.*BC* 160–65 with *Phars.* 1.201–2). Petronius adds some omens to underline the importance of the action to follow (*BC* 126–41): the horrendous descent from the Alps, a description longer and more elaborate but less effective than Lucan's description of Caesar's crossing of the swollen Rubicon (cp. *BC* 177–208 with *Phars.* 1.213–24). A point to notice, however, is that whereas Lucan compares Caesar to a Libyan lion—and Africa is an ill-omened area for Lucan—Petronius likens him to Jupiter and also to Hercules (*BC* 206). Lucan, for his part, had subtly attempted to link Cato with that demigod and Stoic saint.[24]

There follows a description of Fama, heavily dependent on Vergil's description in the first book of the *Aeneid*; Rome is panicked by her. The description of this frenzy at Rome corresponds in its structural location to Lucan's picture of Caesar's effect on Ariminum, the first town he captured, but he is really emulating Lucan's later description of the tumult in the capital city (*BC* 210–37; *Phars.* 1.231 ff., 2.16 ff.). Next comes the pointed attack on Pompey for his flight from the city with both consuls; two lines are especially damning by contrast with Lucan's sympathetic, if still critical, treatment of Pompey and his flight (*Phars.* 1.121 ff.; 2.275 ff.):

24. For discussion of Hercules and Cato, see Ahl (1976) 271.

pro pudor, imperii deserto nomine fugit,
ut Fortuna levis Magni quoque terga videret.
(BC 243–44)

For shame, he fled, abandoning the title of commander, so that
fickle Fortuna might see also the back of Pompey the Great.

Petronius then reverts to the mythological plane with a somewhat forced description of the flight of Peace, Loyalty, and Con-
cord and the emergence of the deities of destruction. Most significant, in terms of Augustan propaganda and Neronian court
politics, is the partisan division among the Olympians. Naturally, Venus (here given the title of Dione) takes the side of Caesar, as do Minerva and Mars, the two most warlike deities.[25]
Apollo, Diana, Mercury, and Hercules follow Pompey, who had
once been, after all, hailed as *Hercules invictus* himself. The court
audience would be well aware that Apollo had been given much
of the credit by Augustus for his victory at Actium and that
Horace had compared Augustus to Mercury (*Carm.* 1.2.41 ff.).
Petronius tries to be superficially evenhanded, but on balance
Caesar is given better divine help in his warfare than the Republican side and Pompey.

Eumolpus' mini-epic ends on a plane where the divine and
human intersect. Discord encourages some of the human partic-
ipants in the struggle, Marcellus, Curio, Lentulus, Caesar, and
Pompey, to play their historic parts. Even here the pro-Caesarian
partisanship is clear. Discord addresses Caesar as *divus*, inciting
him to capture cities and treasuries; Pompey is almost sneered
at for his inability to defend Rome and urged on to Dyrrachium
and Thessaly, where decisive and gratifyingly bloody battles will
be fought and lost by the Republicans.

This analysis and comparison should make it more obvious
that Petronius' *Bellum Civile* is simultaneously a literary and political attack on Lucan's *Pharsalia* and that it would be appre-

25. BC 264 ff. Bücheler (1965) 3.338 argued that *Mavortius* is Romulus; if so, then
Romulus, the founder of Rome, is also on Caesar's side.

ciated as such by Nero and his artistic intimates. If the already alienated Lucan knew of it, it would have been an additional incitement to write his *famosum carmen* against Nero and his newer associates[26] and to drive him further along the road to the Pisonian conspiracy.

This attack on Lucan, however, is a digression in the *Satyricon*. Far more pervasive, and therefore integral to the work, is the allusion to and frequent parody of Seneca's writings.[27] Objections have been raised to this interpretation of the parallels between Seneca and Petronius.[28] Two contemporary authors might after all easily allude accidentally to similar contemporary characters, issues, and philosophical commonplaces; alternatively, they might both draw on common sources. If, however, these parallels are to be construed as accidental, the coincidences would surely be found throughout the whole Senecan corpus, just as the parallels between Lucan's *Pharsalia* and the *Bellum Civile*, if accidental, should be evenly distributed over all the ten books, not mainly confined to Books 1–3. But if the *Apocolocyntosis* is excluded,[29] most of the Petronian parallels are with the *Epistulae Morales*, one of the latest of Seneca's writings, which seems to have been published, several books at a time, in the final three years of his life. This period coincides with the rise of Petronius to his unofficial position as Nero's *arbiter elegantiae* and, one may assume, an influential consular member of the *consilium principis*. Why otherwise would Tigellinus be jealous of his influence with Nero?

As for the objection, which of course can never be entirely discounted, that the parallels between the two authors are due

26. Suet. *Vit. Lucan.: sed et famoso carmine cum ipsum tum potentissimos amicorum gravissime proscindit.*

27. See Studer (1843) 89; Gottschlich (1863) 26, and the reexamination of the evidence in Collignon (1892); Thomas (1905) 11, 17; Gaselee (1909); Schnur (1957) 123; Rose (1971) 69; Sullivan (1968) 193.

28. For the objections, see George (1974) 199, Smith (1975), 214.

29. The parallels between the *Satyricon* and the *Apocolocyntosis* are most fully tabulated by Bagnani (1954) 80. Their explanation, however, is generally sought in the Menippean and Varronian tradition that they share or in the colloquial language adopted by the two authors for their separate purposes; nevertheless, some deliberate echoes or even allusions by Petronius to the satire cannot be ruled out.

to their drawing, each for his very different purposes, on a common source (or sources), the reply must be again that it is more plausible in the abstract than in the concrete. In the Neronian context it makes little sense. If we postulate some large mass of Stoic writing upon which Petronius and Seneca draw, then Petronius is casting too wide a net—Collignon's percipient remark that to parody everybody is to parody nobody is again relevant here. Moreover, the parallels are not merely of thought or exemplary incident; in some of the most important cases, the resemblance is stylistic also. It is surely too much to imagine that other Stoics were writing in Seneca's unique style. It is undeniable that Petronius could be familiar from other sources with the incidents, doctrines, and allusions he shares with Seneca, but the essential point is topicality, the recognition by his hearers of such parallels. It is precisely because it *is* Seneca's material that Petronius' use of it becomes topical (and indeed malicious) for his court audience. The opening of the *Satyricon*, which should not be taken too seriously as criticism or an educational program, in view of the opportunistic character of Encolpius, might be similarly construed as a parody of the Elder Seneca's prefaces to his *Controversiae*,[30] although here the argument that both authors are using commonplaces seems more valid.

The uses to which Petronius puts his Senecan material may be classified in three ways.[31] The first is straight parody, consisting of fairly long passages which read like a pastiche of Senecan prose and Seneca's Stoic meditations. They concern such matters as the effeteness of the age; the vanity of human wishes and man's subjugation to Fortune; the uneasy conscience of the evildoer.[32] They are revealed as parody by the ridiculous contexts in

---

30. See Fairweather (1981) 132 for a summary of the Elder Seneca's views; cf. Petr. *Sat.* 1–5 and 88; also Sussman (1972) 195 and (1978) 94.

31. This is leaving out of account for the moment the poem on the capture of Troy (*Sat.* 89), which is written in the meter and style of Senecan tragedy; see Walsh (1968) 210. For an examination of Seneca's tragic style in the most relevant play, see Tarrant (1977) passim.

32. Cp. *Ep.* 115.10–12; *Nat. Quaest.* 7.31.1 ff. with *Sat.* 88; *Ep.* 92.34–35; 99.8–9, 31; 101.4, 6 with *Sat.* 115.8–9; and *Ep.* 105.7–8 with *Sat.* 125.4.

which they appear or by the disreputability of the characters voicing the sentiments. The lofty discourse on the age's decadence is put into the mouth of the pederastic poet Eumolpus just after he has recounted the humorous story of his seduction of his host's son at Pergamum (*Sat.* 88; 85).

The second classification, not to be distinguished too sharply from the first, is the dramatic use of Senecan material to throw scorn on its philosophical implications. This is generally found in the *Cena Trimalchionis* and a couple of examples should suffice. Seneca's famous *Epistle* 47 on the proper treatment of slaves makes several points: slaves are fellow human beings; Fortune has the same power over masters and slaves; and there is nothing wrong with dining with one's slaves, at least on a selective basis. In the *Cena*, Trimalchio's drunken invitation to his household to join the company at table (*Sat.* 70.10), his maudlin remarks about their common humanity despite their ill fortune, all make good literary sense as straight satire on a vulgar and pretentious freedman, but how much more point do they gain if the listener has Seneca's letter in mind? Encolpius' disgust is here more heavily underlined than usual and Trimalchio's bad taste more explicitly exposed. Petronius in real life, incidentally, had no truck with this sort of egalitarianism. In his last hours he handed out to his slaves, according to their deserts, either lashings or rewards (Tac. *Ann.* 16.19).

The third type of parallel between Petronius and Seneca may explain why the theory of parody has been denied in favor of the explanations of chance and common sources. These last instances cannot be construed as straight parody, stylistic or otherwise; they are rather a subtler deployment of Senecan themes and materials for other and more amusing purposes, in order to show Petronius' artistic superiority as well as his ironic rejection of Seneca's philosophical posturings and stylistic exuberance. By comparison with Seneca, Petronius' style is Atticist in some sense of that abused term, and his artistic *credo* stressing simplicity, pleasure, and the acceptance of life as it is (*Sat.* 132.15) would be diametrically opposed to all that Seneca stood for in his life and writings. Petronius takes material in which Seneca may be seen at his best, namely in vivid, satirical, or indignant description, and turns it to quite different uses. The portrait of Trimalchio, for example, seems deliberately fleshed out with much Senecan material.[33]

The intentions underlying such literary methods are not unfamiliar in ancient authors; they provide a typically Greco-Roman pleasure in the recognition of allusions and further amusement from their radically different deployment. But in the Neronian context invidious emulation is the key. Petronius could show to what better, or more sophisticated, use he could put even serious material, while rejecting its strenuous moralism. This note would sound well in Nero's ears, now that any affection for his old tutor had long since evaporated or turned to resentment. Had Petronius' dealings with Seneca been merely conventional parody, there might have been less doubt about the date and intentions of the *Satyricon*, but the very sophistication of Petronius' methods in incorporating contemporary material has obscured the issue.

The *Troiae Halosis* (*Sat.* 89) calls for a similar explanation. The most likely purpose of Petronius' poem was to parody Seneca's tragic style, and vv.406–57 of Seneca's *Agamemnon* may be recommended for comparison. Petronius' brief poem contains a number of Seneca's favorite words and a fair proportion of verbally pointed *sententiae*, and it is also very tolerant of repetition. I protested earlier against a tendency to date the composition of all Seneca's tragedies to his exile in Corsica. This may be motivated by a pious wish on the part of scholars to fill in Seneca's time profitably, but some of them at least could have been written after his return, in the light of the charges that he had been writing more verse (*carmina*) since Nero developed an interest in

---

33. For example, Trimalchio's posthumously assumed *agnomen* is to be *Maecenatianus* (*Sat.* 71.12); cf. the harsh remarks on Maecenas in *Ep.* 19.9, 101.10 ff., 114.4 ff., 120.19.

this activity.[34] Nor should it be forgotten that Nero was especially interested in dramatic recitation and performances.[35]

The literary feud between the rising, or now established, arbiter of elegance and the two most brilliant ex-members of Nero's court circle, Lucan and Seneca, is susceptible of many explanations. A dominant motive will have been to cater to Nero's
artistic jealousy and general *Schadenfreude* but there was also an
obvious antipathy between the styles of life and thought favored
by Seneca and Lucan on the one hand and by Petronius on the
other.

The feud was not one-sided. The content of Lucan's libelous
poem of 65 against the emperor and the most powerful of his
friends has not been recorded in detail, but it is unlikely that
Petronius was overlooked. Seneca's more oblique response,
however, seems to have survived. In *Epistle* 122 there is a sustained tirade on the *turba lucifugarum*, the crowd of night-owls,
who turn darkness into day with their lengthy potations. Seneca
attacks at length their material luxury, their desire for notoriety,
their eagerness to appear different, and the elaborate elegance of
their table and their way of life, although, as is customary, only
names from the past are cited.[36] The description squares very
closely with Tacitus' account of Petronius' elegance, luxury, and
his custom of turning night into day. Significant also is that in
these later letters Seneca suddenly adopts a hostile tone towards

34. For discussion of the dating of the plays, see Chapter 1 and note 51.

35. For Nero's dramatic activities, see Chapter 1. Supposedly Nero had even
composed a tragedy himself (Philostr. *Vit. Apoll.* 4.39); he performed in tragedies
or at least gave tragic recitals up to the end of his life (Dio 62.14.4); Suet. *Nero* 21;
cf. Dio 63.22.5–6. Although appearances on stage such as those of C. Calpurnius
Piso (Tac. *Ann.* 15.65), those of other prominent citizens for the *Ludi Maximi* (Dio
62.17.3), and the emperor himself (Suet. *Nero* 11) were looked down on, the writing
of plays was popular and respectable, as is clear from Seneca's own tragedies, the
pseudo-Senecan *Octavia*, the evidence for Annaeus Cornutus' plays (*RE* s.v.), Curiatius Maternus' political drama (Tac. *Dial.* 11.3), and the *praetexta* from the pen of
Persius (Suet. *Vit. Pers.*). Even Thrasea Paetus had trodden the boards, but this was
out of town (Tac. *Ann.* 16.21).

36. See Faider (1921) 15. It should be added that this way of living is not uncommon in Rome under various emperors: Seneca singles out individuals from the age
of Tiberius, but as usual with Seneca, one has to look at the depth of his vehemence
rather than the examples he chooses.

Epicureanism in general, which stands in sharp contrast to his earlier sympathetic references to Epicurean doctrine in the first three books.[37]

The last piece of evidence to be adduced is admittedly tenuous and hypothetical, but deserves attention nonetheless. Certain epigrams from the *Anthologia Latina* (396 ff.) are attributed to Seneca, and their authenticity, on various grounds, is not impossible.[38] Some of these poems would clearly belong to the period of his exile if they are his, but his poetic activity was not limited to this period. The arbitrary collocation and dislocation of various groups of epigrams in the collection provoke the surmise that they were anthologized from all the four books that Priscian (*lib.* 7.759) mentioned as making up Seneca's poetic oeuvre.[39]

Of the epigrams attacking personal enemies, some seem appropriate to the period in Corsica, but others (notably 412 and 416) read as though Seneca's reputation was being traduced by personal enemies at court. These could therefore belong to this later period around 62. The two poems in question are complaints of the malicious, if witty, backbiting of an enemy. One (416) is addressed to a certain Maximus, perhaps a fictitious name,[40] who has been injuring Seneca's reputation:

> famam temptasti nostram sermone maligno
> laedere fellitis, invidiose, iocis.
>
> (*Anth.* 416 vv. 3–4)

37. For Petronius' Epicureanism (or at least the sophisticated Roman interpretation of it), see Tac. *Ann.* 16.18; Petronius' artistic credo, *Sat.* 132.15; Raith (1963); and Sullivan (1968) 98. The hostile references in Seneca are especially noticeable in *Ep.* 88.5 and 123.10–11.

38. See Prato (1964) and the bibliography there given; more recently Shackleton Bailey (1979) does not exclude the possibility of Senecan authorship.

39. For example, 432 (on Cato) seems to belong with the short cycle on the same subject, 397, 398, prompted perhaps by the upsurge of interest in Cato at this period, as seen in Lucan's epic, Thrasea Paetus' biography, and even in Martial who, perhaps drawing on prentice work for later productions, uses him both as a symbol of puritanism and a Republican hero (cf. 1. *praef.*, 8, 78; 2.89; 6.32; 9.28; 10.19; 11.2, 5, 15, 39; 12.6). This epigram is one of several unexpected interruptions in the sequence of erotic poems, 427–39, which may be those that justify his inclusion in the list of indecent writers compiled by Pliny the Younger (*Ep.* 5.3.5).

40. Maximus is used eight times as a fictitious name by Martial.

You have tried to hurt my reputation in your vicious talk, you envious creature, with poisonous witticisms.

But more to our purpose is 412, for the enemy invoked here is not only verbally malignant, but he writes satirical poems as well:

> carmina mortifero tua sunt suffusa veneno,
> at sunt carminibus pectora *nigra* magis.
> *(Anth.* 412 vv. 1–2)

Your poems are full of deadly venom, but your heart is more *black* than your poems.

Was this enemy's *name* also as black as his heart? Was Seneca covertly alluding to T. Petronius Niger? Certainly the description might suit the courtier:[41]

> bellus homo es? valde. capitalia crimina ludis.
> deque tuis manant *atra* venena iocis!
> (vv. 13–14)

You're a smart fellow, aren't you? Very well. You are playing deadly games and from your quips *black* venom drips.

The epigrams, if they are authentic, would provide further evidence of the literary feuds, or political quarrels conducted in verse, that were a feature of court life in Seneca's time. The poems would indicate that Seneca fought back in verse as well as in prose. Other possible examples of his responses to such sniping are *Anth.* 396 and 410.

This tenuous web of evidence reveals a not unexpected literary and personal feud between Nero's newer and more *louche* friends and his old Stoic counselor Seneca, and those, for example Lucan, associated with him. Petronius was apparently for a time the victor, until he himself fell victim to the more unscrupulous machinations of Tigellinus.

41. Adopting the emended text of Shackleton Bailey (1979) 58.

Literary life in the Neronian period was intimately connected with patronage, political power, and status, unless, in the manner of Persius, one lived a life of seclusion, concerning oneself only with the principles of art and writing itself. Even Persius had found himself attacking the literary establishment, which at this time coincided with the political establishment. Art and politics, art and economics, cannot be separated as much as the New Critics might wish. Too many literary works have been produced by authors whose prime interest was their present circumstances and not the perennial themes unrelated to contemporary life. Unexpectedly, through sheer artistry, such writers manage to transcend their temporal and personal objectives and produce classics that survive beyond their intended audience. That is the critical point I have tried to make, but a knowledge of the historical matrix of literary classics should increase, rather than detract, from our appreciation of the Neronian literary renaissance.

Literature and Politics
in the Flavian Era

I have tried in the preceding pages to present a coherent picture of Neronian literature and its political background. Inevitably it will strike some readers as impressionistic, if not downright *pointilliste*. But few today would deny the highly political nature of Augustan literature and it should therefore occasion little surprise that Neronian literature should show similar, but not of course identical, features. The two eras do have in common the court as a center of literary patronage and the expectation that the image of the reigning princeps would be appropriately burnished and his policy goals depicted in a favorable light. From the opposition side, the debate about the desirability in general of the principate itself went on as before. Lacking, as far as we can see, on the Augustan literary scene was the flagrant use of literature as a means to personal power and influence, as a way of settling scores and successfully denigrating one's opponents. In the Neronian era the pressure was greater to conform to a court-inspired aesthetic, which drew literary battle lines far more clearly than they were drawn in the more tolerant atmosphere of Maecenas' cultural ministry. To a large degree the difference is to be attributed to the greater or lesser personal involvement of each emperor in the artistic process itself. Augustus' Ajax soon fell on his sponge; but Nero's Bacchantes continued to dance to the very end.

The Flavian era, also rich in literary talent, differs interestingly from the two preceding literary periods; therefore a cursory sketch of literary politics between 69 and 96 may help to highlight the special quality of the Neronian renaissance, and also allow us to glance at a perennial Roman cultural quarrel that had been largely muted because of Nero's personal and political predilections.

There is an interesting contradiction in the *Dialogus* of Tacitus, written around the turn of the century to signalize the author's decision to abandon political oratory in favor of the more influential and poetic genre of historiography. Here Curiatius Maternus argues that poetry is superior to oratory partly because of the poet's freedom from anxiety (*remotum a sollicitudinibus et curis*, 13.5). This from the lips of a dramatist who boasts elsewhere in the work of smashing the power of Nero's repulsive courtier, the cobbler Vatinius (11.2; cf. *Ann.* 15.23). Maternus insists that he will continue his political criticism despite his friend's concern for his safety after the recent public reading of his *Cato*. What that play and his *Domitius* could not say, he would utter in his *Thyestes*. Historians suspect that his friend's worries were not unjustified and that Maternus, sooner or later, joined the ranks of those who, like Lucan, became martyrs of *la littérature engagée*.

The awesome power, the rich rewards, and the personal security that successful oratory brings are vigorously delineated by Aper:

quid est tutius quam eam exercere artem qua semper armatus praesidium amicis, opem alienis, salutem periclitantibus, invidis vero et inimicis metum et terrorem ultro ferat, ipse securus et velut quadam perpetua potentia ac potestate munitus? (5.6)

What is safer than the exercise of that art with whose durable weapons one brings at will security to friends, aid to strangers, and safety to those in danger, but fear and terror to jealous and hostile opponents, while remaining oneself unintimidated and shielded by an enduring potency and power.

Not unnaturally Aper draws many of his examples from the age of Nero and the list of prominent, powerful and accomplished speakers could be easily extended: to the names of Eprius Marcellus, Vibius Crispus, Domitius Afer, and Julius Secundus (from Quintilian, *Inst.* 10.1.118; 12.10.11) may be added those of Seneca, the vigor of whose invective is to be glimpsed at the end of the *De Vita Beata*; Julius Africanus, who delivered the loyal address to Nero after Agrippina's murder; and Galerius Trachalus, who was consul with the eloquent Silius Italicus in 68 and speech writer for Otho in 69. More names, such as Curtius Montanus, Fabricius Veiento, and Aquilius Regulus, may be supplied from the pages of Tacitus and elsewhere.

Messala is only partially right when he says:

longa temporum quies et continuum populi otium et adsidua senatus tranquillitas et maxima principis disciplina ipsam quoque eloquentiam sicut omnia alia pacaverat. (*Dial.* 38.2)

The long tranquility of the times, the undisturbed relaxation of the populace, the uninterrupted calm of the senate, and the supreme discipline of the emperor had imposed peace on eloquence itself, as on everything else.

Loyalty to the Republic and enmity toward partisan foes had been substituted by loyalty to the emperor and hostility toward his adversaries. Personal ambition and avarice remained in place on each side of the equation. If issues of foreign and domestic policy were deliberately and necessarily burked by the senate, the dominating question of loyalty to a dynasty, or rather its current incarnation, easily and rapidly took their place. *Salus reipublicae* became *salus principis* and so the problems of evidence were correspondingly less than those facing Torquemada or Senator Joseph McCarthy. For this purpose, the senate became a Star Chamber.

The pessimistic doubts of the *Dialogus* about the current state of the oratorical art are directed more toward the ends of eloquence rather than the proficiency achieved by its contemporary practitioners. Oratory had not decayed, unless the orchid is seen as the decadence of the lily. The imperial glasshouse fostered more specimens of the *vir malus dicendi peritus* than did the gardens of the Republic, but this may be the verdict of an idealistic orator who preferred after A.D. 100 to retire to the judicial bench of historiography rather than put his talents to forensic use. Quintilian's verdict is different: he judges orators, not the causes they serve or the ideals they profess.

An examination of Neronian oratory, then, could do no more than document individual styles and cases; catalogue victories and defeats; and record reversals and survivals. The evidence is neither scanty nor hard to read as is the case with literary feuds, cultural subversion, and poetic propaganda, black or white. That story continues in the years after Nero's death, but the plot is less complex and the evidence somewhat more visible and easier to interpret.

Image making was, not unexpectedly, a characteristic of the Year of the Four Emperors. There was the negative propaganda against the Julio-Claudians, particularly Nero, that surfaces most openly in the *Octavia*, just as there were attempts by Otho and Vitellius to capitalize on their connections with Nero and gain at least the popular support still clinging to the memory of the great *artifex*. The propaganda battles were waged mainly on coins with slogans aimed at winning the hearts and minds of the people by tributes to its *genius*, *signa*, *aeternitas*, or to the domestic symbol of Vesta. Sometimes the coinages promised *victoria*, *concordia*, *libertas*, *securitas*, or *pax*, along with the dutiful tag *P.R.*[1]

1. It must strike the modern reader as odd that the often feared threat of a popular rising against the senatorial oligarchy or an emperor never materialized. Parallels to the English, French, and Russian revolutions are absent from Roman history once the lower orders achieved their modest political goals by 287 B.C. This reflects not the docility of the people of Rome or the Roman Empire, which is disproved by various local uprisings and massacres of unpopular elements, but rather the lack of an ideology other than nationalism and the immense care traditionally taken by

Coins are more convenient than literature to get one's ideological claims across quickly to the appropriate audience because they circulate more readily than writings, but once a pretender or a dynasty was established it would look to the time-honored ways of establishing its legitimacy, worth, and permanence; first, by erecting material monuments of stone such as aqueducts and arches, baths and basilicas, amphitheatres, circuses, and temples, then through the commissioning or financial encouragement of works more durable, the *monumenta aere perenniora* that writers of talent, if not genius, could marshal against contemporary criticism and, from a longer perspective, the encroachments of time and the tarnish of history.

Although the Flavian emperors (69–96) did not go to the extravagant lengths of Nero, they were all interested in fostering literature, especially Domitian. As in most human affairs, this encouragement had mixed motives. Nevertheless, despite all the grumbling wistfulness of Martial for the great days of Augustan and Neronian patronage, imperial sponsorship and favor still offered substantial rewards. Vespasian appointed Quintilian the first professor to be paid from public funds, and he also encouraged other literary men with generous grants of money. The young epic poet Saleius Bassus was given half a million sesterces (Tac. *Dial.* 5.2; 9.8), although he was not to enjoy it long and the sum is small compared to the five million sesterces given Eprius Marcellus by Nero for his part in the prosecution of Thrasea Paetus.

Titus, who had belonged to Nero's literary circle, was presumably suitably pleased by Martial's sometimes tiresome *Liber de Spectaculis*, written to celebrate his official inauguration in 80 of the great Flavian amphitheatre begun by Vespasian. Commissioned or not, official favor for this no doubt helped to propel Martial to the international fame he boasts of in his first book of epigrams.

---

most emperors to conciliate the masses by amenities and amusements, military and legal security, welfare and engineering programs, and personal largesse, a lesson not yet learned by the authoritarian regimes of Central and South America.

Domitian, like Nero, was a poet himself, particularly in Greek, and he gave public recitals of his work (Tac. *Hist.* 4.86; Suet. *Dom.* 2). There is no reason to believe that when he no longer practiced the art, he turned against its practitioners. His institution of the Capitoline games is proof enough of that, since they incorporated literary and musical contests. Juvenal's description of him as the *calvus Nero* (*Sat.* 4.38) is therefore apt—he himself may well have recognized his affinity to that artistic emperor; after all, he did have Epaphroditus, Nero's secretary *a libellis*, executed for his part in Nero's suicide. The art of the period, at least of portraiture in busts and on coins, reverted to the rich and exuberant Neronian styles. Domitian did not however have Augustus' tolerance of, or Nero's pleasure in, *Spottgedichte*; he punished impolitic historical writing and theatrical satire alike (Suet. *Dom.* 8.10). Still, anonymous satire circulated as in Nero's reign: a squib in Greek on his regulation of excessive viticulture in Italy alludes to him as a goat (Suet. *Dom.* 14).

Domitian needed more help from his panegyrists than did his predecessors, particularly as he grew more and more unpopular after the revolt of Saturninus (88–89). His personal campaigns against the Chatti, the Dacians, and the Sarmatians may seem to the modern historian victories for prudence and common sense, including the settlement with the Dacian king Decebalus, who was bought off with subsidies and practical aid in the shape of a corps of engineers. But to Tacitus and Suetonius they were all pathetic shams and failures, whatever the triumphs and honors demanded for them. Martial and Statius may have been aware of this and they take pains to stress the emperor's military achievements wherever possible (e.g. Stat. *Theb.* 1.16 ff.; *Silv.* 1.25 ff., 79 ff.; 4.1.11 ff., 39 ff.; 4.2.14, 66–67; Mart. 1.22; 2.2; 4.3; 5.3; 6.4; 7.1, 2; 8.1, 2, 82; 9.1, 6, 101, and so on). The epigrammatist especially tries to present Domitian as being sorely missed by the city whenever he is away campaigning (e.g. Mart. 7.2.5) or highly popular with the mob on his frequent appearances at the games (Mart. 6.34.5–6).

Naturally as the poets fed the vanity and alleviated the in-

[185]

security of the emperor, so prose fueled the blazing self-righteousness of the members of senatorial order as they saw their shaky position and privileges further eroded by Vespasian's dilution of their elite number with provincials, Domitian's increasing reliance on equestrians for important posts and even for the governance of a senatorial province. Domitian's assumption of the censorship *in perpetuo* alarmed them further. So the war of the pamphlets did not cease altogether and was to prove more dangerous than ever for Helvidius Priscus, author of a *Life of Cato* and a eulogy of Arulenus Rusticus, and then for Herennius Senecio, who in turn worked on a memoir of Helvidius. On the other hand, revisionist and hostile histories of Nero were produced, and positive accounts of his reign were suppressed or neglected. The claims of the Flavians to be the proper rulers of Rome were magnified by contrast.

Even Domitian's social and moral reforms did not cut much ice with senatorial writers. The Younger Pliny goes to great length to disparage even reforms of which he approved (*Pan.* 46). As usual it was left to the poets to provide the approbation Domitian wanted for his attempts to improve morality, on which he so prided himself (Mart. 6.4).[2]

But these are minor genres in Roman estimation, and it is to the *exordia* of epics on whatever subject that the reader must look for deferential or fulsome compliments to the current ruler. It is worthwhile comparing the different imperial compliments introduced into the four epics that have survived from the Flavian era. If we believe Quintilian, the untimely death of Saleius

2. This sometimes led to curious results. Somewhat strange, for example, are the verses written on Domitian's ordinance against castration (Suet. *Dom.* 7; Dio 67.2.3). Statius, rather indelicately, introduces the theme into the poem commissioned in 94 by Domitian on the occasion of Earinus' dedication of his shorn hair to the Temple of Aesculapius in his native city of Pergamum (*Silv.* 3.4.73–77). Earinus of course was himself a eunuch. The subject recurs in his poem on the construction of the Via Domitiana (*Silv.* 4.3.13–15). Earinus was a favorite subject of Martial's also, as we might expect (9.11–13, 16, 17), and his references to castration (9.6, 8) are closely juxtaposed to his encomiums of the emperor's favorite. This may indicate that it was an open subject for discussion and that the ban, though enacted earlier (cf. Mart. 2.60; 6.2), was somehow connected with Earinus. Dio (67.2.3) claims that the ban was to dishonor the memory of Titus, who was also fond of eunuchs.

Bassus was a great intellectual loss (*Inst.* 10.1.96; cf. Juv. 7.80), so his flattery of Vespasian may have been skilful as well as rewarding. C. Valerius Flaccus (d. 93), however, seems to have been comfortably well off and independent since he, like another rich poet, L. Arruntius Stella, was *quindecemvir sacris faciundis* (*Arg.* 1.5; 8.239–41). His epic, the *Argonautica*, which follows Vergil in many other respects, incorporates at the very beginning the expected compliments to the ruling house along with summary references to its achievements. In addressing Apollo, the poet links the Flavian house to the god by his invocation of the deified Vespasian, whose vicarious victories in Wales, Northern Britain, and Scotland (won by Cerealis, Frontinus, and Agricola), he suggests, would be splendid material for a historical epic. Valerius then suggests that the poetic genius of Domitian should recount the overthrow of Judea and Titus' destruction of Jerusalem (1.7–14); it is he who will raise temples and institute divine cults in his father's honor. Yet this is hardly showering compliments on the Flavian house; it puts him in the company of Silius Italicus rather than Statius as a flatterer.

Silius (c. 25–101) probably thought of himself as continuing the *Aeneid*, his devotion to Vergil being notorious. He was to narrate in the *Punica* the consequences of Dido's curse upon Aeneas' descendants and describe its fulfillment in the Punic War— a noble theme and occasionally Silius rises to it. Only the first six books may have appeared in Domitian's time, as there appears to be a modest compliment to Nerva at the end of Book 14.

If the Julian house was good enough for Vergil it was certainly so for Silius, who may have belonged to Nero's poetic circle and ended up as consul in the year of his demise. How was he to deal with Nero's Flavian successors? He had wisely retired from public life to live down a certain malodorous reputation acquired through association with Nero. An emperor, avid for praise from contemporary authors, would at least trifle with the *exordium* of a new epic poem. Silius, however, with all the confidence of a man with nothing to lose, simply invokes the Muse on opening his poem and closes it (17.650–55) with a salutation to Scipio

Africanus, true scion of Capitoline Jupiter. His cautious praise of Domitian is left until quite late in the work and seems almost an afterthought.

How different from the openings of the two epics by Papinius Statius (c. 45–96)! In the proem of the *Thebais*, the poet protests that he must confine himself to the limits of the house of Oedipus, because he would not as yet dare tackle subjects such as Domitian's defense of the Capitol in 69 or his northern triumphs on the Rhine, the Danube, and in Dacia. He prays that Domitian will refuse to join the other gods in all their urgings and that the time will then come when he can with greater strength and expertise do justice to his great achievements (1.16–33).[3]

The unfinished *Achilleis* had not yet received its final polish and the praise of Domitian in the opening lines is uncharacteristically brief and couched in the *recusatio* form. The *Achilleis*, says the poet, will be merely a prelude to some long, though still unworthy, poem on an emperor who has won laurels in the arts of both poetry and war (*Achil.* 1.14–19).

But it is to Statius' *Silvae* and to ten books of Martial's epigrams that the fastidiously curious turn to discover the sort of praise that the latest and last heir of the Flavian house, though not the modern reader, would find congenial. The longest piece of this kind is Statius' ecphrastic poem on the great equestrian statue of Domitian erected in the Forum Romanum. It was, like the statue, a commissioned piece and was dashed off in less than forty-eight hours.

The themes emphasized in the poem are external war and internal peace (vv.37, 51). Domitian's puissance in both are symbolized by the statue of Pallas Minerva, his favorite goddess, who is perched on his left hand. The groaning of the mighty plinth beneath the weight of Domitian's genius might remind the uncharitable of Lucan's description of Nero's weight as a threat to the heavens (*sentiet axis onus, Phars.* 1.57). His German con-

---

3. There is, in fact, a pathetic fragment in hexameters surviving from a work by Statius on Domitian's *Bellum Germanicum* (Morel [1963] 132).

quests are represented by the trodden locks of the captive River Rhine, a theme further emphasized in his address by the tutelary deity of the area, Romulus, who adds for good measure a reference to the civil wars ended by the Flavian dynasty. A favorable comparison of Domitian with Julius Caesar is managed by contrasting their two equestrian statues. Domitian's is the gift of the people and the senate. The poem concludes with a prayer to the ruler to delay his departure to heaven so that his wards may grant him divine honors on earth.

This poem and the *Eucharisticon* (*Silv.* 4.2) on the great splendor of Domitian's lavish feast to which the poet was invited are adequate illustrations of how far poets were prepared to go in their presumably acceptable adulation. G. W. E. Russell once remarked to Matthew Arnold, "Everyone likes flattery; and when it comes to Royalty you should lay it on with a trowel." Statius seems to have anticipated the advice.

Martial confirms our ideas of what conventions and subjects were agreeable to the reigning autocrat. Book 8 of the epigrams is in fact dedicated *Imperatori Domitiano Caesari Augusto Germanico Dacico*. This book, in keeping with Domitian's pretensions to be the great reformer of Roman morality, is free of the more licentious epigrams on which Martial's reputation is unfortunately (and wrongly) based. These would be inconsistent with the majesty of his main subject. The book presents, however, an adequate selection of suitable motifs, and needs little supplement from elsewhere. Martial for one has no objection to Domitian's insistence on such honorific addresses as *Dominus et Deus*; he does what he can to weave the concept into his verses (e.g. 8.4); only later will he regret this (10.72.3: *dicturus dominum deumque non sum*).

As in Julio-Claudian times, so in the Flavian era, the pursuit of imperial largesse and social advancement went in tandem with the chase after private patronage and profitable friendships. Not surprisingly, Martial and Statius had several benefactors in common. Among the most prominent of these were the poet Arruntius Stella, the freedman Claudius Etruscus, Atedius Melior, and

Lucan's widow, Argentaria Polla. The different ways the quest for patronage and benefits takes in the case of each poet deserve some brief notice.

Stella may be singled out as the first example, particularly because of the ingenious poems written by the two authors on the subject of his marriage (after a long courtship) to Violentilla. Statius' *epithalamium* (*Silv.* 1.2) is a playful and elaborate piece of 277 lines on a consummation devoutly to be wished between a worthy lady and a devoted poet. The baroque humor of the debate between Venus and one of her cupids is Alexandrian in inspiration, owing much to Apollonius Rhodius' treatment of mythological characters in the *Argonautica*. The eulogistic motifs within the conventions of the marriage song are therefore subtler and more acceptable to the modern ear than Statius' more blatant flatteries of Domitian.

Martial's lines on the same event (6.21) fit readily into the pattern of his other poems relating to Stella (1.7, 44, 61; 4.6; 5.11, 12, 59; 6.21, 47; 7.14, 36; 8.78; 9.42, 55, 89; 10.48; 11.52; 12.3). Martial had put Stella's poetry above that of Catullus (1.7) and equal to Horace (1.61.3–4), but, in general, his verses addressed to Stella are light and humorous, even when they are begging letters, and so the piece on the union of the pair maintains the same vein of lightness. The epigram (8.78) praising him for his games in celebration of Domitian's ending of the Sarmatian War in 93 demands more of his powers, but this is to be explained by its concentration on the emperor who, in the last line, is welcomed home. The stress on Stella's modesty and loyalty is a deft gesture that a patron would appreciate, as he would Martial's prayer to Apollo for his consulship (9.42).

From the comparison the reader may deduce that Statius was much closer to Stella than was Martial; Statius tries to write more as a friend than as a client, whereas Martial is more forthright about the true relationship. This makes more rewarding an inspection of the poems addressed by both to Argentaria Polla, Lucan's widow, on the occasion of the birthday of the dead poet (Mart. 7.21–23; *Silv.* 2.7). These are more impersonal and ap-

propriately combine the anti-Neronian motifs of Flavian propaganda with genuine regret for a great genius and delicately subdued praise of an important woman patron. One of Martial's
three is worth quoting as illustration:

> haec est illa dies, quae magni conscia partus
> Lucanum populis et tibi, Polla, dedit.
> heu! Nero crudelis nullaque invisior umbra,
> debuit hoc saltem non licuisse tibi.
>
> (7.21)

This is that day which, aware of its great nativity, gave Lucan to
the world and to you, Polla. Ah! cruel Nero and for no death
more hated, this at least should not have been in your power.

This epigram is short and to the point. Statius' poem (*Silv.* 2.7)
by contrast is much more ambitious. Addressing Lucan, he exclaims:

> sic et tu (rabidi nefas tyranni!)
> iussus praecipitem subire Lethen,
> dum pugnas canis arduaque voce
> das solacia grandibus sepulchris
> (o dirum scelus! o scelus!) tacebis.
>
> (100–104)

And so [*like other short-lived heroes*] you were ordered—the
wickedness of the mad tyrant!—to go down in precipitious haste
to Lethe, and while you are singing of battles and in your lofty
tones bring comfort to imposing sepulchres, you will fall silent.
Monstrous, monstrous crime!

Statius' attack is more sustained because he attributes the burning of Rome to the emperor and pictures Nero pursued in hell
by the avenging torch of his murdered mother Agrippina (vv.60–
61; 118–19).[4] He is also more fulsome about Polla's own merits
(vv.83–88). In short, it is a bravura piece as usual.

---

4. Obviously the burning of Rome was attributed to Nero in Lucan's *De Incendio
Urbis* and Statius seems to be suggesting that the pseudo-Senecan *Octavia* was writ-

Poems such as these combine flattery, propaganda, and hopes of reward, but the rewards expected are conventional: friendship with the great, grants, rewards, and commissions, all suited to the situations and expectations of professional poets and other eulogists. Obviously a dimension is lacking in the Flavian literary picture; namely, the use of literature as a weapon in the fight for real power at court and in the *consilium principis*. The senatorial historians, biographers, and memoirists, even Maternus in his *Fabulae togatae* and his tragedies, see themselves as critics of the regime, not pretenders to power. It would seem then that none of the Flavians encouraged senatorial literary activity and none of them was so star-struck by literary gifts as to attribute to such writers political talents. Moreover, even Domitian, who welcomed delation, apparently disliked the venting of venom under artistic guises—unlike Nero at least in this. He was in any case too suspicious to encourage any jockeying for influence or prestige by such means, which may explain the reluctance of contemporary patrons to play Maecenas. Martial's chagrin at such caution (8.55) is understandable, but so is their reluctance.

This is not to say that there were no personal or literary vendettas at all, but that reasons other than political must be sought. Martial and Statius were antagonistic. This is unremarkable, for here were two great poets who were very close contemporaries, neither rich (cf. Stat. *Silv.* 5.3.117–18) nor Roman by birth, and both in need of imperial and other patronage. Genius and talent do not always go hand in hand with magnanimity or even tolerance.

The evidence is to be found in the ominous silence about each other, despite their many common friends. Statius pointedly omits Martial from his list of Spanish luminaries (*Silv.* 2.7.24–35). Such silence implies dislike more than indifference and shows the usual

---

ten by the same author (*ingratus Nero dulcibus theatris . . . tibi proferetur,* vv. 58–59). The portrayal of Agrippina as a vengeful fury (vv. 118–19) is to be found also in the *Octavia* (vv. 593 ff.). Statius also has sneering remarks on Nero's lake for the *Domus Aurea* (*Silv.* 4.3.8) and his cruelty (5.2.44). Martial's other attacks on Nero are found in 4.63 (his attempt on Agrippina's life) and in 7.34, 44, 45.

determination to grant no posthumous fame or contemporary notoriety to one's rival. If allusion is unavoidable, it is oblique or in the form of sobriquets.

Moving in such elevated and dignified circles, the contending poets found themselves "willing to wound and yet afraid to strike." Critical darts could be their only weapon. So Statius, in the dedicatory letter to Atedius Melior prefacing Book 2, refers to his lighter poems on Melior's tree and his parrot (*Silv.* 2.3, 4) as *leves libellos quasi epigrammatis loco scriptos*, a delicate slighting of the art and potential seriousness of the epigrammatist's mode. Martial's apparent reply is to be found in the famous *apologia pro opere suo*:

> qui legis Oedipoden caligantemque Thyesten,
> Colchidas et Scyllas, quid nisi monstra legis?
> quid tibi raptus Hylas, quid Parthenopaeus et Attis,
> quid tibi dormitor proderit Endymion? . . .
> non hic Centauros, non Gorgonas Harpyiasque
> invenies: hominem pagina nostra sapit.
> sed non vis, Mamurra, tuas cognoscere mores
> nec te scire: legas *Aetia* Callimachi.
>
> (10.4.1–4, 9–12)

You who read of Oedipus and Thyestes in darkness, of the woman from Colchis and Scylla, what are you reading of but monsters? What will be the profit for you in the rape of Hylas, Parthenopaeus and Attis, or the sleeper Endymion? In these pages you won't find Centaurs, Gorgons and Harpies: our pages smack of mankind. But you, Mamurra, don't wish to learn about the way you live or know yourself: you should read *Origins* by Callimachus.

The reference to Parthenopaeus, son of Atalanta, one of the seven champions sent against Thebes (*Theb.* 4.246 ff.) can hardly be accidental. Indeed to have dropped in the *exemplum* casually, or not to have eschewed delicately, such an obvious reference to an important epic by one of the most distinguished Flavian poets would be a sign of a carelessness in Martial that strains belief. After all, Parthenopaeus is brought on stage last in Statius' parade of the seven champions and more attention is devoted to him than to the rest. The extended examination of his complex psychology may have struck Martial as altogether too Callimachean, and he knew as well as we do that Statius, like his father, was an admirer of Callimachus (cf. *Silv.* 5.3.155 ff.).

The two had entree to Domitian through different court personages, although nothing political seems to stem from this. Flavius Abascantus, the emperor's *libertus ab epistulis*, was the particular patron of Statius, whose *epicedium* on Flavius' dead wife Priscilla is prefaced by a letter referring to the closeness of their wives' friendship and mentioning the poet's own loyalty to the court. Martial's intermediary was Parthenius, the palace chamberlain and *libertus a libellis* (Mart. 4.45; 5.6; 8.28; 9.49; 11.1; 12.11). Significantly enough, Abascantus is not mentioned by Martial and Statius is silent about Parthenius.

Statius died near the end of Domitian's reign and for a considerable time after the emperor's assassination his work in general was ignored. The event was more fraught with consequences for Martial. What was the Spanish poet to do with the sudden departure of his imperial patron, whose memory was now damned by the senate? Cocceius Nerva (96–98), the new emperor, had been the Tibullus of his day in Nero's eyes (Mart. 8.70.7), but he had abandoned his learned Alexandrian elegies as soon as they ceased to be valuable to him in politics. He had turned his attention to the law, becoming a respected jurist and a sound member of the senatorial body. There can be little doubt that Martial's close literary associations with Domitian and the Flavian house was detrimental to him in his search for imperial patronage. Moreover, Nerva had taken over from Domitian a very tight fiscal situation and financial exigencies as well as personal modesty may have made him less generous towards literature than previous rulers. Small wonder then that Martial reluctantly decided to return to his native Bilbilis in 98. Pliny the Younger helped him with travel money and in his condescending obituary (*Ep.* 3.21) prudently makes no mention of the shifts Martial had had to make in order to gain imperial patronage.

The poet's discontent with his enforced retirement makes itself felt in the preface to Book 12. His attempts to get into the good graces of Nerva and Trajan (98–117) had presumably proved futile although he had done his best; Book 11 contains eulogies of the new emperor and his general popularity, particularly with the senate who had so quickly embraced one of their own. His lack of censoriousness is appropriately commended (11.4, 5, 2). Martial's epigram to Nerva in his twelfth book (12.6), published finally in 101, acclaims him as the gentlest man ever to occupy the imperial *aula*; a poet who has brought back *fides, clementia, cauta potestas*, banished fear, and, more importantly for Martial, restored to senators the once dangerous right to be financially generous to others. He ventures to compliment him on his steadfast honesty in the black days of Domitian's rule: *sed tu sub principe duro / temporibusque malis ausus es esse bonus* (vv. 11–12). Martial had of course already joined the senatorial order in damning Domitian's memory. A fragment of his verse preserved by a scholiast on Juvenal and mislocated in our editions partly reads:

> Flavia gens, quantum tibi tertius abstulit heres!
>   paene fuit tanti, non habuisse duos.
>   (*Lib. de Spect.* 33)

> How damned was the Flavian line by that third heir!
> Was it worth the benefits of the earlier pair?

Other minor attacks, which had to be somewhat muted to avoid the obvious charge of hypocrisy, were inserted in the revised edition of Book 10 published in 98, where prayers for Trajan's speedy return from Germany (10.6; 7) are found in company with a plea for greater liberties for patrons and greater support for clients (10.34). Nevertheless, the praise of Trajan's military reputation (12.8) and the donation of Domitian's treasures to the Capitoline (12.15) seem rather perfunctory in comparison with his verses to Domitian and his satellites. Martial may have felt that to compose more was hardly worth the effort, so tainted was he by his associations with the disgraced ruler. Even Nerva had presumably preferred the more subdued praise of one of Martial's friends, the conscientious Sextus Julius Frontinus. His compliment to Nerva is casual (*Nerva Augusto, nescio quo diligentiore an amantiore rei publicae imperatore, Aq.* 1), and not unlike the brisk thanks for his honest administration that Silius Italicus had inserted into his epic.

This brief survey of the interaction between literature and politics is intended to show only that the Flavian period differed from the Neronian in significant ways, but deserves further exploration which may be left for a future occasion. In particular I have made no attempt to show how political dialogue about the system, about the nature of the principate and its relationship to liberty and justice, continued on the symbolic plane in both mythological and historical epic. However bound a writer such as Statius was to the patronage system, imperial and private, and the duties that entailed, reflections on matters civic and political and the nature of kingship and dominance in society are to be found throughout the *Thebais*. These elements deserve the same subtle and close analysis that has usually been given mythic themes in Neronian drama. The politics of myth do not lose their fascination once they leave the inspired hands of Vergil. It is a mistake therefore for modern or ancient critics to dismiss the mythical epics of the Silver Age as incompetent imitations of the great classical masterpieces or, alternatively, as monstrous productions with no relation to contemporary life and thought.

Chronology of
the Neronian Age[*]

POLITICAL EVENTS	LITERARY EVENTS
	Before A.D. 54

3 B.C. Seneca b. Cordoba, Spain
14 A.D. Augustus d.
37 (15 Dec.) Nero b. (Anzio)   37–41 Elder Sen. *Controv., Suas.*
40 Cn. Domitius Ahenobarbus d.;
    Octavia b.
    Martial b. Bilbilis, Spain
41 (Jan.) Claudius succeeds Calig-   41 Sen. *Ad Marc.*
    ula; (Mar.) Britannicus b.; Sen-
    eca e.

                                            42 Sen. *Ad. Helv.*
                                            43 Sen. *Polyb.*
                                            44–49 Sen. *Epigrammata de exilio*
                                          45 Sen. *De Ira* 1–2 (45–48)
48 Messalina d.   48 Sen. *Const. Sap.*
49 Claudius m. Agrippina; Seneca
    recalled to tutor Nero
50 Nero adopted by Claudius

---

[*]Any literary chronology of the Neronian age must be speculative in many areas
and I have signaled my doubts where necessary. Abbreviations used are:

b. = born; d. = died; m. = married; e. = exiled; div. = divorced; cos. = consul.

POLITICAL EVENTS	LITERARY EVENTS
51 Burrus praetorian prefect	51 Sen. *De Ira* 3 (49–52)
53 Nero m. Octavia	

A.D. 54–69

54 (13 Oct.) Nero succeeds Claudius; Parthian War begins	54 Sen. *Apoc.* (Dec.?)
55 Britannicus d.; Nero cos. and *pater patriae*; Pallas dismissed; Agrippina out of power	55 (Jan.) *Commentarii* of Agrippina; (or 56) Sen. *Clem.*
56 Seneca cos.	56 Calp. Sic. *Ecl.* (56–58)
	57 Sen. *Ben.*; Calp. Sic. *Ecl.* 7
58 Tacitus b.; Poppaea mistress of Nero	58 Columella, *de Arboribus; Laus Pisonis*
59 (Mar.) Agrippina d.; Nero's literary circle founded; *Ludi Iuvenales*; Augustiani formed	59 Sen. *Vit. Beat.*; Nero's *Attis* and shorter poems
60 Uprising in Britain under Boudicca; Puteoli *colonia Claudia Neronensis*; Neronia I	60 Columella, *Rust.* (60–64?); Sen. Tragedies (59–65); Nero performs *Attis*; begins *Troica*; Luc. *Phars.* 1–3 (60–62); *Carm. Einseid.*; Pers. *Sat.* (60–62)
61 Nero's gymnasium built	61 Annaeus Cornutus *Epitome of Greek Theology* (?); Sen. *Tranq. An.*
62 Burrus d.; Tigellinus, Faenius Rufus praetorian prefects; treason trials; Seneca retires; Octavia div., e. and d.; Nero m. Poppaea. T. Petronius Niger suffect cos. (May–Aug.); joins Nero's literary circle; *arbiter elegantiae*	62 Sen. *De Otio.*; Persius d. (Nov.)
63 Nero's daughter Claudia Augusta b. & d.; end of Parthian War and revolt in Britain	63 Sen. *Nat. Quaest.* (63–64); *De Prov.*; Lucan banned from publication; Luc. *Phars.* 4
64 Nero on stage at Naples; fire of Rome (18 July); persecution of Christians; *Domus Aurea* begun; fire of Lyon (Aug.); Pontus annexed	64 Petr. *Sat.* (64–66); Sen. *Tranq. An.*; *Ep. Mor.* (64–65); Nero's *Troica* finished

POLITICAL EVENTS	LITERARY EVENTS
65 Pisonian conspiracy (Apr.); Piso, Lucan, Seneca, Faenius Rufus, etc., d.; Musonius Rufus e.; Nymphidius Sabinus copraetorian prefect; *Neronia* II	65 Lucan, Seneca d.; Elder Pliny, *Dubius Sermo*; *Studiosi*; Martial arrives in Rome; finds patron in Lucan's widow, Argentaria Polla
66 Thrasea Paetus, Barea Soranus d.; Petronius d.; closure of Temple of Janus; Nero m. Statilia Messalina; conspiracy of Vinicianus; Nero leaves for tour of Greece (Sept.–early Oct.)	66 Petronius d.; *Epigrams* of Lucillius (63–68); Curiatius Maternus, *Domitius*, *Medea*, *Cato*, and *Thyestes* (66–75)
67 Nero at Corinth (Nov.); triumphant tour of Greece; Greek freedom proclaimed; Corbulo, Scribonii d.; Vespasian fights Jewish revolt; Nero returns to Italy (Dec.)	
68 Entry of Nero into Naples (Jan.); revolt of Vindex (Mar.); Galba in arms against Nero (Apr.); Verginius defeats Vindex at Vesontium (May); Nero d. (9 June)	
69 Galba (68–69), Otho, Vitellius, Vespasian (69–79) emperors; Nero's *cantica* performed for Vitellius	69 Cluvius Rufus, *History of Nero's Reign* (?); pseudo-Senecan *Octavia* circulated (late 68–early 69)

Selected Bibliography

Ahl, Frederic M. *Lucan: An Introduction*. Ithaca, N.Y., 1976.
———. "Lucan and Statius." In *Ancient Writers*. Ed. T. J. Luce. New York, 1982, 917.
Athanassakis, Apostolos N. *Senecae Apocolocyntosis Divi Claudii*. Lawrence, Kans., 1973.
Bagnani, Gilbert. *Arbiter of Elegance*. Toronto, 1954.
Baldwin, Barry. "Seneca's *Potentia*." *CP* 65 (1970) 187.
———. "Seneca and Petronius." *AC* 24 (1981) 133.
Bardon, Henri. *La Littérature latine inconnue II, l'époque imperiale*. Paris, 1956.
Barnes, Timothy D. "The Date of the *Octavia*." *MH* 39 (1982) 215.
Bauman, Richard A. *The Crimen Maiestatis in the Roman Republic and the Augustan Principate*. Johannesburg, 1962.
———. *Impietas in Principem*. Munich, 1974.
Becker, Karl, *Opposition im frühen Prinzipat*. Diss., Tubingen, 1950.
Benario, Herbert W. "The 'Carmen de bello Actiaco' and Early Imperial Epic." *ANRW* II.33.3 (1983) 1656.
Bickel, Ernst. "Zur Senecasschrift über die Freundschaft." *RhM* 60 (1905) 505.
Bishop, J. David. "Seneca's *Oedipus*: Opposition Literature." *CJ* 73 (1978) 289.
Boethius, Axel. *The Golden House of Nero*. Ann Arbor, Mich., 1960.
Boissier, Gaston. *L'Opposition sous les Césars*[7]. Paris, 1913.
Bradley, Keith R. "'*Tum Primum Revocata Ea Lex*.'" *AJP* 94 (1973) 172.
———. *Suetonius' Life of Nero: An Historical Commentary*. Brussels, 1978.
Bramble, J. D. *Persius and the Programmatic Satire: A Study in Form and Imagery*. Cambridge, 1974.

Brink, C. O. *Horace on Poetry.* Cambridge, 1963.

Browne, G. M. "Withdrawal from Lease." *BASP* 5 (1968) 17.

Brunt, P. A. "The Revolt of Vindex and the Fall of Nero." *Latomus* 18 (1959) 531.

————, and J. M. Moore, eds. *Res Gestae Divi Augusti.* Oxford 1967.

Bücheler, F. "Coniectanea." *RhM* 35 (1880) 390.

————. *Kleine Schriften.* Osnabruck, 1965.

Calder, William M. III. "Seneca's *Agamemnon.*" *CP* 71 (1976a) 27.

————. "Seneca: Tragedian of Imperial Rome." *CJ* 72 (1976b) 1.

Cameron, Alan. *Circus Factions.* Oxford, 1976.

————. "The *Garland* of Philip." *GRBS* 21 (1980) 43.

Champlin, E. "The Life & Times of Calpurnius Siculus." *JRS* 68 (1978) 95.

Cizek, Eugen. *L'Époque de Néron et ses controverses idéologiques.* Leiden, 1972.

————. *Néron.* Paris, 1982.

Clarke, Howard W. *Homer's Readers: An Historical Introduction to the Iliad and the Odyssey.* Wilmington, Del., 1980.

Clausen, Wendell V. *A. Persi Flacci et D. Iuni Iuvenalis Saturae.* Oxford 1959.

————. "Callimachus and Roman Poetry." *GRBS* 5 (1964) 181.

Collignon, Albert. *Étude sur Petrone.* Paris, 1892.

Conington, John. *The Satires of A. Persius Flaccus².* Oxford, 1874.

Costa, C.D.N. *Seneca, Medea.* Oxford, 1973.

Cowley, Abraham. *The Country Mouse, A Paraphrase upon Horace, Book 2, Satyr. 6 in Several Discourses by Way of Essays in Verse and Prose.* London, 1663.

Crawford, Dorothy J. "Imperial Estates." In *Studies in Roman Property.* Ed. M. I. Finley. Cambridge, 1976, 35.

Crook, J. A. "*Strictum et Aequum*: Law in the Time of Nero." *The Irish Jurist 5 (1970) 357.*

Dessen, Cynthia S. *Iunctura Callidus Acri.* Ann Arbor, Mich., 1968.

Dihle, Albrecht. "Der Beginn der Attizismus." *A&A* 23 (1977) 162.

D'Israeli, Isaac. *Quarrels of Authors.* London, 1814.

Duckworth, George E., *Vergil and Classical Hexameter Poetry.* Ann Arbor, Mich., 1969.

Eck, W. "Miscellanea Prosopographica." *ZPE* 42 (1981) 227.

Faider, P. *Études sur Sénèque.* Ghent, 1921.

Fairweather, Janet. *Seneca the Elder.* Cambridge, 1981.

Fears, J. Rufus. *Princeps A Diis Electus: The Divine Election of the Emperor as a Political Concept at Rome.* Rome, 1977.

Ferrill, Arthur. "Seneca's Exile and the *Ad Helviam*: A Reinterpretation." *CP* 61 (1966) 253.

Fitch, J. G. "Sense-Pauses and Relative Dating in Seneca, Sophocles and Shakespeare." *AJP* 102 (1981) 289.

Fortey, Stuart, and John Glucker. "*Actus Tragicus*: Seneca on the Stage." *Latomus* 34 (1975) 699.

Fraser, P. M. *Ptolemaic Alexandria*. Oxford, 1972.

Friedrich, W. H. "Cato, Caesar und Fortuna bei Lucan." *H* 73 (1938) 391.

Fuchs, Harald. "Der Friede als Gefahr: Zum Zweiten Einsiedler Hirten-gedichte." *HSCP* 63 (1958) 363.

Gallivan, P. A. "Some Comments on the Fasti for the Reign of Nero." *CQ* 24 (1974) 290.

Gaselee, Stephen. Some unpublished materials for an edition of Petronius. Cambridge University Library, 1909.

Gelzer, Matthias. *Kleine Schriften*. Vol. 2. Wiesbaden, 1963.

George, P. A. "Petronius and Lucan, *de Bello Civili*." *CQ* 24 (1974) 119.

Giancotti, Francesco. *L'Octavia attribuita a Seneca*. Turin, 1954.

———. *Cronologia dei Dialoghi di Seneca*. Rome, 1957.

Gillis, Daniel J. "The Portrait of Afranius Burrus in Tacitus' *Annales*." *PP* 38 (1963) 5.

Ginsburg, Judith R. "Nero's Consular Policy." *AJAH* 6 (1981) 51.

Gottschlich, J. "De parodiis Senecae apud Petronium." In *Miscellaneorum Philologicorum libellus zu Friderici Haase Jubilaüm*. Breslau, 1863.

Grant, Michael. *Roman Anniversary Issues*. Cambridge, 1950.

———. *Roman History from Coins*. Cambridge, 1958.

———. *Nero*. London, 1970.

———. *The Twelve Caesars*. London, 1975.

Griffin, Miriam T. *Seneca, a Philosopher in Politics*. Oxford, 1976.

Grimal, Pierre. "Le *Bellum Civile* de Pétrone dans ses rapports avec la *Pharsale*." In *Neronia 1977*. Ed. J. M. Croisille, and P. M. Fanchère. Clermont-Ferrand, 1982, 117.

Hannestad, N. *Romersk Kunst som Propaganda*. Copenhagen, 1976.

Heitland, W. E. Introduction to Haskins, C. E., *Lucani Pharsalia*. London, 1887.

Herington, C. J. "*Octavia Praetexta*: A Survey." *CQ* 11 (1961) 18.

———. "Senecan Tragedy." *Arion* 5 (1965) 422.

Heuvel, H. "De inimicitiarum quae inter Martialem et Statium fuisse dicuntur." *Mn.* 4 (1937) 299.

Hubaux, M. *Les Thèmes bucoliques dans la poésie latine*. Brussels, 1930.

Huss, W. "Die Propaganda Neros." *AC* 47 (1978) 129.

Hutchinson, A. D. "Petronius and Lucan," *LCM* 7 (1982) 46.

Imperatore, G. F. *Saggio di Analisi Critica della Bibliographia Neroniana dal 1934 al 1975*. Milan, 1978.

Jahn, O. *Aules Persius Flaccus Satirarum Liber cum Scholiis antiquis*. Leipzig, 1843.

Kamp, H. W. *A Critical Biography of Lucius Annaeus Seneca*. Diss., Univ. of Ill., 1930.

Kenney, E. J. "The First Satire of Juvenal." *PCPhS* 8 (1962) 36.

———. Review of A. Seel, *Laus Pisonis* (1969). *CR* 22 (1972) 279.

Keydell, Rudolph. "Bemerkungen zu Griechischen Epigrammen." *H* 80 (1952) 497.

Kindt, B. "Petron und Lucan." *Philologus* 51 (1892) 355.

Klein, Theodore M. "The Role of Callimachus in the Development of the Concept of the Counter-Genres." *Latomus* 33 (1974) 217.

Kopp, A. *Staatsdenken und politisches Handeln bei Seneca und Lucan.* Diss., Heidelberg, 1969.

Korzeniewski, Dietmar. "Die 'Panegyrische Tendenz' in den Carmina Einsiedlensia." *H* 94 (1966) 344.

———. *Hirtengedichte aus neronischer Zeit.* Darmstadt, 1971.

Kragelund, Patrick. *Prophecy, Populism, and Propaganda in the 'Octavia.'* Copenhagen, 1982.

Lana, Italo. *Lucio Anneo Seneca.* Turin, 1955.

Leach, Eleanor Windsor. "Corydon Revisited: An Interpretation of the Political Eclogues of Calpurnius Siculus." *Ramus* 2 (1973) 53.

Levi, Mario Attilio. *Nerone et i suoi Tempi.* Milan, 1949.

McAlindon, D. "Senatorial Opposition to Claudius and Nero." *AJP* 77 (1956) 113.

McDermott, William C. "Fabricius Veiento." *AJP* 91 (1970) 129.

MacMullen, Ramsay. *Enemies of the Roman Order: Treason, Unrest and Alienation in the Empire.* Cambridge, Mass., 1966.

Manning, C. E., "Acting and Nero's Conception of the Principate." *G&R* 22 (1975) 164.

Marti, Berthe M. "Seneca's Tragedies, a New Interpretation." *TAPA* 76 (1945) 216.

———. "Seneca's *Apocolocyntosis* and *Octavia*: A Diptych." *AJP* 73 (1952) 24.

Martin, René. "Quelques remarques concernant la date du *Satiricon*." *REL* 53 (1975) 182.

Marx, F. "Tacitus und die Literatur der exitus illustrium virorum." *Philol.* 92 (1937) 83.

Mattingly, Harold. *The Coins of the Roman Empire in the British Museum.* Vol. 1. London, 1965.

———, and E. A. Sydenham. *The Roman Imperial Coinage.* London, 1923.

Maxwell-Stuart, P. G. "Strato and the *Musa Puerilis*." *H* 100 (1972) 215.

Mayer, Roland. "Calpurnius Siculus: Technique and Date." *JRS* 70 (1980) 175.

Momigliano, Arnaldo. *Claudius: The Emperor and His Achievements.* Oxford, 1934.

———. "Literary Chronology of the Neronian Age." *CQ* 38 (1944) 96 = *Secondo contributo alla storia degli studi classici.* Rome, 1960, 454.

———. Review of C. Wirszubski, *Libertas* (1950) *JRS* 41 (1951) 146.

———. "Seneca between Political and Contemplative Life." In *Quarto contributo alla storia degli studi classici*. Rome, 1975.

Mooney, G. W. *Index to the Pharsalia of Lucan*. Dublin and London, 1927.

Morel, Willy. *Fragmenta Poetarum Latinorum*. 2d. ed. Leipzig, 1975.

Motto, Anna L. "Seneca on Trial: The Case of the Opulent Stoic." *CJ* 61 (1966) 254.

Mueller, Lucien. "Homerus Latinus." *Philologus* 15 (1860) 481.

Münscher, Karl. "Senecas Werke." *Philologus* supp. 16 (1922) 481.

Newman, J. K. *The Concept of Vates in Augustan Poetry*. Brussels, 1967.

Nicolova-Burova, A. "On the Chronology of Seneca's Philosophical Dialogues." *Revue* (organisation internationale pour l'étude des langues anciennes par ordinateur) 2 (1975) 1.

Pathmanathan, R. S. "The Parable in Seneca's *Oedipus*." *Nigeria and the Classics* 10 (1967/8) 13.

Pecchiura, P. *La figura di Catone uticense nella letteratura latina*. Turin, 1965.

Pfeiffer, Rudolph. *Callimachus*. Vol. 1 *Fragmenta*. Oxford, 1965.

Plessis, Frédérique Édouard. *Italici Ilias Latina*. Paris, 1885.

Prato, Carlo. *Gli epigrammi attribuiti a L. Anneo Seneca*. Rome, 1964.

Praz, Mario. *The Romantic Agony*. Oxford, 1951.

Pugliese Carratelli, G. "Tabulae Ceratae Herculanenses." *PP* 3 (1946) 381.

Raith, Oskar. *Petronius ein Epikureer*. Nuremburg, 1963.

Reckford, Kenneth J. "Studies in Persius." *H* 90 (1962) 283.

Reeve, M. D. "The Addressee of *Laus Pisonis*." *ICS* 9 (1984) 42.

Robson, W. W. *The Definition of Literature and Other Essays*. Cambridge, 1982.

Rogers, Robert S. "The Tacitean Account of a Neronian Trial." In *Studies Presented to David M. Robinson*, vol. 2. St. Louis, Mo., 1953, 711.

———. "Freedom of Speech in the Empire—Nero." In *Laudatores Temporis Acti*. The James Sprunt Studies in History and Political Science, vol. 46. Chapel Hill, N.C., 1964, 91.

Roper, T. K. "Nero, Seneca and Tigellinus." *HH* 28 (1979) 346.

Roscher, W. H. *Ausführlicher Lexicon der griechischen und römischen Mythologie*. Leipzig, 1890–1897.

Rose, K.F.C. "Problems of Chronology in Lucan's Career." *TAPA* 97 (1966) 379.

———. *The Date and Author of the Satyricon*. Leiden, 1971.

Rosenmeyer, Thomas G. *The Green Cabinet: Theocritus and the European Pastoral Lyric*. Berkeley, Calif., 1969.

Ross, David O. *Style & Tradition in Catullus*. Cambridge, Mass., 1969.

———. *Backgrounds to Augustan Poetry—Gallus, Elegy, and Rome*. Cambridge, 1975a.

———. "The *Culex* and *Moretum* as Post-Augustan Literary Parodies." *HSCP* 79 (1975b) 235.

Rostovtzeff, M. I., *The Social and Economic History of the Roman Empire.* 2d ed. Oxford, 1957.

Sarpe, G. *Quaestiones Philologicae.* Rostock, 1819.

Sattler, P. "Augustus und der Senat." In *Untersuchungen zur römischen Innenpolitik zwischen 30 und 17 vor Christus.* Berlin, 1960.

Schmid, D. *Der Erbschleicher in der antiken Satire.* Tubingen, 1951.

Schnur, Harry C. *The Age of Petronius Arbiter.* Diss. New York Univ. Ann Arbor, Mich., microfilm, 1957.

Seel, Arno. *Laus Pisonis.* Erlangen, 1969.

Shackleton Bailey, D. R. *Cicero's Letters to Atticus.* Vol. 1. Cambridge, 1965.

———. *Towards a Text of 'Anthologia Latina.'* Cambridge, 1979.

Sheavyn, Phoebe. *The Literary Profession in the Elizabethan Age.* 2nd ed. Manchester, 1967.

Sinclair, Brent W. "Encolpius and Asianism (*Satyricon* 2.7)." In *Classical Texts and their Traditions.* Chico, Calif., 1984.

Smith, Martin S. *Petronii Arbitri Cena Trimalchionis.* Oxford, 1975.

Smith, R. E. "The Law of Libel at Rome." *CQ* n.s. 1 (1951) 169.

Stewart, Zeph. "Sejanus, Gaetulicus, and Seneca." *AJP* 74 (1953) 70.

Studer, G. "Über das Zeitalter des Petronius Arbiter." *RhM* 2 (1843) 89.

Sullivan, J. P. *The Satyricon of Petronius: A Literary Study.* London, 1968.

———. "Petronius, Lucan, and Seneca: A Neronian Literary Feud?" *TAPA* 100 (1969) 453.

———. "Ancient Satire." In *Literature and Western Civilization: The Classical World.* Ed. D. Daiches, and A. Thorlby. London, 1972a, 233.

———. "In Defence of Persius." *Ramus* 1 (1972b) 48.

———. *Propertius: A Critical Introduction.* Cambridge, 1976.

———. "Asses's Ears and *Attises*: Persius and Nero." *AJP* 99 (1978) 159.

———. "Martial's Sexual Attitudes." *Philologus* 123 (1979) 88.

———. "Petronius' *Bellum Civile* and Lucan's *Pharsalia*: A Political Reconsideration." In *Neronia* 1977. Ed. J. M. Croisille, and P. M. Fanchère. Clermont-Ferrand, 1982, 151.

———. "The Background of Petronius Fr. xxviii." *PSNL* 15 (1983) 7.

———, trans. *Petronius The Satyricon and Seneca The Apocolocyntosis.* Rev. ed. Harmondsworth, 1977.

Sussman, Lewis A. "The Elder Seneca's Discussion of the Decline of Roman Eloquence." *CSCA* 5 (1972) 195.

———. *The Elder Seneca.* Leiden, 1978.

Sutherland, C.H.V. *Coinage in Roman Imperial Policy 31 B.C.–A.D. 68.* London, 1951.

———. *Roman Coins.* London, 1974.

Sutton, Dana F. *The Dramaturgy of the Octavia.* Königstein, 1983.

Syme, Ronald. *The Roman Revolution.* Oxford, 1939, 1960.

———. *Tacitus.* Oxford, 1958.

———. *History in Ovid.* Oxford, 1978.

————. *Some Arval Brethren*. Oxford, 1980.

Tamm, Birgitta. *Neros Gymnasium in Rom*. Stockholm, 1970.

Tarrant, Richard J. *Seneca Agamemnon*. Cambridge, 1977.

Taylor, Lilly Ross. *Party Politics in the Age of Caesar*. Berkeley, Calif., 1949.

Thomas, Paul. *L'Age et l'auteur du Satyricon*. Ghent, 1905.

Townend, Gavin B. "Calpurnius Siculus and the *munus Neronis*." *JRS* 70 (1980) 166.

Toynbee, J.M.C. *Nero Artifex: The Apocolocyntosis* Reconsidered." *CQ* 36 (1942) 83.

Tränkle, H. *Die Sprachkunst des Properz und die Tradition der lateinischer Dichtersprache*. Wiesbaden, 1960.

Verdière, Raoul. *Calpurnius Siculus: De Laude Pisonis et Bucolica et M. Annaei Lucani de Laude Caesaris Einsiedlensia quae dicuntur Carmina*. Brussels, 1954.

Vermaseren, M. T. *Cybele and Attis: The Myth and the Cult*. Leiden, 1977.

Vogel-Weidemann, U. "The Opposition under the Early Caesars." *AC* 22 (1979) 91.

Walsh, P. G. "Eumolpus, the *Halosis Troiae*, and the *De bello civili*." *CP* 63 (1968) 208.

Waltz, René. *La Vie politique de Sénèque*. Paris, 1909.

Ward Perkins, J. B. "Nero's Golden House." *Antiquity* 30 (1956) 209.

Warmington, B. H. *Nero: Reality and Legend*. London, 1969.

White, Peter. "*Amicitia* and the Profession of Poetry in Early Imperial Rome." *JRS* 68 (1978) 74.

————. "Positions for Poets in Early Imperial Rome." In *Literary and Artistic Patronage in Ancient Rome*. Ed. Barbara K. Gold. Austin, Tex. 1982, 50.

Williams, Gordon. *Change and Decline: Roman Literature in the Early Empire*. Berkeley, Calif., 1978.

————. "Phases in Political Patronage of Literature in Rome." In *Literary and Artistic Patronage in Ancient Rome*. Ed. Barbara K. Gold. Austin, Tex. 1982, 3.

Wimmel, Walther. *Kallimachos in Rom*. Wiesbaden, 1960.

Wirszubski, Charles. *Libertas as a Political Ideal at Rome During the Late Republic and Early Principate*. Cambridge, 1950.

Wiseman, James R. *The Land of the Ancient Corinthians*. Studies in Mediterranean Archaeology, vol. 50. Goteborg, 1978.

————. "Corinth and Rome I: 228 B.C.–A.D. 267." *ANRW* 2.7 (Berlin, 1979) 438.

Wiseman, Timothy Peter. "Calpurnius Siculus and the Claudian Civil War." *JRS* 72 (1982) 57.

Wistrand, Erik. *Politik och Litteratur i Antikens Rom*. Upsala, 1962.

Yavetz, Zvi. *Plebs and Princeps*. Oxford, 1969.

Zorzetti, Nevio. *La pretesta e il theatro latino arcaico*. Naples, 1980.

Index

abstract art, 109–110
Accius, 97
Achilles, 151
Acratus, 28 n
Acte, 26
Actium, 168, 171
Aeacus, tribunal of, 49, 54
Aegialus, 28
Aeneas, 149, 151
Aeschylus, 156
aes coinage, 28
Afer, Domitius, 182
Afranius Quintianus, 47, 90, 155
Africa, 170
Agamemnon, 30 n
Agricola, 187
Agrippina: and Claudius, 62, 71; and
  coinage under Nero, 28; death of, 26,
  154 n, 182; epigrams to, 99; influence
  of, 29; as a Julian, 53; in pseudo-
  Senecan *Octavia*, 61, 63, 64, 66, 67,
  70, 192 n; and Seneca, 49, 49 n, 126,
  136, 158; Statius on, 191
Ajax, 88
Alcibiades, 141
Alcmaeon, 31
Alexandria: literature of, 76–77
Alexandrianism, 74, 79, 80, 85, 86, 88,
  190; and elegy, 96; in Nero's poetry,
  90–91
Amphitrite, 90
Andromache, 88
Annaean family, 44, 106

Annii, the, 71 n
Anthologia Latina, 158, 161, 177
Antichrist, the, 27 n
Antigone, 31
Antiochus Epiphanes, 45 n
Antipater of Thessalonica, 85
Antiphanes, 84
Antiphilus, 79 n, 98 n
Antistius Sosianus, 42, 98 n, 106, 130 n
Antony, Mark, 147
Apamea, 42
Aper, 181–182
Apollo, 50, 58, 81, 82, 187; and Augus-
  tus, 150; in Lucan's *Pharsalia*, 146; in
  Petronius' *Bellum Civile*, 171
Apollonius Rhodius, 76, 82, 88, 151,
  190
Apollophanes, 99
Aratus, 78, 79
Archias, 30 n
architecture, under Nero, 27
Areus, 122
Argo, 78
Argonauts, 90
Ariadne, 96
Ariminum, 170
Aristarchus, school of, 85
Aristophanes, 108
Aristotle, 14
Armenia, Lesser, 51
Armenian question, 51
army, Roman, purges of, 25
Arria (the elder), 39

[209]

Artabanus, 25 n
Astyanax, 88
Atedius Melior, 189, 193
Athens, 28 n
Atlas, 125
Atticism, 74
Atticus, M. Julius Vestinus, 32
Attis, 103, 193
Augustus: and Apollo, 150, 171; and
    enemies, 65; governance of, 24, 65,
    117, 134, 135; and Mercury, 171; as
    patron of the arts, 105 n; propaganda
    under, 55, 147, 150; in pseudo-
    Senecan Octavia, 61, 71, 171; and
    senate, 40; Seneca on, 49, 50, 53, 71,
    129, 134, 135; as symbol of govern-
    ance, 148
aula Neronis, 37

Bacchantes, 104
Bacchus (Dionysus), 81, 104
Baiae, Piso's villa at, 36
Bassarids, 98, 103, 104
Baucis, 87 n
Belloc, Hilaire, 73, 94
Bilbilis, 194
bisexuality, 26
Bithynia, 39, 159
Boissier, Gaston, 115
Bononia, 42
Borges, Jorge Luis, 19
Britain, 187
Britannicus, 26, 33, 50, 62, 63, 64
Brutus, 65, 118, 149
Bull of Marathon, 77
Burrus, 31, 44, 136, 154 n, 156

Caecilius, 103
Caesar, Julius: and Cato the Younger,
    118; and the Civil War, 166, 171;
    death of, 65; governance of, 116,
    133, 135; Lucan on, 150–151, 167,
    169, 170; Petronius on, 165, 168,
    169, 171; and Republican ideology,
    143; Seneca on, 129; speeches of,
    165 n
Caesennius Paetus, 46
Caesius Bassus, 37, 37 n, 39, 104
Caligula, 24, 49
Callimacheanism, 74, 75, 80, 84; defini-
    tions of, 75; influence of, 78, 83; and
    elegy, 96; in Nero's poetry, 91–92;

and periphrases for time, 81, 82; as
    passing trend, 93; in Persius' satires,
    95
Callimachus: Aetia, 80, 90; and Apollo-
    nius Rhodius, 77; on Aratus, 78; crit-
    icism of, 79–81, 84, 85, 86; on epics,
    91 n, 151; on Euphorion, 78; Hecale,
    77, 86, 87, 90; on Heraclitus of Hali-
    carnassus, 78; on Hesiod, 78; Hymns,
    90; influence of, 75, 76; on the Lock
    of Berenice, 89; and Nero, 28, 104;
    Origins, 193; and Statius, 194; and
    Telchines, 156; on Theocritus, 78
Callirhoe, 102
Callistratus, 100
Calpurnii, 46
Calpurnius Siculus: Bucolica, 30 n; Ec-
    logues, 37, 47, 48, 51–57, 54 n, 59,
    84; and Laus Pisonis, 36; and Nero,
    57, 58, 146; parody of, 59; pastorals
    of, 96; and Piso, 48 n
Calvia Crispinilla, 28 n, 159
Calvus, 75
Canace, 30
Capaneus, 31, 31 n
Capito, Cossutianus, 42, 106
Capitoline games, 185
captatio, 137 n
Carmina Einsiedlensia, 30 n
Cato the Censor, 118 n
Cato (the Younger): and the Civil War,
    150; and Hercules, 170; and libertas,
    117, 149; Lucan on, 120, 148, 150,
    151, 152; Petronius on, 166–167; as a
    Stoic, 143–144, 169; suicide of, 150;
    symbolism of, 118, 118 n, 119, 144;
    wealth of, 140
Cato, Valerius, 75
Catullus, 76, 96, 103, 108; on bisexual-
    ity, 26; and Callimachus, 75, 89; and
    Cybebe, 104; as a Neoteric, 75, 94;
    and Nero, 104; Peleus and Thetis, 77;
    poetry of, 90, 190
Cebren, River, 102
Celer (architect), 27
Cerealis, 98 n, 187
Cerealius, 22, 98, 98 n
Chaeremon, 28
Chatti, 185
Christians, persecution of, 27 n, 40
Cicero, 43, 75, 118
Cinna, 75, 77, 134, 149
Ciris, 96

Civil War: causes of, 166; in literature, 146, 147, 163, 165, 168, 170; Lucan on, 164; omens of, 165 n, 169; propaganda during, 149

Claudius: and Agrippina, 62, 71; death of, 81, 154 n; flattery of, 123; governance of, 54–55, 116–117; in pseudo-Senecan *Octavia*, 63; and senate, 54; and Seneca, 49 n, 117, 120, 126, 127, 130, 158; in Seneca's *Apocolocyntosis*, 48 n, 49, 50, 54, 64, 155; in Seneca's *Consolatio ad Polybium*, 124–126

Claudius Etruscus, 189

clementia, 53

Cluvius Rufus, 35–36

Cocteau, Jean, 157

coinage: under Nero, 28; propagandistic value of, 184

Collignon, Albert, 173

Columella, 48 n, 83, 84

Corbulo, 25, 117

Cordus, A. Cremutius, 122

Corinth, Isthmus of, 44 n; proposed canal at, 90, 90 n

Cornutus, Annaeus, 39, 42, 46, 73, 106, 119, 176 n

Corsica, 121, 158

Corybants, 104

Corydon, 52, 56

Cowley, Abraham, 82, 100

Crassus, 167

Crispinus, Rufrius, 67, 68

Crispus, Vibius, 46, 182

Curio, 171

Curtius Montanus, 155, 182

Cybebe (Cybele), 103–104

Cynicism, 120

Cynthius, 91

Dacians, 185

Datus, 154 n

De Bello Actiaco, 147

Decebalus, 185

Democritus, 141

Demophilus, 99

Diana, 171

Didactic poetry, 83

Dido, 151, 187

Dio Cassius, 27, 41 n, 102, 104

Dio Chrysostom, 25 n

Dis (Pluto), 168

Domitian: criticism of, 195; flattery of, 188, 190; governance of, 25 n, 186;

Juvenal on, 157 n, 185; libel suits under, 35 n; as literary patron, 42, 184, 192, 194; military campaigns of, 185, 188; and Pallas Minerva, 188; paranoia of, 25; as poet, 185, 187; and senate, 107 n; social reforms of, 186 n; statues of, 188

Domitii, 71 n

Domitius Ahenobarbus, 145

Domus Aurea, 27

Domus Transitoria, 27

Donne, John, 35 n, 100, 111, 114

Douglas, Norman, 153

Drusus, 122

Dryden, John, 114, 153 n

Dyrrachium, 171

Earinus, 186 n

Egypt, 65, 168

Einsiedeln Eclogues, 56–59, 91

elegy, 96

Elizabethan age, 19

Encolpius, 173

Endymion, 193

Ennius, 74, 88 n, 93, 111

Epaphroditus, 185

Epicureanism, 45, 46, 142, 143

Epigoni, 31

epigrams, 22, 79, 99, 189

Eprius Marcellus, 46, 182, 184

epyllion, 77, 78, 89

Eteocles, 151

Eumolpus, 30 n, 162, 164–166, 171, 174

Euphorion, 78, 81

Euripides, 43 n, 91

Eutychides, 99

extempore composition, 30, 30 n

Fabricius, A. Veiento, 34, 34 n, 35, 35 n, 162, 182

Faenius Rufus, 45, 156

Fama, 170

Fannius, C., 106 n

Fates, 49

Flaccus, C. Valerius, 152, 187

Flavian amphitheatre (the Colosseum), 21, 22

Flavian dynasty, 72

Flavius Abascantus, 194

Flavus, Verginius, 41 n

Fortuna, 168, 169, 171, 173

Freud, Sigmund, 26

Frontinus, Sextus Julius, 187, 196
Fronto, 31

Galba, 67, 72, 72 n, 117, 167 n
Gallio, 138
Gallus, 75, 76, 77, 96, 118
Gaul, 160
Gauls, 149
Germanicus, 79, 137
Giraudoux, Jean, 157
Golden Age of Augustus, 53, 56, 60
Golden Age of Nero, new, 51, 52,
    52 n, 55, 56, 144
Golden Fleece, 90
Greece, 23, 25 n, 31, 41, 90 n

Hadrian, 105 n
Hannibal, 149
Hector, 88, 91, 102, 151
Hegelochus, 99
Helen of Troy, 68, 102
Helicon, 93, 163
Heliodorus, 100
Helios, 23
Helvidius Priscus, 144, 186
Heraclitus of Halicarnassus, 78
Hercules, 30, 49, 170, 171
Herennius Senecio, 186
Hesiod, 78, 83, 84, 93, 152
Hesione, 88
Hiero II of Syracuse, 59
Hirtius, Aulus, 118
Homer, 85; in *Einsiedeln Eclogues*, 58;
    Iliad, 88, 89, 91, 102, 151; influence
    of, 89; and periphrases for time, 82;
    in Persius' satires, 93; and Vergil, 20
Horace: and archaizing, 97; *Ars Poetica*,
    79, 79 n; and Augustus, 105 n; on
    Callimacheanism, 75, 79 n; on the
    Civil War, 147; as critic, 101; on el-
    egy, 96 n; *Epistulae*, 111; on literary
    forms, 79; and lyric poetry, 76; on
    neo-Callimacheanism, 78; *Odes*, 118;
    and Persius, 94, 110, 112; poetry of,
    111; and Propertius, 20 n, 108, 156;
    on Punic Wars, 88 n; and satire, 113;
    Sermones, 111
Housman, A. E., 85
Hylas, 78, 90, 193
Hypsipyle, 95, 96

Ibis, 156
Ilias Latina, 33, 33 n, 34, 87, 88, 89,
    89 n

Ilium, 42
incest, 63 n, 66, 68, 70, 71, 157 n
Index Librorum Prohibitorum, 107 n
Ireland, Northern, 187
Isodorus the Cynic, 154 n
Isthmian games, 99
Iulus, 149
Iuvenalia, 92
Ixion, 81

Jason, 151
Jerusalem, destruction of, 187
Johnson, Samuel, 111, 153 n
Josephus, 25, 35, 36, 73
Judea, 33, 187
Jugurtha, 149
Julia Augusta, 70, 122
Julia Livilla, 123
Julian dynasty, 33, 52, 53, 122, 149,
    150, 187
Julio-Claudian dynasty, 71 n; incest
    among, 63 n, 68, 70, 71, 157 n; Lu-
    can on, 145, 148; morals of, 26; op-
    position to, 115, 115 n, 183; in
    pseudo-Senecan *Octavia*, 61, 63, 70,
    72
Julius Africanus, 182
Juno, 64, 150
Jupiter, 49, 64, 146, 150, 170
Juvenal: and Callimacheanism, 92; cau-
    tiousness of, 107; on contemporary
    writing, 105 n; as critic, 101; on
    Domitian, 107 n, 157 n, 160, 185; on
    Messalina, 62; satire of, 113; on so-
    cial welfare, 40

Ladas, 58
Laus Pisonis, 36, 48 n
Lentulus, 171
Leonidas of Alexandria, 99
Leucothea, 90
lex maiestatis, 42, 154
Lex Roscia, 52 n
libertas, 117, 118, 132, 147–149; defini-
    tion of, 115–116; in Lucan's *Pharsalia*,
    150
Libya, 168
literature: under the Antonines, 19 n;
    under Augustus, 19 n, 92, 180; under
    Domitian, 185; under the Flavians,
    19 n, 181, 184, 189, 192, 196; under
    Nero, 19–21, 27, 57, 59, 74, 75, 87,
    93, 179, 180
Livia, 70, 122

Livy, 88 n, 166

Lock of Berenice, 89, 104

Lucan: *Adlocutio ad Pollam*, 38; career of, 164 n; on Cato the Younger, 118, 120, 165; criticism of, 164; *De Incendio Urbis*, 40 n; and extempore composition, 30 n; forgeries of, 155; *Iliacon*, 38, 88; and *Ilias Latina*, 33 n; *Laudes Neronianae*, 38; and *Laus Pisonis*, 48 n; literary circle of, 22; on Nero, 145, 155, 188; Nero's hostility toward, 44, 90, 162; in Nero's literary circle, 31, 37, 38, 42; and Persius, 95, 107; and Petronius, 176; *Pharsalia*, 30 n, 38, 87, 107, 118–120, 143–152, 162 n, 163 n, 165 n, 166–172; and Pisonian conspiracy, 107, 148 n; as political writer, 20, 119; as a Republican, 148, 164, 165; scholiast on, 91; and Silius Italicus, 88 n; *Silvae*, 38; as a Stoic, 120, 143, 169; suicide of, 107; and Vergil, 164

Lucian, 81

Lucilius: and extempore composition, 30 n; and Persius, 94, 100, 105, 107, 108, 110; style of, 111, 112

Lucilius Iunior, 73

Lucillius, 74; on bad poets, 99–100; epigrams of, 22, 85; and Persius, 104; on philology, 85

Lucretia, 64

Lucretius, 111, 152

Ludi Iuvenales, 30, 41, 102

Ludi Maximi, 176 n

Lusitania, 45, 68

Lycophron, 78

McCarthy, Senator Joseph, 182; McCarthyism, 107 n

Machiavelli, 131

Maecenas, 56, 105 n, 175 n, 180, 192

Maenads, 98, 103, 104

Mamurra, 79, 193

Marcellus, 122, 171

Marcia, 122

Marcus, 100

Marius, 147, 149

Mars, 150, 171

Martial, 108; on bisexuality, 26; and Callimacheanism, 92; on Callimachus, 79; career of, 21; on Domitian, 185, 189, 195; epigrams of, 85, 105 n, 188, 189; on Horace, 190; *Liber de Spectaculis*, 21, 184; on literary patronage, 184, 192; on Nero, 22, 25, 30, 89, 192 n; on Nerva, 32, 195; political satire of, 52 n; on Polla, 191; and Statius, 19 n, 156, 192, 193, 194; on Stella, 190; and Trajan, 195

Massilia, seige of, 145

Maternus, Curiatius, 157 n, 176 n; *Cato*, 155, 181; *Domitius*, 181; *Fabulae togatae*, 192; *Thyestes*, 181; and Vatinius, 45, 47

Melanippe, 31

"Meliboeus," 48, 48 n, 52, 56

Melicerta, 90

Melito, 99

Menecrates, 45

Menippean satire, 49

Mercury, 49, 150, 171

Messala, M. Valerius Corvinus, 48 n, 182

Messala, Valerii, 71 n

Messalina, 62, 63, 70, 120

Metaphysical poetry, 111

Midas, 57

Milton, John, 145, 151

Minerva, 171, 188

Mithriades, 90

Montanus, Julius, 82

Munatius Rufus, 118

munus Neronis, 51 n

Muses, 52

Musonius Rufus, 143

Mycenae, 58

Mystes, 56, 57

Naples, 41

Nauplion, 99

Nauplius, 31

neo-Callimacheanism, 74, 80, 89, 108; and archaizing, 97; definition of, 76; and elegy, 96; influence of, 86; Persius' satire of, 95

Neotericism, 74, 77, 79, 80, 89; and archaizing, 78; and Callimachean theory, 75; definition of, 75; mannerisms of, 100; and neo-Callimacheanism, 76; and Nero's poetry, 91; themes of, 103; vocabulary of, 95

Nero: and Afranius Quintianus, 47; and Apollo, 56, 57; as artist, 27, 41, 159; *Attis (The Bacchantes)*, 92, 102, 103; and Augustus, 50; and Callimachus, 104; and Catullus, 104; and Christians, 27 n, 40; court of, 161, 171;

Nero (*continued*)
criticism of, 119, 120, 144, 154, 154 n, 157 n; death of, 25 n, 61, 185; dramatic performances of, 22, 30, 31, 31 n, 176 n; education of, 28; in *Einsiedeln Eclogues*, 57, 58; and Fabricius' exile, 35; flattery of, 29, 29 n, 37, 51, 57, 58, 59, 129, 131, 145, 146, 159; foreign policy under, 23, 23 n; governance of, 25, 41 n, 54–55, 117, 131 n, 132, 133, 135, 136 n; and great fire of Rome, 40, 40 n, 58, 69, 91, 191, 191 n; and Greece, 23, 24, 25 n, 31, 41, 90 n; historical treatment of, 25, 186; as homosexual, 26 n; impersonators of, 25 n, 41; inaugural speech of, 24; and incest, 66; as a Julian, 52, 53; as a Julio-Claudian, 70 n, 71; and libel, 35 n, 42, 106, 107; literary circle of, 29, 31–39, 44, 45, 89, 105, 155, 176; and Lucan, 38, 107, 164; in Lucan's *Pharsalia*, 42, 145, 146; *Luscio*, 103; marriages of, 60; and the masses, 25 n, 26, 40, 41, 66, 69, 72; and Midas, 57; and the military, 23; as musician, 30; as a neo-Callimachean, 102; and oratory, 40 n; as pacifist, 51; paranoia of, 51; as patron of the arts, 23, 28, 28 n, 184; and Persius, 109; and Petronius, 159, 160, 172; plots against, 106; poetry of, 28–30, 89–91, 101, 103 n, 104–106, 106 n, 108, 110, 111, 113, 142; and Poppaea Sabina, 26, 36 n, 45; propaganda against, 73, 183, 191; in pseudo-Senecan *Octavia*, 27, 40 n, 60–71, 73; and senate, 23, 24, 26, 40, 53, 65, 107 n; and Seneca, 24, 28–31, 42–44, 127, 131, 142, 158; in Seneca's *Apocolocyntosis*, 50, 51, 73, 146; sexual excesses of, 26; and Stoicism, 146; *Troica*, 88, 91, 92, 102, 106 n, 159; and Troy, 58. *See also entries for individual writers*
Neronia, 30, 30 n, 32, 41
Neronian literary renaissance, 179, 181
Nerva: flattery of, 195, 196; governance of, 194; as literary patron, 194; and Nero, 32, 89, 159; and Pisonian conspiracy, 32; poetry of, 32 n, 35, 105 n
Nicander, 78
Nicarchus, 22
Nigidius Frigulus, 147, 169

Niobe, 31
Nonianus, Servilius, 39
Numa, 54
Numitorius, 86

Octavia: exile of, 61; as a Julian, 122; murder of, 26; and Nero, 60; in pseudo-Senecan *Octavia*, 62–66, 68, 70, 72
Odysseus, 88
Oedipus, 30, 193
Oenone, 102
Oenothea, 86, 87 n
Olympia, 28 n
Olympian games, 90
oratory, 181–183
Orestes, 30
Ornytus, 52
Orwell, George, 20
Otho: coinage of, 72 n; expensive tastes of, 96; and the masses, 72; and Nero, 26, 45, 68, 154 n, 183; and Poppaea Sabina, 36 n
Ovid, 76, 108; *Ars Amatoria*, 84; on Callimachus, 77, 88 n; on Ciris, 96; and elegies, 96; *Epistulae ex Ponto*, 123; exile of, 120; *Heroides*, 96; *Ibis*, 90, 156; and *Ilias Latina*, 34; influence of, 88; *Medea*, 156; *Medicamina*, 84; *Metamorphoses*, 77, 84, 87 n; and neo-Callimacheanism, 76; in Petronius' *Satyricon*, 86

Pacuvius, 97
Palatine Anthology, 99
Palladas, 98 n
Paneros, 46
Papinius (the Elder), 89 n, 90 n
Paris, 91, 92, 102
Parnassus, 93
Parthenius, 76, 79, 81, 194
Parthenopaeus, 193
Parthia, 51; Parthians, 25 n, 149
pastoral poetry, 59
Paullinus, 127 n
Pausanias, 25 n
Pergamum, 28 n, 174; Temple of Aesculapius at, 89, 186 n
Persius, 74; on archaizing, 97, 99; and Callimacheanism, 92, 93, 108; on contemporary poets, 93, 110; education of, 39; on elegy, 96; and Horace, 78, 111, 112; and *Iliad*, 102; on liber-

Persius (*continued*)
 tas, 149; on literary circles, 47; and
 Lucan, 107; and Lucilius, 100, 105,
 107, 108; and Lucillius, 104; on neo-
 Callimacheanism, 80, 96, 97, 104,
 108; on Neoterics, 93–94; on Nero,
 100–106, 108, 113; on oratory, 46;
 praetexta of, 176 n; satires of, 92–98,
 100, 101, 103–105, 107–109, 112–
 114, 179; and Stoicism, 46; style of,
 111–112; themes of, 110
Petronius: *Bellum Civile*, 34, 107, 162–
 172; on bisexuality, 26; on Callimachus, 87; career of, 159; on Cato (the
 Younger), 166–167; *Cena Trimalchionis*, 174; on the Civil War, 147;
 Codicilli, 34, 34 n, 35 n; as an Epicurean, 45, 177 n; expensive tastes of,
 96, 160; and forgeries, 155; on Julius
 Caesar, 168, 170; and Lucan, 161,
 162, 164, 172, 176; and Nero, 20,
 136, 154 n, 160, 161, 172, 175, 178;
 in Nero's literary circle, 38–39; on
 Nero's sexual excesses, 35 n; Persius'
 satires of, 95; *Satyricon*, 21, 30 n, 34,
 34 n, 49 n, 86, 161–163, 165, 172–
 175; and Seneca, 161, 172–176; *Troiae
 Halosis*, 34, 88, 175
Petronius Turpilianus, 46
Phaedrus, 141
Philemon, 87 n
philhellenism, under Nero, 23, 24, 79
Philip of Macedon, 129
Philip of Thessalonica, 79 n, 84
Philippi, 65, 168
Philostratus, 25 n
Phyllis, 95, 96
Pierian Muses, 83, 93
Pindar, 85
Piso, Calpurnii, 71 n
Piso, C. Calpurnius: as archconspira-
 tor, 46; as artist, 36, 37 n; and Cal-
 purnius Siculus, 48 n; as an Epicu-
 rean, 45; dramatic performances of,
 176 n; flattery of, 48, 59; literary
 circle of, 57; marriage of, 36 n; and
 Nero, 36, 57
Pisonian conspiracy, 25, 32, 36, 67,
 107, 107 n, 133, 142, 145, 148 n,
 155, 160
Plato, 108, 141
Plautus, Rubellius, 64–65
Playboy, 107 n

Pliny (the Elder), 158, 160
Pliny (the Younger), 19, 108, 132; and
 Bithynia, 159; on Domitian, 186; *Ep-
 istulae*, 105 n, 106 n, 177 n; and Mar-
 tial, 194; poetry of, 90
Plutarch, 25 n, 119
Polla, Argentaria, 22, 190, 191
Pollio, Asinius, 55
Pollio, Clodius, 90, 103
Polybius, 123, 123 n, 124, 124 n
Polyclitus, 28 n
Polynices, 151
Pompey, 118, 165 n, 167; and Hercules,
 170, 171; in Lucan's *Pharsalia*, 150,
 151
Pontus Polemoniacus, 51
Pope, Alexander, 89, 114
Poppaea Sabina: hair of, 89, 104; and
 Nero, 26, 36 n, 45; in pseudo-
 Senecan *Octavia*, 60, 63, 65–70
popular uprisings. *See* Rome
Poseidon, 90
Potamon, 100
Praetorian Guard, 116
Priscian, 177
Priscilla, 194
Private Eye, 107 n
Proculus, Scribonius, 25
Propertius, 100; and Callimachus, 80,
 96; on the Civil War, 147; elegies of,
 78; and Horace, 20 n, 108, 156; and
 neo-Callimacheanism, 76; Persius'
 satire of, 93
pseudo-Senecan *Octavia*, 60–73, 176 n;
 Julio-Claudians in, 148, 157 n, 183.
 See also entries for individual writers
pseudo-Vergilian *Culex*, 86
pseudo-Vergilian *Moretum*, 86
Ptolemies, 24
Ptolemy Philadelphus, 59
Ptolemy Philopator, 23
Punic Wars, 88 n
Pythagoras, 26
Pythian games, 99

Quinquennium Neronis, 73
Quintilian, 37, 96, 156, 183, 184, 186

Rabirius, 147
Reckford, Kenneth, 110, 113
recusatio, 78, 92
Regulus, 149, 151, 152, 182
Republican ideology, 143

Rhea, 104
Rhianus, 79
Rhine River, 189
Rhodes, 42
Rome: great fire of, 23, 27, 70 (*see also* Nero*)*; popular uprisings in, 183–184 n
Romulus, 54, 189
Rubicon, Caesar's crossing of, 170
Russell, G. W. E., 189
Rusticus, Arulenus, 186

Sabinus, Nymphidius, 116
Saleius Bassus, 184, 186, 187
Sarmatians, 185
Sarmatian War, 190
Satria Galla, 36 n
Saturninus, revolt of, 185
Scaevinus, Flavius, 160, 160 n
Scamander, River, 102
Scapula, P. Ostorius, 42
Scaurus, M. Aemilius, 157, 157 n
scholia antiqua, 101, 102
Scipio Africanus, 187, 188
Scribonius Rufus, 25
Secundus, Julius, 182
Secundus, Pedanius, 41 n
Secundus, Pomponius, 156
Sejanus, Aelius, 116, 120, 122
senate, Roman, 25; in Calpurnius Siculus' *Eclogues*, 54; Domitian and, 186; Nero and, 23, 24, 26, 40, 53, 65, 107 n; Vespasian and, 186
Seneca: *Agamemnon*, 175; and Agrippina, 49, 49 n, 126, 136, 158; *Apocolocyntosis*, 30 n, 48–55, 59, 64, 71, 73, 84, 117, 130, 146, 155, 172 n; on Augustus, 49, 50, 53, 71, 117, 129, 134, 135; on Cato (the Younger), 118, 144, 177 n; and Claudius, 49 n, 117, 120, 126, 127, 130, 158; *Consolatio ad Helviam*, 122, 122 n, 123, 158; *Consolatio ad Marciam*, 121, 122, 122 n, 128; *Consolatio ad Polybium*, 123–126, 158; on contemporary writing, 105; *Controversiae*, 173; *De Beneficiis*, 130, 144; *De Brevitate Vitae*, 127; *De Clementia*, 55, 130–135, 148, 158; *De Ira*, 126–130, 158; *De Otio*, 136, 137, 142; *De Providentia*, 156 n; *De Tranquillitate Animi*, 137, 142, 156 n; *De Vita Beata*, 138–141, 155, 182; on Epicureanism, 142, 177, 177 n; epigrams of, 177, 177 n, 178; epistles of, 108, 109, 174, 176; *Epistulae Morales*, 82, 140, 142–144, 156 n, 172; exile of, 64, 120, 121, 123, 158, 175; on governance, 64, 128, 134, 143, 158 n; *Hercules Furens*, 157 n; literary circle of, 22; lost works of, 43 n; *Naturales Quaestiones*, 44, 142, 156 n; and Nero, 29, 42, 43, 44, 142, 154 n, 156, 158; as Nero's speechwriter, 49; as Nero's tutor, 24, 28, 30, 31, 42, 127; on Nero, 89, 131, 133, 154 n; *Oedipus*, 157 n; on oratory, 46; and Petronius, 173–176; as political writer, 119, 120, 122 n, 126, 136 n, 148; and pseudo-Senecan *Octavia*, 60, 64, 65, 66, 71, 73; and Stoicism, 138, 139, 142, 143; *Thyestes*, 71, 157 n; tragedies of, 43, 43 n, 44 n, 60, 147, 156 n, 157, 158, 158 n, 173 n, 176 n; wealth of, 44 n, 137 n, 139
Serenus, Annaeus, 136, 137
Servius, 91, 102
Severianus, 80
Severus (architect), 27
Sheavyn, Phoebe, 19
Shelley, Percy Bysshe, 156
Ship of Death, 61, 70
Sicilian War, 65
Silani, 71 n
Silanus, Junius, 62
Silia, 46, 159
Silius Italicus: career of, 88, 88 n; on Domitian, 188; and *Ilias Latina*, 33, 87; and Julian dynasty, 187; literary tastes of, 88 n; and Nero, 33, 34; *Punica*, 33, 33 n, 34, 151, 163 n, 166, 187; and tradition, 152; and Vitellius, 33
Silver Age, 196
Silver Poets, 75
Silvinus, Publius, 83, 84
Socrates, 141
Soviet Union, 109–110
Spain, 168
Spiculus, 46
Sporus, 26, 159
Statius: *Achilleis*, 188; on Agrippina, 191; on Argentaria Polla, 191; and Atedius Melior, 193; on Callimachean theory, 75; on Callimachus, 194; *Capilli Flavi Earini*, 89; on

Statius (*continued*)
  Domitian, 185, 186 n; *Epithalamium*, 89 n; *Eucharisticon*, 189; and Martial, 19 n, 156, 192, 193, 194; on mythology, 157 n; on Nero, 191, 192 n; *Silvae*, 188–190; and Stella, 190; *Thebais*, 188, 196; and tradition, 152
Stella, L. Arrontius, 187, 189, 190
Stoicism, 108, 112, 113, 115, 118, 119, 148, 149; and doctrines of happiness, 138; and Lucan, 146, 169; as political philosophy, 120; Seneca on, 138, 139, 142, 143
Stoic literary circles, 46, 106
Straton, 22
Suda, 80
Suetonius: on Domitian, 185; on Lucan, 38; on Nero, 26, 27, 29, 106, 159; on Otho, 26; on Vitellius, 32; on wills, 35 n
Suillius, P. Rufus, 137, 138, 139, 141, 155
Sulla, Cornelii, 71 n
Sulla, Faustus Cornelius, 64, 65, 147, 149
Sutorius Macro, 157 n
Swift, Jonathan, 20

Tacitus: on Claudius, 127 n; on *codicilli*, 34 n; *Dialogus*, 181–183; on Domitian, 185; on literature, 19; on Messalina, 62; on Nero, 26, 27, 41, 106, 120, 135–136, 159; on Nero's literary circle, 31, 37; on Nero and the masses, 66; on Nero's poetry, 29–30; on oratory, 46, 181–183; on Petronius, 159, 160, 176; on Roman Republic, 166; on Seneca, 35 n, 137; on Vatinius, 44
Tantalus, 81
Telchines, 156
Terentius Maximus, 25 n
Terpnus, 30, 45
Testamentum Porcelli, 35 n
Thamyras, 58
Theban cycle, 151
Thebes, expedition against, 31
Theocritus, 52, 59, 77, 78, 82
Theseus, 77, 87, 90
Thespiae, 28 n
Thessaly, 171
Thrasea Paetus, 106, 155; as actor, 176 n; *Life of Cato*, 119, 144; prosecution of, 46, 184; as a Republican, 132; as a Stoic, 143
Thyestes, 31, 193
Tiberius, 35 n, 41, 79, 157 n
Tibullus, 26, 32, 76, 90, 96
Ticidas, 75
Tigellinus, Ofonius, 29 n, 116; and Nero, 29, 45, 136, 156, 159; at Nero's court, 45; and Petronius, 39, 160, 172, 178; and pseudo-Senecan *Octavia*, 72; as prosecutor, 65
Timagenes, 129
Titus, 21, 30 n, 33, 184, 186 n, 187
Titus Vinius, 72
Toller, Ernst, 25
Torquatus, L. Junius Silanus, 63 n
Torquemada, 182
Trachalus, Galerius, 182
Trajan, 73, 132, 195
Trimalchio, 174, 175, 175 n
Tros, 102
Troy, 38, 53, 58, 91
Tullia, 64
Turnus, 151

Utica, 150

Vacca, 162
Varius, 156
Varro, 35 n, 49
Vatinius, 28 n, 44, 45, 47, 155, 181
Vaughan, Henry, 100
Velleius Paterculus, 166
Venus, 149, 150, 171, 190
Vergil: *Aeneid*, 20, 118, 145, 148, 150, 151; and Alexandrian literature, 77; and Augustus, 105 n; on Callimachean theory, 75; on the Civil War, 147; early works of, 80; *Eclogues*, 52, 55, 76, 86; in *Einsiedeln Eclogues*, 58; epics of, 91; *Georgics*, 76, 83, 84, 152; and *Ilias Latina*, 34; influence of, 88, 187; and Lucan, 164; and Maecenas, 56; and pastoral tradition, 59; in Petronius' *Satyricon*, 86; on Punic Wars, 88 n; and Silius Italicus, 88 n; on Trojan games, 91
Verginia, 64
Vespasian, 72 n, 184, 187
Vesta, 150, 183
Vestinus, 154 n, 160
Vesuvius, eruption of, 37 n
Villon, François: *Testaments*, 35 n

Vindex, Julius, 160
Violentilla, 190
Vita Persi, 100, 107
Vitellius, Aulus: coinage of, 72 n; and the masses, 41, 72; and Nero, 32, 148, 183; and Silius Italicus, 33
Volusius, 78

Year of the Four Emperors, 66, 133, 183

Library of Congress Cataloging in Publication Data

Sullivan, J. P. (John Patrick).
  Literature and politics in the age of Nero.

  "Based on the Charles Beebe Martin Lectures delivered at Oberlin Col-
lege in March, 1976"—Pref.
  Bibliography: p.
  Includes indexes.
  1. Latin literature—History and criticism. 2. Politics and literature—
Rome. 3. Politics in literature. 4. Rome—History—Nero, 54-68. I. Title.
PA6029.P64S85   1985   870'.9'001   84-14278
ISBN 0-8014-1740-6 (alk. paper)